HIGH PRAISE FOR BEN MACINTYRE'S
SPECTACULAR NATIONAL BESTSELLER
THE NAPOLEON OF CRIME

"ENTERTAINING . . . THIS TRUE-CRIME DRAMA IS AS
INTERESTING FOR THE PERSONALITIES IT CAPTURES AS
FOR THE CAPERS IT DISSECTS."
—*Newsday*

"A carefully researched and smoothly narrated tale."
—*The Washington Post*

"[A] VASTLY ENTERTAINING SAGA . . . the ingenious
details of his most memorable heists are hilariously recounted
in comic fashion by an author who expresses genuine affection
and admiration for his flawed subject. This fascinating and
amusing biography will delight true-crime buffs."
—*Booklist*

"COMPELLING."
—*USA Today*

"DELIGHTFUL, GRIPPING, TOUCHING, EXOTIC, peopled
with highly colorful characters and written with
humor and brilliant polish."
—James Lord, author of *Some Remarkable Men*

Please turn the page for more extraordinary acclaim. . . .

Also by Ben Macintyre

Forgotten Fatherland: The Search for Elisabeth Nietzsche

THE
NAPOLEON
OF
CRIME

THE
NAPOLEON
OF
CRIME

The Life and Times of Adam Worth, Master Thief

BEN MACINTYRE

Delta
Trade Paperbacks

A Delta Book
Published by
Dell Publishing
a division of
Bantam Doubleday Dell Publishing Group, Inc.
1540 Broadway
New York, New York 10036

Grateful acknowledgment is made for permission to reprint the following: Photographs of William Pinkerton, Adam Worth, Charles Bullard, Charles Becker, Max Shinburn, and Henne Alonzo courtesy of Pinkerton's, Inc. Photographs of Kitty Flynn courtesy of Katharine Sanford. Excerpts from "Macavity the Mystery Cat" by T. S. Eliot, from "Old Possum's Book of Practical Cats," with permission of Harcourt, Brace & Co. Excerpts from "Macavity the Mystery Cat" by T. S. Eliot reprinted in Canada with permission of Faber & Faber. Copyright © 1939 by T. S. Eliot, renewed 1967 by Esme Valerie Eliot.

ISBN: 0-385-31993-2

Reprinted by arrangement with Farrar, Straus and Giroux

Manufactured in the United States of America
Published simultaneously in Canada

August 1998

10   9   8   7   6   5   4   3   2

BVG

For Kate

Preface

I had come to Los Angeles to cover the latest installment in the Rodney King case, that grimly defining saga of modern times. But I left the city with a very different tale of cops and robbers.

The white Los Angeles policemen who had been filmed by an amateur cameraman beating up a black motorist were in court for a second time, stolidly proclaiming their innocence. It was confidently predicted that the city was on the verge of another riot. One afternoon, when the jury had retired to consider its verdict, I decided to drive out to the suburb of Van Nuys to explore the archives of the Pinkerton Detective Agency, thinking I might write an article for *The Times* about American law enforcement in another, sepia-tinted age, a world away from the thugs on trial downtown, or those in the ghetto who would take to the streets if they escaped justice again.

The Pinkertons. The name itself summoned up hard lawmen with comic facial hair and six-shooters, riding out after the likes of Jesse James, the Reno gang, Butch Cassidy and the Sundance Kid. Shown into the basement archive by a bored secretary popping bubble gum, I immediately realized there was far more here than could possibly be digested in a year, let alone an afternoon. The rows of cabinets literally overflowed with files, a testament to the painstaking methods of America's earliest detectives. After an hour or so of random delving, I picked up a bound scrapbook, dated 1902. Leafing through it, I came across this fragment of newsprint:

SUNDAY OREGONIAN, PORTLAND, JULY 27, 1902.

ADAM WORTH

GREATEST THIEF OF MODERN TIMES; STOLE $3,000,000

This is the story of Adam Worth. If a fiction writer could conceive such a story, he might well hesitate to write it for fear of being accused of using the wildly improbable.

The sober, cold, technical judgment passed upon Adam Worth by the greatest thief-hunters of America and Great Britain is that he was the most remarkable, most successful and most dangerous professional criminal ever known to modern times.

Adam Worth, in a life of crime covering almost half a century, looted at least $2,000,000, and most probably as much as $3,000,000.

He cruised through the Mediterranean on a steam yacht with a crew of 20 men, and left a trail of looted cities behind him.

He was caught only once, and then through a blunder by a stupid confederate.

He ruled the shrewdest criminals, and planned deeds for them with craft that bade defiance to the best detective talent in the world.

The police of America and Europe were eager to take him for years, and for years he perpetrated every form of theft—check-forging, swindling, larceny, safe-cracking, diamond robbery, mail robbery, burglary of every degree, "hold-ups" on the road and bank robbery—under their very noses with complete immunity.

There were three redeeming features in the life of this lost human creature.

He worshiped his family and regarded and treated his loved ones as something sacred. His wife never knew that he was a criminal. His children are living in the

United States today in complete ignorance of the fact that their father was the master-thief of the civilized world.

He never was guilty of violence, and would have nothing to do under any circumstances with any one who did.

He never forsook a friend or accomplice.

Because of that loyalty he once rescued his band of forgers from a Turkish prison and then from Greek brigands, reducing himself to beggary to do it.

Because of that loyalty he became "The Man Who Stole the Gainsborough."

The reason for that theft will be told here for the first time. Until now, all who knew it were under binding obligations of silence. The motive that caused the deed was unique in the history of modern crime.

And Adam Worth, who had millions, who once flipped coins for £100 a toss, who at one time had an interest in a racing stable, had a steam yacht and a fast sailing yacht, died a few weeks ago as he had begun—a poor, penniless thief.

He towered above all other criminals of his time; he was so far in advance of them that the man who hunted him weakened before his masterful intellect; but the inexorable fate that pursues the breaker of moral law caught him and finished him at last where the man-made law was powerless.

When Adam Worth died he was as much a mystery—aside from certain officials and detective inspectors of Scotland Yard, the Pinkertons, and a very few American police officials—even to the great majority of the police officials of the world as he had been throughout his life. If he had not become prominent recently as the man who stole and returned the Gainsborough portrait, the public probably never would have heard of him at all. Only a very few of the most able detectives of the world knew him even by sight. Still less knew anything about him. The story that follows is an absolute and minutely exact history, verified in every particular and vouched for by the men who spent almost half a century in trying to hunt him down.

Nothing in this history is left to conjecture.

The rest of the promised article, infuriatingly, had not been pasted into the book. Time and again I read this clipping, extravagant in its claims even by the journalistic standards of the day, and a small L.A. riot of excitement began building somewhere in the back of my mind. Then my electronic pager sounded, bringing me hurtling back to the present with the news that a verdict in the Rodney King trial was imminent. By the next afternoon, two of the cops had been found guilty, the inhabitants of South Central Los Angeles had obligingly decided not to go on a rampage, and I was back in Van Nuys, combing the Pinkerton archive for every scrap of material I could find on Adam Worth. The detectives, I soon learned, had hunted Worth across the world for decades with dogged perseverance, and the result was a wealth of documentation: six complete chronological folders, tied together with string and bulging with photographs, letters, newspaper articles, and hundreds of memos by the Pinkerton detectives, each one written in meticulous copperplate and relating a tale even more intriguing and peculiar than the nameless *Sunday Oregonian* writer had implied.

For Adam Worth, it transpired, was far more than simply a talented crook. A professional charlatan, he was that most feared of Victorian bogeymen: the double man, the charming rascal, the respectable and civilized Dr. Jekyll by day whose villainy emerged only under cover of night. Worth made a myth of his own life, building a thick smokescreen of wealth and possessions to cover a multitude of crimes that had started with picking pockets and desertion and later expanded to include safecracking on an industrial scale, international forgery, jewel theft, and highway robbery. The Worth dossiers revealed a vivid rogues' gallery of crooks, aristocrats, con men, molls, mobsters, and policemen, all revolving around this singular man. In minute detail the detectives described his criminal network, radiating out of Paris and London and stretching from Jamaica to South Africa, from America to Turkey.

I left the Pinkerton archive elated but tantalized. The material was vast but incomplete. Like any sensible crook anxious to avoid detection, Worth had not written his memoirs and had left behind only a handful of coded letters. My initial researches had raised more questions than they answered. How had Worth evolved his contradictory moral code? How had he escaped capture for so many years? How had he transformed himself from a penniless German-Jewish emigrant from Cambridge, Massachusetts, into an English milord in the aristocratic heart of London?

One mystery intrigued me more than all the others. In the early summer of 1876, at the height of his criminal powers, Worth stole from a London art gallery, in the dead of night, *The Duchess of Devonshire,* Thomas Gainsborough's famous portrait and then the most expensive painting ever sold. What had possessed him? And why, still more bizarrely, had he kept the great painting, in secret, for the next twenty-five years? The Gainsborough portrait, I was already certain, held the key to unlocking the secret of Adam Worth.

California proved to be only the first stop on a long trail. Slowly I assembled a fuller picture, from letters, diaries, published memoirs by other criminals, newspaper accounts, and the archives of Scotland Yard, the Paris Sûreté, Agnew's art gallery, and Chatsworth House. Other, quite unexpected discoveries followed.

Worth invented his own life as a dramatic romance. When the *Portland Oregonian* had talked of his piquant history as the very stuff of fiction, the newspaper was telling the literal truth. The English detective Sherlock Holmes was already a household name when Sir Arthur Conan Doyle first learned of Worth's villainous deeds. The great English writer, it turns out, had used Worth as the model for none other than Professor Moriarty, Holmes's evil, art-collecting adversary, and one of the most memorable criminals in literature. Conan Doyle was not alone in his debt to Worth, for writers as diverse as Henry James and Rosamund De Zeer Marshall, an author of wartime bodice-rippers, also found inspiration in Worth's activities.

My quarry led me on some unlikely pilgrimages: to the grand building in Piccadilly near Fortnum & Mason's that was Worth's criminal headquarters; to the Civil War battlefield where he first reinvented himself; to the London art gallery where he stole his most prized possession, and to a room in Sotheby's auction house where, for the first time, I encountered that indelible image face-to-face. As I write, from the Paris office of *The Times* (London), I can look across the Place de l'Opéra to the Grand Hotel, where Worth ran an illegal casino and held court with his mistress in the 1870s. I am still not sure whether I have been following Worth for the last four years or whether he has been shadowing me.

I had set off to hunt down "The Greatest Thief of Modern Times." What I found turned out to be an unlikely reflection of those times, and our own: a Victorian gentleman and master thief who merged the highest moral principles with the lowest criminal cunning. What follows is a story that has never been told before; it is a story of dual personalities, double standards, and heroic hypocrisy.

This is the story of Adam Worth.

Adam Worth was the Napoleon of the criminal world. None other could hold a candle to him.

—Sir Robert Anderson, Head of Criminal Investigation,
Scotland Yard, 1907

He is the Napoleon of crime, Watson. He is the organizer of half that is evil and of nearly all that is undetected in this great city. He is a genius, a philosopher, an abstract thinker. He has a brain of the first order. He sits motionless, like a spider at the centre of its web, but that web has a thousand radiations, and he knows well every quiver of each of them. He does little himself. He only plans. But his agents are numerous and splendidly organized . . . the central power which uses the agent is never caught—never so much as suspected.

—Sherlock Holmes on Professor Moriarty, in
The Final Problem by Sir Arthur Conan Doyle

I hope you have not been leading a double life, pretending to be wicked and being really good all the time. That would be hypocrisy.

—Oscar Wilde, *The Importance of Being Earnest*

ONE

The Elopement

On a misty May midnight in the year 1876, three men emerged from a fashionable address in Piccadilly with top hats on their heads, money in their pockets, and burglary, on a grand scale, on their minds. At a deliberate pace the trio headed along the thoroughfare, and at the point where Piccadilly intersects with Old Bond Street, they came to a stop. Famed for its art galleries and antiques shops, the street by day was choked with the carriages of the wealthy, the well-bred, and the culturally well-informed. Now it was quite deserted.

The three men exchanged a few words at the corner of the street before one slipped into a doorway, invisible beyond the dancing gaslight shadows, while the other two turned right into Old Bond Street. They made an incongruous pair as they walked on: one was slight and dapper, some thirty-five years in age, with long, clipped mustaches, and dressed in the height of modern elegance, complete with pearl buttons and gold watch chain. The other, ambling a few paces behind, was a towering fellow with grizzled mutton-chop whiskers, whose ill-fitting frock coat barely contained a barrel chest. Had anyone been there to observe the couple, they might have assumed them to be a rich man taking the night air with his unprepossessing valet after a substantial dinner at his club.

Outside the art gallery of Thomas Agnew & Sons, at number 39, Old Bond Street, the two men paused, and while the aristocrat extinguished his cheroot and admired his own faint but stylish reflection in the glass, his brutish companion glanced furtively up and down the street. Then, at a word from his master, the giant flattened himself against the wall and joined his hands in a stirrup, into which the smaller man placed a well-shod foot, for all the world as if he were climbing onto a thoroughbred. With a grunt the big man heaved the little fellow up the wall and in a moment he had scrambled nimbly onto the window ledge some fifteen feet above the pavement. Balancing precariously, he whipped out a small crow bar, wrenched open the casement window, and slipped inside, as his companion vanished from sight beneath the gallery portal.

The room was unfurnished and unlit, but by the faint glow from the pavement gaslight a large painting in a gilt frame could be discerned on the opposite wall. The little man removed his hat as he drew closer.

The woman in the portrait, already famed throughout London as the most exquisite beauty ever to grace a canvas, gazed down with an imperious and inquisitive eye. Curls cascaded from beneath a broad-brimmed hat set at a rakish angle to frame a painted glance at once beckoning and mocking, and a smile just one quiver short of a full pout.

The faint rumble of a night watchman's snores wafted up from the room below, as the little gentleman unclipped a thick velvet rope that held the inquisitive public back from the painting during daylight hours. Extracting a sharp blade from his pocket, with infinite care he cut the portrait from its frame and laid it on the gallery floor. From his coat he took a small pot of paste, and using the tasseled end of the velvet rope, he daubed the back of the canvas to make it supple and then rolled it up with the paint facing outward to avoid cracking the surface, before slipping it inside his frock coat.

A few seconds later he had scrambled back down his monstrous assistant to the street below. A low whistle summoned the lookout from his street corner, and with jaunty step the little dandy set off back down Piccadilly, the stolen portrait pressed to his breast and his two rascally companions trailing behind.

The painted lady was Georgiana, Duchess of Devonshire, once celebrated as the fairest and wickedest woman in Georgian England. The painter was the great Thomas Gainsborough, who had executed this, one of his greatest portraits, around 1787. A few weeks before the events just recounted, the painting had been sold at auction for 10,000 guineas, at that time the highest price ever paid for a work of art, causing a sensation. Georgiana of Devonshire, née Spencer, was once again the talk of London, much as her great-great-great-grandniece Diana, Princess of Wales, née Spencer, would become in our age.

During Georgiana's lifetime, which ended in 1806, her admirers vied to pay tribute to "the amenity and graces of her deportment, her irresistible manners, and the seduction of her society." Her detractors, however, considered her a shameless harpy, a gambler, a drunk, and a threat to civilized morals who openly lived in a ménage-à-trois with her husband and his mistress. No woman of the time aroused more envy, or provoked more gossip.

The sale of Gainsborough's great painting to the art dealer William Agnew in 1876 had been the occasion for a fresh burst of Georgiana mania. Gainsborough's vision of enigmatic loveliness, and the extraordinary value now attached to it, became the talk of London. Victorian commentators, like their eighteenth-century predecessors, heaped praise once more on this icon of female beauty, while rehearsing some of the fruitier aspects of her sexual history.

When the painting was stolen, the public interest in Gainsborough's *Duchess* reached fever pitch. The painting acquired huge cultural and sexual symbolism. It was praised, reproduced, and parodied time and again, the Marilyn Monroe poster of its day, while Georgiana herself was again held up as the ultimate symbol of feminine coquetry.

The name of the man who kidnapped the *Duchess* that night

in 1876 was Adam Worth, alias Henry J. Raymond, wealthy resident of Mayfair, sporting gentleman about town, and criminal mastermind. At the time of the theft Worth was at the peak of his powers, controlling a small army of lesser felons in an astonishing criminal industry. Stealing the picture was an act of larceny, but also one of hubris and romance. Georgiana and her portrait represented the pinnacle of English high society. Worth, by contrast, was a German-born Jew raised in abject poverty in America who, through an unbroken record of crime, had assembled the trappings of English privilege and status, and every appearance of virtue. The grand duchess had died seventy years before Worth decided, in his own words, to "elope" with her portrait, beginning a strange, true Victorian love affair between a crook and a canvas.

TWO

A Fine War

Fourteen years earlier, at the end of August 1862, the armies of the Union and the Confederacy had come to grips in a muddy Virginia field and blasted away at each other for two days in an encounter known to history as the Second Battle of Bull Run, one of the bloodiest engagements of the American Civil War.

According to official war records, more than three thousand soldiers died in that carnage, including one Adam Worth, who was just eighteen at the time.

Bull Run was the scene of Worth's first death and first reincarnation. Reports of his death were, of course, greatly exaggerated. Far from perishing on the Virginia battlefields, the young Worth survived the war in excellent health with a new identity, a deep aversion to bloodshed, and a wholly new career as an impostor stretching out before him. The Civil War almost destroyed America, but after the bloodletting the country fashioned itself anew, and so did Worth. Over the next forty years he would vanish and then reappear under a new name with a regularity and ease that baffled the police of three continents.

Worth was notoriously reticent when it came to discussing the years before his strange renaissance at Bull Run—the better, perhaps, to preserve the myriad myths that clustered around them. Some later accounts insisted that he was the product of a wealthy

Yankee family and an expensive education, a gentleman criminal in the Raffles tradition. Another stated, categorically and without corroboration, that "his father was a Russian Pole and his mother a German." The great detective William Pinkerton, a man who came to know Worth better than any other, insisted that he was the child of a rich Massachusetts burgher who had sent his son to a private academy to learn an honest business, only to see him seduced into crime by bad company in the stews of New York. "Had he continued an upright life, he undoubtedly would have become famous as a businessman," the worthy Pinkerton lamented. Another important figure in Worth's life, a notorious thief and gangster's moll named Sophie Lyons, concurred in the belief that Worth had come from good stock, reporting that he was "born of an excellent family and well educated, [but] formed bad habits and developed a passion for gambling."

Worth himself was the last person to deny such glamorous beginnings, which were, like so many aspects of his existence, a very considerable distance from the truth. Adam Worth (or Wirth, or even, occasionally, Werth) was born in 1844 somewhere in eastern Germany. His father and mother were German Jews who emigrated to the United States when Worth was just five years old. Speaking no English and almost destitute, Worth père set up shop as a tailor in Cambridge, Massachusetts. No other details about Worth's mother and father have survived, but one may surmise that their parenting skills, particularly in the area of ethical guidance, were distinctly lacking: not only did Adam Worth take to crime at an early age, but his younger brother, John, quickly followed suit, and his sister, Harriet, continued the family tradition by marrying a more than usually crooked lawyer.

Worth's first lesson in swindling was apparently learned in a Cambridge school playground. Pinkerton liked to tell the story of how Worth "entered school when six years of age, and was very soon after, as he himself stated, drawn into a trade with a boy larger than himself, who offered to give him a brand-new penny for two old ones." The child Worth, finding the newly minted coin a more attractive object than his two old ones, agreed to the swap and returned home to show his father, who "gave him a most unmerciful whipping," thus "impressing on him the value of the new penny as against his two old ones."

"From that day until his death, no one, be he friend or foe, honest or dishonest, Negro or Indian, relative or stranger, ever got the better of Adam Worth in any business transactions, regular or irregular," Pinkerton concluded.

The young Worth grew up, or rather did not grow up, to be small in stature, measuring between five feet four and five feet five, according to police records. Contemporaries made much of his lack of height, and his criminal colleagues, who were nothing if not literal when it came to the allocation of sobriquets, called him "Little Adam." In reality, for an age when human beings were appreciably smaller than they are now, he was not much below average height, but it suited the purposes of those who could not help admiring him to make our man out to be a midget, for thus his evil-doing was magnified and his ability to thwart authority appeared the more remarkable. When the Scotland Yard detective Robert Anderson called him "the Napoleon of the criminal world," he was referring not only to the man's nefarious accomplishments and criminal stature but also to his lack of inches. The undersized Worth quickly developed an outsized Napoleonic complex.

Worth's height was the first physical feature noted by the various detectives, policemen, crooks, and lovers who came into contact with him. The second was his eyes, which were dark, almost black, penetrating voids beneath shaggy eyebrows, suggestive of intelligence and determination. When he became enraged, which was seldom, they bulged unpleasantly. He had thick hair, which he wore short and combed to one side, a prominent curved nose, and, in later life, a long mustache which curled across his cheeks to meet a pair of mighty side-whiskers.

If Worth's tough childhood left him with a cynical determination to outdo his peers by guile, it also seems to have imbued him with an intense romanticism. As his father scraped together a living to keep his brood alive in the malodorous hovel that was the Worth family home, his oldest son's imagination released him to a world of grand dinners, fine apparel, and civilized conversation.

In the Harvard students who paraded through Cambridge, the immigrant Jewish urchin had ample opportunity to observe the outward shows of wealth and privilege. The brighter the penny, he saw, the easier the counterfeit. Ashamed of his lowly origins, frustrated by impecunity, the young Worth clearly felt himself to be the equal of the fine young gentlemen strutting Boston Common. Their wealth and sophistication provoked ambivalent feelings of envy, resentment, and anger, and also of admiration and desire. Worth resolved to "better" himself.

Among the student body in the 1850s, for example, was Henry Adams, just a few years Worth's senior, but a young man so far his social superior as to represent a wholly different species. Wealthy, aristocratic, sophisticated, the scion of one of America's oldest and grandest families, bloodstock of Presidents, "never in his life," as Adams noted in his *Education,* "would he have to explain who he was." But Adams also knew that his ancient class was under threat from just such as Worth. "Not a Polish Jew fresh from Warsaw or Cracow—not a furtive Yacoob or Ysaac still reeking of the Ghetto, snarling a weird Yiddish to the officers of the customs—but had a keener instinct, an intenser energy, and a freer hand than he—American of Americans, with heaven knew how many Puritans and Patriots behind him." Reflecting on the advantages of his birth, Adams observed that "probably no child, born in the same year, held better cards than he," and wondered "whether life was an honest game of chance, or whether the cards were marked." The hand dealt to Adam Worth contained no such aces. But with an instinct and energy second to none, he resolved to mark the deck himself.

America, then as now, promised all things to all men, even if it did not always deliver. It was a time when "ambition," as Cardinal Newman wrote, "sets everyone on the lookout to succeed and to rise in life, to amass money, to gain power, to depress his rivals, to triumph over his hitherto superiors, to affect a consequence and a gentility which he had not before." Worth shared those aspirations, and would eventually realize them. His methods alone would set him apart from other "self-made men," for what others had earned, inherited, or bought, he would simply steal, winning respectability by robbery, effrontery, and fraud. Where his father had toiled to make clothes for the vanity of rich men, Worth would spin himself the dazzling outfit of a pretender, from pilfered cloth.

But it would be wrong to see the young Worth as merely a creature of immorality, a natural-born wrecker of the social fabric. From an early age he espoused many of the worthiest principles: allegiance to family and friends, the virtues of hard work, perseverance, generosity, charity, and courage. As he entered his teens, Little Adam was already evolving into a character of many and conflicting parts: selfish, greedy and also generous to a fault, at once ruthless and sentimental. He regarded his fellowmen, and particularly his social superiors, with undiluted cynicism, yet he would never swindle a friend, rob a poor man, or harm the harmless. He was acutely aware of the difference between right and wrong and evolved a code of behavior that he held with the same resolute conviction as would any pillar of society, while turning society's codes upside down. Adam Worth had plenty of time for morals; it was laws he disdained. The hard, uncertain circumstances of Worth's early life left him with the deep conviction that it was possible to be a "good" man, at least in his own estimation, while pursuing a life of calculated deceit.

The "Old Boston" described by Henry James and others was probably the most socially divided city in the United States, where power and money were still retained by a handful of white, Protestant families of Anglo-Saxon lineage with a genetic tendency toward snobbery, self-consciousness, and genteel self-righteousness. Boston is the only place in America with a name for its own uppercaste, but the puritanical elite of Boston Brahmins with its "serious poetry [and] profound religion," which "knelt in self-abasement before the majesty of English standards" and nothing else, was already being undermined by the immigrant invasion.

Worth could only gaze from an unbridgeable distance on the Boston power elite, the handful of city gentry communicating only with their peers and the Almighty, having utterly expunged their own ordinary immigrant origins. As one wit observed later:

> *So this is dear old Boston,*
> *The Land of the Bean and the Cod*
> *Where the Cabots talk only to Lowells*
> *And the Lowells talk only to God.*

If the snooty, anglophile Brahmins stood at the pinnacle of Boston's social scale, Worth represented precisely the other extreme.

As Henry James later observed in *The Bostonians,* this was "a nervous, hysterical, chattering, canting age, an age of hollow phrases and false delicacy and exaggerated solicitudes and coddled sensibilities." There was something fraudulent and hollow in the Brahmins' social superiority. This may have enraged the young Worth, excluded from their civilized ranks, but it also inspired him. As Henry Adams noted: "The Bostonian could not but develop a double nature. Life was a double thing."

As he emerged from a deprived childhood into an adolescence that offered little better, Worth took the fateful decision to rid him self of his first, unglamorous life. At the age of fourteen, he ran away from home, leaving behind his humble parents and their status as social outcasts. The idea of a career in crime and imposture may not yet have formed in his young mind, but Worth knew what he did not want. He never again set foot inside his childhood home, but a need for family love, and perhaps also for the strong father figure that his own father never was, marked the rest of his restless existence.

After some months of leading "a vagabond life in the city of Boston," he drifted to New York, where he took, for the first and only time, an honest job as a clerk "in one of the leading stores in New York City." Worth never offered any details of this brief flirtation with paid work, master criminals being notoriously touchy about that sort of thing, and the experiment was, anyway, cut short by the start of the Civil War. At the age of eighteen, the store clerk from Massachusetts promptly abandoned the tedious job of filling in ledgers and joined a New York regiment in the Union Army, preparing to march south for battle.

Worth's name first appears in the register of the 34th New York Light Artillery, better known as the Flushing or "L" Battery, which assembled in Long Island. He was officially mustered into the regiment in New York City on November 28, 1861, and received a "bounty of $1,000," according to Pinkerton. Many young recruits inflated their ages upon joining up, to appear more mature than they were and thus hasten possible promotion. The seventeen-year-old Worth gave his age as twenty, his first recorded lie.

The commander of the Flushing battery was a German-born shoemaker named Jacob Roemer, who had emigrated to New York in 1839. Captain Roemer was a fussy, irascible man with a thrusting beard, crossed eyes, and the bristling face of a natural martinet. Vain, blustering, and courageous to the point of insanity, Roemer wrote a massively self-inflating memoir many years later, apparently intended to prove that the author was himself primarily responsible for winning the war. Young Worth, Roemer's fellow countryman by birth, seems to have caught the eye of his commander, for he was soon promoted to corporal and then, on June 30, 1862, to the rank of sergeant in command of his own cannon and five men. Worth was well on his way to becoming a successful soldier, but he had by now fallen into bad—and thoroughly congenial—company. "He became associated with some wild companions, whom he had met at dances and frolics" while in New York, Pinkerton later recorded.

The life of the Flushing Battery was anything but frolicsome. For several months, the soldiers drilled on Long Island, learning to wheel the field guns under the obsessively critical inspection of Captain Roemer. Then, in early summer, Captain Jacob Roemer, five commissioned officers, Sergeant Adam Worth, 150 men, 110 horses, 12 baggage mules, and a laundry woman packed up and headed south to join the Union Army under the command of that dithering incompetent, General Pope, deservedly one of the least remembered generals of the Civil War. In Washington they drilled some more, around the unfinished Capitol building. Worth clearly hated every moment, and even Roemer admitted that Camp Barry was a "mud hole."

"All we wanted was a chance to prove our devotion and our loyalty to our country," the prickly and patriotic Roemer stated. Worth already had other ideas. Indeed, his first taste of army life compounded a blossoming disrespect for authority.

During the early part of August the Union Army and the Confederates under the command of Stonewall Jackson warily circled each other in the fields and hills of Virginia. The Flushing Battery took part in several skirmishes but it was not until late August that Roemer's men tasted the full horror of battle when the two sides met head-on, for the second time in the war, near the stream known as Bull Run.

On the evening of August 28, thanks largely to Captain Roemer's absurd determination to cover himself and his men in glory and blood, the Flushing Battery found itself engaged at close quarters with the enemy in the middle of Manassas Valley. Roemer enjoyed every moment. "Shot and shell flew thick and fast," he recalled, as the gunners fired off 207 rounds and somehow beat the enemy back. "I was triumphant," wrote Roemer. One of his terrified lieutenants, however, was found hiding under a bush and had to be removed, gibbering, from the field. The battery commander was in his element, belting around the battlefield expecting, perhaps even hoping, to be shot by the enemy, and leaving a trail of appropriately heroic last words as he went. On the thirtieth he gave a pep talk to his troops. "Boys, it is no longer of any use to keep from you what may be in store for us," he announced gleefully. "Before the sun sets to-night, many of you may have given up your lives; perhaps I myself will have to, but all I have to say is— Die like men; do not run like cowards. Stick to your guns, and, with the help of God and our own exertions, we may get through. Forward march." What Worth made of Roemer's epic oratory may be deduced from his subsequent actions.

A few hours later, "L" Battery was caught up in the fiercest engagement so far. "Bullets, shot and shell fell like hail in a heavy storm . . . bullets were dropping all around and shells were ploughing up the ground. Men were tumbling, horses were falling and it certainly looked as though 'de kingdom was a-comin'," recalled Roemer, who had his horse shot out from under him and received, to his transparent delight, a flesh wound in the right thigh. Finally the enemy retreated. The Union Army was soundly defeated at Bull Run, but the unstable Captain Roemer regarded the battle as an immense personal victory.

From Adam Worth's point of view, the most intriguing fact about the engagement at Bull Run is that he did not, officially speaking, survive it.

Roemer was unemotional in recording the passing of young Worth: "During this battle, generally known as the Second Battle of Bull Run or Manassas, August 29–30, 1862, the casualties in Battery L were fourteen enlisted men wounded (including Sergeant Adam Wirth, mortally wounded) besides myself, three horses killed and 21 wounded." According to his army records, Adam Worth died at the Seminary Hospital, Georgetown, on September 25, from wounds received three weeks earlier.

What really happened to Adam Worth at Bull Run must be a matter of speculation, for, unlike Roemer, and for obvious reasons, he did not write his war memoirs. Certainly he was wounded during the engagement. He later boasted of the fact, yet the injury does not appear to have been serious. At some point between August 30, when he was carried from the battlefield, and September 25, when he was officially listed as dead, Worth successfully made his escape. Perhaps he swapped his identification with another, mortally wounded soldier, or perhaps in the confused aftermath of battle when so many injured and dying were crammed into the nation's capital, he merely ended up as a fortuitous clerical error, marked down on the wrong list. Either way, Worth emerged from the battlefields of Virginia with only a superficial wound and an entirely new identity. Adam Worth was officially no more, and thus could move on without fear of pursuit. For the first time, but not the last, he reinvented himself and became a professional bounty jumper.

Over the coming months Worth established a system: he would enlist in one regiment under an assumed name, collect whatever bounty was being offered, and then promptly desert. Thus he drifted from one part of the sprawling army to another, changing his alias at every stop and developing a talent for masquerade that would later become a full-time profession. William Pinkerton, who was himself a young soldier in the Union Army, reported that Worth, after his first desertion and reenlistment, was "stationed for a time on Riker's island, N.Y. and from there he was conveyed by steamship to the James River in Virginia, where he was assigned to one of the New York regiments in the Army of the Potomac." Although the war convinced Worth of the futility of violence, his desertions were prompted by avarice rather than cowardice, and he repeatedly found himself in the thick of battle, including, according to Pinkerton, the Battle of the Wilderness in May 1864, an engagement scarcely less ferocious than the Battle of Bull Run.

Desertion was a lucrative but highly risky business. "On his third enlistment," according to one of his criminal associates, "he was recognized as a bounty jumper, and was in consequence sent, in company with others of his class, chained together, to the front of the Army of the Potomac." Once more, Worth somehow emerged unscathed; he promptly deserted and reenlisted again. There was clearly a limit to how long Worth could get away with changing regiments, so, in a remarkable act of brass cheek, he now decided to change sides. As a contemporary stated: "About this time General Lee of the Southern Army issued a proclamation to the effect that all Federal soldiers who would desert from the Federal armies to the Confederate lines, bringing their arms with them, would receive thirty dollars from the Confederate Government, and also receive a free pass to cross the frontier back into the United States by way of the adjoining States of West Virginia and Kentucky."

The aspiring crook, untroubled by niceties such as loyalty to

the Union cause, immediately "took advantage of these exceptionally liberal terms, and deserted one night in company with
some others, while doing picket duty." He did not linger in the
South and, having collected his thirty dollars, traveled back
"through the Confederate States on foot, in order to gain the
frontier of the Northern States." He would doubtless have repeated the process several more times, but before he could do so,
the war came to end, and so did the first phase of Worth's criminal career.

Worth was just one of thousands of young soldiers to find themselves at loose ends with the declaration of peace. William Pinkerton, who came to play a defining role in Worth's life and was to
become his most reliable chronicler, was another. Before long,
the two men would become adversaries on opposite sides of the
law, then grudging mutual admirers, then co-conspirators, and
finally, most bizarrely, friends. Their paths did not cross until the
war's end, but already they were dark and light reflections of each
other. Like the bright and tarnished pennies of Worth's childhood, they were similar in value but utterly different in luster.

The elder son of Allan Pinkerton, a Scotsman who had
founded the great detective agency in Chicago in 1850, William
Pinkerton was Worth's exact contemporary and had enrolled in
the Union Army at much the same time. Where Worth's early life
had been marked by material want and a complete absence of
ethical guidance, Pinkerton was brought up in well-to-do Chicago
under a regime of the strictest moral rules.

Allan Pinkerton was a superb detective but a brutal father and
a fantastic prig who hammered the virtues of honesty, integrity,
and raw courage into his children and employees with something
close to fanaticism. William did his best to live up to these exacting standards, but could never be quite good enough. Working
with his father, Abraham Lincoln's official spymaster, William
Pinkerton not only ran agents across the border into Confederate
territory but was also present on the first flight of an observation
hot-air balloon during the Civil War. Brave, bluff, and energetic,

Pinkerton was wounded in the knee by an exploding shell at the Battle of Antietam, having already "gained experience that was invaluable to him in the vocation which he was to follow." He attended Notre Dame College in Indiana for a year and then joined his father's fast-growing detective agency, where he soon established a reputation as a tireless lawman, one of the first and perhaps the greatest of the American detective breed. The Pinkertons chose as their symbol an unblinking human eye and the motto "The Eye That Never Sleeps," from which the modern term "private eye" has evolved.

The lives and subsequent careers of Worth and Pinkerton starkly demonstrate the moral duality that so obsessed Victorians. They shadowed and echoed one another, the detective playing Holmes to Worth's Moriarty, yet they were birds of a feather in their tastes, attitudes, and opinions. Both, to a remarkable degree, represented typical American stories of self-created men from immigrant stock, rugged in their opportunism, sturdy in their beliefs, but at opposite poles of conventional morality. Worth would have made an outstanding detective; Pinkerton, a talented criminal. The Civil War was a grimly leveling experience, but its end allowed the country to begin to rebuild and reinvent itself once more. The two men emerged from the battlefields determined, like thousands of others, to make their mark. They took diametrically opposed routes to that goal, but a lifetime later the bounty jumper and the war hero would end up, in a way neither could have predicted, as allies.

Pinkerton's had been a remarkable war, but then the official military record of Sergeant Adam Worth was also one of unblemished bravery and tragic heroism: a young and promising soldier mortally wounded while defending the Union at Bull Run. In truth, of course, he had spent the war dodging the authorities, swapping sides, abandoning the flags of two rival armies, and collecting a tidy profit along the way.

THREE

The Manhattan Mob

After the Civil War, Worth drifted, like so many veterans, to New York City, which by the mid-1860s was already one of the most concentratedly criminal places on earth. The politicians were up for sale, the magistrates and the police were corrupt, the poor often had little choice but to steal, while the rich sometimes had little inclination not to, since they tended to get away with it. Seldom has history conspired to assemble, on one small island, such a vivid variety of pickpockets, con men, whores, swindlers, pimps, burglars, bank robbers, beggars, mobsmen, and thieves of every description. Some of the worst professional criminals occupied positions of the greatest authority, for this was the era of Boss Tweed, probably the most magnificently venal politician New York has ever produced. Corruption and graft permeated the city like veins through marble, and those set in authority over the great, seething metropolis were often quite as dishonest as those they policed, and fleeced. As human detritus washed into lower Manhattan in the wake of the Civil War, the misery—and the criminal opportunities—multiplied. In 1866 a Methodist bishop, Matthew Simpson, estimated that the city, with a total population of 800,000, included 30,000 thieves, 20,000 prostitutes, 3,000 drinking houses, and a further 2,000 establishments dedicated to gambling. Huge wealth existed cheek-to-cheek with staggering poverty, and crime was endemic.

New York's most famously bent lawyers, William Howe and Abraham Hummel, wrote a popular account of the wicked city, entitled *In Danger, or Life in New York: A True History of the Great City's Wiles and Temptations,* which purported to be a warning against the perils of crime, published in the interests of protecting the unwary. But it basically advertised the easy pickings on offer, and provided a primer on the various methods of obtaining them, from blackmailing to cardsharping to safecracking. Howe and Hummel promised "elegant storehouses, crowded with the choicest and most costly goods, great banks whose vaults and safes contain more bullion than could be transported by the largest ship, colossal establishments teeming with diamonds, jewelry, and precious stones gathered from all the known and uncivilized portions of the globe—all this countless wealth, in some cases so insecurely guarded." The book was an instant best-seller and, according to one criminal expert, "became required reading for every professional or would-be law-breaker."

It was only natural that an ambitious and aspiring felon should make his way to New York and, once there, learn quickly. Determined to avoid returning to work as a mere clerk and hardened by his wartime experiences, Adam Worth took his place in the thieving throng. "On account of his acquaintance with bounty jumpers, he finally became associated with professional thieves and crooked people generally, and from that time on his career was one of wrong doing," Pinkerton glumly recounted.

Worth soon found himself in the Bowery, in Manhattan, an area of legendary seediness and home to a large and thriving criminal community which was divided, for the most part, into gangs: the Plug Uglies, the Roach Guards, the Forty Thieves, the Dead Rabbits, the Bowery Boys, the Slaughter Housers, the Buckaroos, the Whyos, and more. Many of these gangsters were merely exceptionally violent thugs whose criminal specialties extended no further than straightforward mugging, murder, and mayhem, often inflicted on one another and usually carried out under the influence of prodigious quantities of alcohol laced with turpentine, camphor, and any other intoxicant, however lethal, that happened to be on hand.

"Most of the saloons never closed. Or they did for just long enough to be cleaned out and then to begin afresh drinking, fighting, cursing, gambling, and the Lord only knows what," recalled Eddie Guerin, a useless crook but a successful memoirist who would eventually become Worth's friend and colleague. The three thousand saloons noted with distaste by Bishop Simpson and others in post-bellum New York included such euphonious establishments as the Ruins, Milligan's Hell, Chain and Locker, Hell Gate, the Morgue, McGurk's Suicide Hall, Inferno, Hell Hole, Tub of Blood, Cripples' Home, and the Dump. But if the nomenclature of the dives was indicative of the immorality therein, the names of the clientele were still more telling: Boiled Oysters Malloy; Ludwig the Bloodsucker, a vampire who had hair "growing from every orifice"; Wreck Donovan; Piggy Noles; the pirate Scotchy Lavelle, who later employed Irving Berlin as a singing waiter in his bar; Eat-em-up Jack McManus; Eddie the Plague; Hungry Joe Lewis, who once diddled Oscar Wilde out of $5,000 at banco; Gyp the Blood; the psychotic Hop-Along Peter, who tended, for no reason anyone could explain, to attack policemen on sight; Dago Frank; Hell-Cat Maggie, who filed her teeth to points and had sharp brass fingernails; Pugsy Hurley and Gallus Mag, a terrifying dame who ran the Hole-in-the-Wall saloon and periodically bit the ears off obstreperous customers and kept them in a pickling jar above the bar, "pour encourager les autres"; Big Jack Zelig, who would, according to his own bill of fare, cut up a face for one dollar and kill a man for ten; Hoggy Walsh, Slops Connally, and Baboon Dooley of the Whyos gang; One-Lung Curran, who stole coats from policemen; Goo Goo Knox; Happy Jack Mulraney, who killed a saloonkeeper for laughing at the facial twitch which led to his sobriquet; brothelkeepers Hester Jane the Grabber Haskins and Red Light Lizzie, and the unforgettable Sadie the Goat, a river pirate and leader of the Charlton

Street Gang, which occupied an empty gin mill on the East Side waterfront and terrorized farms along the Hudson River.

According to Herbert Asbury, whose 1928 *Gangs of New York* is probably the best book ever written on New York crime, "Sadie [the Goat] acquired her sobriquet because it was her custom, upon encountering a stranger who appeared to possess money or valuables, to duck her head and butt him in the stomach, whereupon her male companion promptly slugged the surprised victim with a slung-shot and they then robbed him at their leisure." (For reasons unknown but not hard to imagine, Sadie fell afoul of the formidable Gallus Mag of the Hole-in-the-Wall, who bit off her ear, as was her wont. But the story has a happy ending: the two women eventually became reconciled, whereupon gallant Gallus fished into her pickle jar, retrieved the missing organ, and returned it to Sadie the Goat, who wore it in a locket around her neck ever afterward.)

Sophie Lyons, the self-styled Queen of the Underworld, whose remarkable memoirs are a crucial source of information on Worth's life, was held by Asbury to be "the most notorious confidence woman America has ever produced." She eventually went straight, began writing her salacious and partly fabricated accounts of New York lowlife for the city newspapers, and ended up as America's first society gossip columnist.

Into this colorful and horrific world, Adam Worth slipped quickly and easily. At the age of twenty, now complete with his own criminal moniker, Little Adam became a pickpocket.

"Picking pockets has been reduced to an art here, and is followed by many persons as a profession," noted the author of *Secrets of the Great City* in 1868. "It requires long practice and great skill, but these, once acquired, make their possessor a dangerous member of the community." Sophie Lyons, who became Worth's close friend and sometime accomplice, described how Little Adam took to the apprentice criminal's art: "Like myself and many other criminals who later achieved notoriety in broader fields, he first tried picking pockets. He had good teachers and was an apt pupil. His long, slender fingers seemed just made for the delicate task of slipping watches out of men's pockets and purses out of women's hand-bags."

As an apprentice pickpocket, Worth found himself in an intensely hierarchical world. The lowest level of pickpocket was a "thief-cadger," inexperienced youngsters often virtually indistinguishable from beggars; of slightly more consequence were the "snatchers," who, as the name implies, made no attempt to avoid detection but simply grabbed and ran, or "tailers," who specialized in extracting silk handkerchiefs from tailcoat pockets. The most developed of the species was the "hook," also known as a "buzzer," for whom picking pockets was an art requiring considerable daring and manual dexterity. Nimble and inconspicuous, Worth began as a "smatter-hauler" or handkerchief thief, but soon the Civil War veteran graduated to a full-fledged "tooler," a master of the art of "dipping." Churches were particularly profitable hunting grounds, as were ferry stations, theaters, racecourses, political assemblies, stages, rat fights, and any other place containing large numbers of distracted people in close proximity.

While lone pocket-dipping could be profitable, the most successful pickpockets worked in gangs, and Worth's talents ensured that "it was not long before he had enough capital to finance other criminals." Teaming up with some like-minded fellows, Worth now established a dipping syndicate, with himself as principal coordinator, banker, and beneficiary. It was, proclaimed Lyons, "the first manifestation of the executive ability which was one day to make him a power in the underworld," a Napoleon of ne'er-do-wells.

The technique for team-dipping, or "pulling," was well established. A prosperous-looking "mark" is selected: he is then jostled or bumped by the "stall"; while the mark is thus distracted, the "hook" (sometimes known as the "mechanic") quickly rifles or "fans" his pockets, immediately passing the proceeds to a "caretaker" or "stickman," who then moves nonchalantly in another direction. Charles Dickens described the maneuver in *Oliver Twist*: "The Dodger trod under his toes, or ran upon his boot accidentally, while Charley Bates stumbled up against him behind: and in that one moment they took from him with extraordinary rapidity, snuff box, note-case, watchguard, chain, shirt-pin, pocket handkerchief, even the spectacle case." The "mark," in this case, was none other than Fagin himself, the paterfamilias of dippers.

With his efficient team of purse snatchers, Worth was fast becoming a minor dignitary in the so-called swell mob, as the upper echelon of the underworld was known, and according to Lyons he soon acquired "plenty of money and a wide reputation for his cleverness in escaping arrest." But no sooner had Worth's criminal career begun to blossom than it came to a sudden and embarrassing halt. Late in 1864, Worth was arrested for filching a package from an Adams Express truck and summarily sentenced to three years' imprisonment in Sing Sing, the notoriously nasty New York jail just north of the city, on the banks of the Hudson River.

Worth's brief incarceration for bounty jumping had not prepared him for the extravagant horror of the "Bastille on the Hudson." In 1825 the prison's first warden, a spectacular and inventive sadist by the name of Elam Lynds, remarked, "I don't believe in reformation of the adult prisoner . . . He's a coward, a willful lawbreaker whose spirit must be broken by the lash." In 1833 Alexis de Tocqueville described Sing Sing as a "tomb of the living dead," so silent and cowed were its inmates.

Clad in the distinctive striped prison garb instituted by Lynds, Worth was sent with the rest of the convicts to the prison quarries, where he was put in charge of preparing the nitroglycerin for blasting. Many years later, Worth recalled how he was instructed by the foreman to heat the explosive when it became cold and brittle in the freezing air. This he did, grateful for the chance to warm his hands, and was lucky not to be blown to pieces, for, as he frankly admitted, he "never had an idea at that time how dangerous it was." Teaching hardened criminals how to handle nitroglycerin was not perhaps the brightest move on the part of the authorities, as Worth's safecracking skills in later years so clearly proved.

The man who had slipped his chains on the Potomac, who had made a craft out of desertion, was not going to suffer Sing Sing a moment longer than necessary, even though the prison's guards, a breed of breathtaking brutality, had orders to shoot anyone attempting to escape. As he worked, Worth calculated the movements of the guards, and after only a few weeks of prison life, he dropped out of sight while the guard shift was changing. He hid inside a drainage ditch, which "discharged itself inside the railway tunnel." Under cover of night, according to a contemporary, "he managed to get a few miles down the river where there lay at a dock some canal boats," in one of which, freezing and covered in mud, Worth hid, and "had the satisfaction a few hours after that, of having himself transported to New York City by a tug boat, which came up to fetch the canal boat in which he took refuge." At dawn, as the tug approached its "lonely dock far up on the West side of the city," Worth clambered into the water and swam back to shore. "He managed, although having his prison clothes on, to get to the house of an acquaintance, where he was provided with a suit of clothes." He immediately plunged back into the protective anonymity of the Bowery.

Worth's later insouciance when recalling this escape belied what must have been a dreadful, if formative, experience. At barely twenty years of age, he had seen the worst the American penal system had to offer, and his contempt for authority was formidable. That Worth did not hesitate to plunge into a churning river at dead of night, clad in prison clothes and aware that apprehension might well mean death, reflected both his physical toughness and a growing faith in his own invincibility. So far from being reformed by his brief and unpleasant experience of prison, Worth concluded that the life of a "dip" did not offer sufficient rewards, given its perils, and the time had come to change direction, to up the stakes in his personal vendetta against society. Reuniting with some of his former gang, Worth began to expand his scope of operations to include minor burglaries and other property thefts as well as picking pockets. His "word was law with the little group of young thieves he gathered around him," remembered Sophie Lyons. "He furnished the brains to keep them out of trouble and the cash to get them out if by chance they got in. Every morning they would meet in a little Canal Street restaurant to take their orders from him—at night they came back to hand him a liberal share of the day's earnings."

So far, Worth's activities had gone no further than what might be called disorganized crime. Henceforth, he would tread more carefully, delegating often and putting himself at risk only when the rewards, or promise of adventure, were greatest. His strict dominance over the gang was the first illustration of a power complex that would grow more pronounced with age. Criminals, it is fair to say, are not the most intellectual of people. Indeed, the class as a whole tends to be characterized by fairly intense stupidity. Worth's highly intelligent approach to the business, and his ability to get results in the form of hard cash, was enough to ensure the obedience, even the reverence, of his underlings.

Solvent for the first time in his life, Worth was determined to beat the odds at every level, and this soon led him to New York's roulette wheels, gambling dens, and the faro tables—that extraordinarily chancy game that was once the rage of gamblers and has since virtually disappeared. Betting heavily in the burgeoning belief that the more he dared, the more fortune would smile, he began to live the life of a "sportsman," moving away from the grim Bowery dives to the brighter, more luxurious, but no less dissipated lights of uptown New York and the famously seedy glamour of the Tenderloin district.

Worth's native intelligence was not the only character trait to distinguish him from his fellow crooks. He was also notable for avoiding strong drink, at a time when alcoholism was endemic and heavy drinking virtually obligatory among the criminal classes. Perhaps still more strange, he regarded violence as uncouth, unnecessary, and, given his limited physical stature, unwise.

Of the 68,000 people arrested in New York in 1865, 53,000 were charged with crimes of violence. Yet Worth made it a rule that force should play no part in any criminal enterprise that involved him, a rule he broke only once in his life. His rejection of alcohol and violence was itself part of a need to control, not just himself, but those within his power. Crooks who drank or fought made mistakes, and for that reason he steered clear of the established gangs, which were often little more than roving bands of pickled hoodlums at war with each other.

Worth was not content merely to organize his minions; he needed to rule, regulate, and reward them as he clawed his way up through the underworld. A sober, resourceful, nonviolent crook marshaling his forces amid a troop of ignorant, drunken brawlers, Worth was also exceptional for the scope of his criminal aspirations, or, to put it another way, his greed. Sophie Lyons took note of his "restless ambition" as he began his ascent into the criminal upper classes.

One of America's senior crooks later recorded that "the state of society created by the war between the North and the South produced a large number of intelligent crooks" of varied talents, but in post-bellum New York bank robbers were considered an aristocracy of their own. James L. Ford, an expert on—by participation in—New York's seamy side, said in his memoirs: "Such operations as bank burglary were held in much higher esteem during the 'sixties and 'seventies than at present, and the most distinguished members of the craft were known by sight and pointed out to strangers." Allan Pinkerton, the father of Worth's future adversary, in his 1873 book *The Bankers, the Vault and the Burglars,* observed that "instead of the clumsy, awkward, ill-looking rogue of former days, we now have the intelligent, scientific and calculating burglar, who is expert in the uses of tools, and a gentleman in appearance, who prides himself upon always leaving a 'neat job' behind."

Worth's friend Eddie Guerin argued that "a successful bank sneak requires to be well-dressed and to possess a gentlemanly appearance." Sophie Lyons concurred, noting also that a certain amount of professional snobbery existed in the upper ranks of crime. "It was hard for a young man to get a foothold with an organized party of bank robbers, for the more experienced men were reluctant to risk their chances of success by taking on a beginner."

Without success, Worth sought acceptance in such established bank-robbing cliques as that of George Leonidas Leslie, better known as "Western George," which was responsible for a large percentage of the bank heists carried out in New York between the end of the war and 1884. Sophie Lyons first encountered Worth when he was "itching to get into bank work," specifically through her husband, Ned Lyons, a noted burglar. But the veteran crooks turned down all advances from the aspiring newcomer.

Worth needed a patron, someone to provide him with an entrée to the criminal elite. He found one in the mountainous figure of Marm Mandelbaum.

FOUR

The Professionals

Contemporary writers reached for superlatives when describing Fredericka, better known as "Mother" or Marm, Mandelbaum. "The greatest crime promoter of modern times," the "most successful fence in the history of New York," and the individual who "first put crime in America on a syndicated basis" are just a few of the plaudits she garnered in a long, unbroken career of dishonesty.

Marm's nickname was a consequence of her maternal attitude toward criminals of all types, for her heart was commensurate with her girth. She was an aristocrat of crime, but unlike the object of Worth's later affections—namely, Georgiana, Duchess of Devonshire—Marm Mandelbaum was no oil painting. "She was a huge woman, weighing more than two hundred and fifty pounds, and had a sharply curved mouth and extraordinarily fat cheeks, above which were small black eyes, heavy black brows and a high sloping forehead, and a mass of tightly rolled black hair which was generally surmounted by a tiny black bonnet with drooping feathers."

Like Worth, Fredericka had emigrated from Germany to the United States in her youth, arriving "without a friend or relative," but far from defenseless. Sophie Lyons, who adored Marm, noted that "her coarse, heavy features, powerful physique, and penetrating eye were sufficient protection and chaperone for anyone," adding unkindly (but no doubt accurately) that "it is not likely that anyone ever forced unwelcome attentions on this particular immigrant."

Soon after she got off the boat, the formidable Fredericka had fixed her beady eye on one Wolfe Mandelbaum, a haberdasher who owned a three-story building at 79 Clinton Street in the Kleine Deutschland section of Manhattan's East Side. A weak and lazy fellow, Wolfe was "afflicted with chronic dyspepsia." A few weeks of Fredericka's voluminous but easily digestible cooking persuaded him to marry her, and "Mrs Mandelbaum forever afterward was the head of the house of Mandelbaum."

While still nominally a haberdasher's, the property on Clinton Street was turned by Marm into the headquarters of one of the largest fencing operations New York has ever seen. She started by selling the "plunder from house to house," and in a few years had built up a vast business which "handled the loot and financed the operations of a majority of the great gangs of bank and store burglars." Warehouses in Manhattan and Brooklyn were used to hide the stolen goods, and the unscrupulous lawyers Howe and Hummel were on an annual retainer of five thousand dollars to ensure her continued liberty, principally through bribery, whenever "the law made an impudent gesture in her direction." Most of Marm's business was fencing, but she was not above financing other crooks in their operations and was even said to have run a "Fagin School" in Grand Street, not far from police headquarters, "where small boys and girls were taught to be expert pickpockets and sneak thieves." A few outstanding pupils even went on to "post-graduate work in blackmailing and confidence schemes."

Marm Mandelbaum is first listed in police records in 1862, and over the next two decades she is estimated to have handled between $5,000,000 and $10,000,000 worth of stolen property. Criminals adored her. As the celebrated thief Banjo Pete Emerson once observed, "she was scheming and dishonest as the day is long, but she could be like an angel to the worst devil so long as he played square with her." As the fame, fortune, and waistline of

Mrs., soon to be the widow, Mandelbaum (Wolfe's dyspepsia having returned with a vengeance) grew, so too did the extravagance of her life-style and her social ambitions. The two floors above her center of operations "were furnished with an elegance unsurpassed anywhere in the city; indeed many of her most costly draperies had once adorned the homes of aristocrats, from which they had been stolen for her by grateful and kind-hearted burglars." There Marm Mandelbaum held court as an underworld *saloniste*, and "entertained lavishly with dances and dinners which were attended by some of the most celebrated criminals in America, and frequently by police officials and politicians who had come under the Mandelbaum influence."

"I shall never forget the atmosphere of 'Mother' Mandelbaum's place," Sophie Lyons recalled wistfully, for here congregated not merely burglars and swindlers, but bent judges, corrupt cops, and politicians at a discount, all ready to do business. Such criminal notables as Shang Draper and Western George came to sit at Marm's feet, and she repaid their homage by underwriting their crimes, selling their loot, and helping those who fell afoul of the law. In a profession not noted for its generosity, Marm was an exception, retaining "an especial soft spot in her heart for female crooks" and others who might need a helping hand up the criminal ladder. Marm was an equal-opportunities employer and a firm believer that gender was no barrier to criminal success, a most enlightened view for the time, of which she was herself the most substantial proof. She did not, however, brook competition, and when one particularly successful thief called Black Lena Kleinschmidt stole a fortune, moved to Hackensack (more fashionable then than now), and began putting on airs and giving dinner parties, Marm was livid. She was thoroughly delighted when Black Lena was exposed as a jewel thief and jailed after one of her dinner guests noticed his hostess was wearing an emerald ring stolen from his wife's handbag a few weeks earlier. "It just goes to prove," Marm Mandelbaum sniffed, "that it takes brains to be a real lady."

At the time that Worth was desperately seeking a way into the criminal big leagues, Marm Mandelbaum was an established legend and arguably the most influential criminal in America. "The army of enemies of society must have its general, and I believe that probably the greatest of them all was 'Mother' Mandelbaum," observed Sophie Lyons, who had taken a shine to young Worth and probably introduced him into Marm Mandelbaum's charmed criminal circle.

Worth became a regular at the Mandelbaum soirées, and it was almost certainly under her tutelage that he made his first, disappointing foray into bank robbery. In 1866 Worth and his brother John broke into the Atlantic Transportation Company on Liberty Street in New York and spent several hours attempting to blow open the safe, before leaving in frustration as dawn broke. Lyons recounts his "great disgust" at the failed heist.

Undaunted, Worth, after a year of organizing some lesser thefts, and now working alone, pulled off his first major robbery by stealing $20,000 in bonds from an insurance company in his home town of Cambridge. Marm Mandelbaum, who could fence anything, from stolen horses to carriages to diamonds, obligingly sold them at a portion of their face value—giving Worth her customary ten percent and pocketing the rest. He was hardly made a rich man by the robbery, but it was a start, and the minor coup effectively "established him as a bank burglar" among his peers. Before long, Worth had gained a reputation as "a master hand in the execution of robberies," and stories of his "sang-froid" began to circulate in the underworld.

Worth seems to have delighted in sailing as close to the wind as he could, and with every near-escape his contempt for the forces of law and order was confirmed and amplified. As the detectives Eldridge and Watts later recounted: "Once, after robbing a jewelry store in Boston, this daring burglar slipped out of the front door, only to meet a policeman face to face. Without an instant of tremor, this man of iron nerve politely saluted the officer and stepped back to re-open the door and coolly call to his confederate within: 'William, be sure and fasten the door securely when you leave! I have got to catch the next car.' So, indeed, he did, after bidding the officer a pleasant good night, but he hopped off the car, a few blocks beyond the store, slipped back stealthily, signalled to his confederate and both escaped with their booty."

An avid pupil, Worth appears to have found in Marm Mandelbaum both an ally and a role model. The easy way she farmed out criminal work to others, her lavish apartments and social graces, were precisely the sort of things he had in mind for himself. Above all, it was perhaps Marm who taught the lesson that being a "real gentleman" and a complete crook were not only perfectly compatible but thoroughly rewarding. Marm's dinner table offered an atmosphere of illicit luxury, where superior crooks could enjoy the company of men and women of like lawless minds.

Two of Marm's guests in particular would play crucial although very different roles in Worth's future. The first was Maximilian Schoenbein, "alias M. H. Baker, alias M. H. Zimmerman, alias The Dutchman, alias Mark Shinburn or Sheerly, alias Henry Edward Moebus (according to the Pinkerton files)," but most usually alias Max Shinburn, "a bank burglar of distinction who complained that he was at heart an aristocrat, and that he detested the crooks with whom he was compelled to associate." For the next three decades, the criminal paths taken by Adam Worth and Max Shinburn ran in tandem. The two lawbreakers had much in common, and they came to loathe each other heartily.

Shinburn was born on February 17, 1842, in the town of Ittlingen, Württemberg, where he was apprenticed to a mechanic before emigrating to New York in 1861. Styling himself "The Baron" from early in life, Shinburn later actually purchased the title of Baron Schindle or Shindell of Monaco with "the judicious expenditure of a part of his fortune." Aloof, intelligent, and insufferably arrogant, the Baron cut a wide swath through New York low society. Even the police were impressed.

Inspector Thomas Byrnes of the New York Police Department considered him "probably the most expert bank burglar in the country," and Belgian police offered this description of the soigné, multilingual felon: "Speaks English with a very slight Ger-

man accent. Speaks German and French. Always well dressed. He
has a distinguished appearance with polished manners. Speaks
very courteously. Always stays at the best hotels." Shinburn's looks
were striking; he had "small blue penetrating eyes, long, straight
nose, moustache and small imperial, both of brownish color
mixed with gray, moustache twisted at the ends, pointed chin . . .
at times wears a full beard and sometimes a moustache and chin
whisker, in order to hide from view the pronounced dimple in
chin." His numerous encounters with the law and a youthful taste
for dueling had left him with numerous other identifying features.
After one arrest, a police officer noted these with grisly exacti-
tude: "on back of left wrist . . . pistol shot wounds running parallel with each other and near the deformity in right leg . . .
pistol or gunshot wound on left side . . . several small scars that
look like the result of buck shot wounds; scar on left side of abdo-
men, appearing as though shot entered in the back and came
through . . ." Shinburn's fraudulent aristocratic claims were full
of holes, and so was the rest of him.

His criminal notoriety sprang principally from the invention
of a machine which he maintained could reveal the combination
of any safe: "a ratchet which, when placed under the combination dial of a safe, would puncture a sheet of calibrated paper
when the dial stopped and started to move in the opposite direction. He would repeat this process until he had the entire combination." According to other police sources, "his ear was so acute
and sensitive that by turning the dial he could determine at what
numbers the tumblers dropped into place."

With his mechanical training, Shinburn also perfected a set of
light and powerful safecracking tools which he was prepared to
sell to others for a price. "Shinburn revolutionized the burglar's
tools and put them on a scientific basis," recorded Sophie Lyons.
The better to perfect his safe-busting technique, the Baron "for
some time took employment under an assumed name in the
works of the Lilly Safe Co. [whose] safes and vaults were considered among the best and most secure." But not for long. Leaving
a trail of empty safes in his wake, Shinburn was eventually penal-

ized through his own competence and the Lilly safe "came into such disrepute that the company was forced into liquidation."

"The safe I can't open hasn't been built," Shinburn once boasted to Sophie Lyons.

By the time Worth encountered Shinburn in the mid-1860s, the latter had developed a name for himself as a man of importance among the bank-robbing fraternity by cleaning out the Savings Bank in Walpole, New Hampshire. Worth was ambivalent about the Baron. He admired his dandified dress and envied his reputation, but found his braggadocio and his air of superiority unbearable.

Far more to Worth's taste was another dark luminary of the underworld, and a Mandelbaum protégé, Charles W. Bullard, a languid and alluring criminal playboy better known as Piano Charley. The scion of a wealthy family from Milford which could trace its ancestry to a member of George Washington's staff, Bullard "had a good common school education," inherited a large fortune from his father while still in his teens, and had gone to the bad immediately and extravagantly. Having squandered his inheritance, Bullard briefly tried his hand in the butcher's trade but gave up the occupation and "devoted his ability to the robbing of banks and safes," for which he inherited a taste from his grandfather, who was said to be a burglar "in a small way." Bullard's "dissipation and a restless craving for morbid excitement made him a 'fly' [skilled] crook" and later an uncommonly daring and wily burglar, and in New York low society he was considered "one of the boldest operators that has ever handled a jimmy or drilled a safe."

"Bullard is a man of good education," recorded one admiring police report, "speaks English, French and German fluently, and plays on the piano with the skill of a professional." Raffish, refined, and handsome, with a wispy goatee and limpid eyes, Bullard had three passions in life, each of which he indulged to the limit: women, music, and gambling. Through constant practice on his baby grand, Piano Charley had developed such "delicacy of touch" that he could divine the combination of a safe simply by spinning the tumblers, while his piano sonatas could reduce the hardest criminal to tears and lure the most chaste woman into bed. "An inveterate gamester," perennially short of funds, often outrageously drunk, but always charming, Bullard was a romantic figure in the New York underworld. Under the benign eye of Marm Mandelbaum, he and Worth established an immediate rapport.

Piano Charley Bullard's crime sheet included jewel theft, train robbery, and jailbreaking. Early in 1869 he teamed up with Max Shinburn and another professional thief, Ike Marsh, to break into the safe of the Ocean National Bank in New York's Greenwich Village after tunneling through the basement. The venture was said to have realized more than $100,000, almost all of which ended up in Shinburn's pockets. "The robbers were nearly a month at the work, and the bank was ruined by the loss," the police reported.

Later that year, on May 4, Bullard had again conspired with Marsh to rob the Hudson River Railroad Express as it trundled from Buffalo in upstate New York along the New York Central Railroad to Grand Central Station. Knowing that the Merchant's Union Express Co. used the train to transport quantities of cash, with the connivance of a bribed train guard they "concealed themselves in the baggage car . . . in which the safe was stored and rifled it of $100,000." Bullard and Marsh then leaped off the train in the Bronx with the cash and negotiable securities stuffed into carpet bags. The guard was found bound and apparently unconscious, with froth dripping down his chin—this turned out to be soap, and the guard was immediately arrested.

The Pinkertons, whose reputation had expanded to the point where they were called in on almost every significant robbery, had traced the thieves to Toronto and found Ike and Charley living in high style in one of the city's most expensive hotels. After a long court battle, Bullard was extradited to the United States and jailed in White Plains, New York, to await trial. Using what little money remained to them, the Bullard family hired an expensive lawyer to defend their wayward son. Like Worth, Piano Charley never passed up a criminal opportunity and arranged for one of his many women friends to extract $1,000 (the entire fee) from his attorney's pocket "as he was returning to New York on the train." It was almost certainly Marm Mandelbaum who decided that Piano Charley, whose music-making was such a popular feature of her dinner parties, should not be allowed to languish in jail. Worth, already a close friend, was selected for the job of getting him out, along with Shinburn. It was the first and only time the two men would work together.

One week after he was imprisoned, Bullard's friends dug through the wall of the White Plains jail and set both Ike and Charley free, whereupon the crooks promptly returned to New York City for a long, and in Bullard's case staggeringly bibulous, celebration. The Baron was immensely pleased with himself. "Shinburn used to take more pride in the way he broke into the jail at White Plains, New York, to free Charley Bullard and Ike Marsh, two friends of his, than he did in some of his boldest robberies," Sophie Lyons recounted.

But the immediate effect of the successful jail break was to cement the burgeoning friendship between Bullard and Worth. Piano Charley had the sort of effortless élan and cultural veneer that Worth so deeply admired and sought to emulate. On the other hand, Worth was clever and calculating, qualities which the suave but foolish Bullard singularly lacked.

They decided to go into partnership.

FIVE

The Robbers' Bride

The Boylston National Bank in Boston was a familiar sight from Worth's youth. The rich burghers of Boston believed their money was as safe as man could make it behind the grand façade of the bank, an imposing brick edifice at the corner of Boylston and Washington streets in the heart of the city. According to Sophie Lyons, Worth "made a tour of inspection of all the Boston banks and decided that the famous Boylston Bank, the biggest in the city, would suit him." Max Shinburn would later claim to have had a hand in planning the robbery, but there is no evidence his expertise was either required or requested. Indeed, Shinburn's exclusion from this "job" may have been the original source of the enmity between him and Worth. Ike Marsh, Bullard's rather dim Irish sidekick in the train-robbery caper, was brought in on the heist, which was, like all the best plans, perfectly straightforward.

Posing as William A. Judson and Co., dealers in health tonics, the partners rented the building adjacent to the bank and erected a partition across the window on which were displayed some two hundred bottles, containing, according to the labels mucilaged thereon, quantities of "Gray's Oriental Tonic." "The bottles served a double purpose," the Pinkertons reported, "that of showing his business and preventing the public looking into the place." Quite what was in Gray's Oriental Tonic has never been revealed, since not a single bottle was ever sold.

After carefully calculating the point where the shop wall adjoined the bank's steel safe, the robbers began digging. For a week, working only at night, Worth, Bullard, and Marsh piled the debris into the back of the shop, until finally the lining of the · vault lay exposed.

"To cut through this was a work of more labor," *The Boston Post* later reported. "So very quiet was the operation that the only sound perceptible to the occupants of adjoining rooms was like that made by a person in the act of putting down a carpet with an ordinary tack hammer. The tools applied were [drill] bits or augers of about an inch in diameter, by means of which a succession of holes were drilled, opening into each other, until a piece of plate some eighteen inches by twelve had been removed. Jimmies, hammers and chisels were used as occasion required for the purpose of consummating the nefarious job." In the early hours of Sunday, November 21, 1869, Worth wriggled through the hole, lit a candle inside the bank safe, and surveyed the loot. "The treasure was contained in some twenty-five or thirty tin trunks," which Worth now handed back out to his accomplices one by one. "The trunks were pried open, their contents examined, what was valuable pocketed and what was not rejected." As dawn broke over Boston, the three thieves packed the swag into trunks labeled "Gray's Oriental Tonic," hailed a carriage to the station, and boarded the morning train to New York.

At nine o'clock on Monday morning, fully twenty-four hours later, bank officials opened the safe and were "fairly thunderstruck at the scene which met their gaze." The entire collection of safe-deposit boxes, and with them the solid reputation of the Boylston National Bank of Boston, was gone.

THE BOSTON POST
TUESDAY MORNING, NOVEMBER 23, 1869
Yesterday morning Boston was startled. There is no discount on the word. A robbery of such magnitude as that of the Boylston

National bank—amounting to from $150,000 to $200,000, in fact—which was perpetrated sometime between Saturday afternoon and Monday morning, is something quite out of the ordinary run in the municipal affairs of this city, and nearly if not quite too much for ready credence. But the robbery stands indisputably a robbery; and, taken as an exploit, considered in its aspect as a job, as one artist considers the work of another, it is one of the most adroit which it has ever been the fortune or misfortune of the press to record. The almost uniformly successful manner in which this class of burglary has been carried on throughout the country during the past few months may lead to the inference that the party or parties in the present case will escape the arm of the law, although it is true that the prime originator is as well known as any criminal need to be. The infinite cleverness with which his operations have been conducted from beginning to end, indicate him to be a man of no ordinary ability, and it seems very probable that, having so far succeeded in eluding police, he may escape altogether. Should he do so, he will find himself a richer man, even, than he had perhaps anticipated . . . The name by which the criminal is known is William A. Judson.

The Boston Post, barely able to suppress its admiration, was conservative in its estimate. The Pinkertons believed that "nearly one million dollars in money and securities" had been stolen by Worth and his accomplices, a sum confirmed by Sophie Lyons. In the premises of William A. Judson and Co. police found "a dozen bushels or more of bricks and mortar," about thirty disemboweled tin trunks, and two hundred bottles of Gray's Oriental Tonic. For a week the Boylston Bank robbery was Boston's sole topic of conversation. "Everyone continues to talk about the robbery of Boylston Bank," *The Boston Post* reported gloomily a few days later. "But nobody—or nobody that has anything real to say—communicated anything new. On all sides it is admitted to be a very neat job, all the way from the Oriental Tonic clear through to the Bank safe."

It was indeed Worth's neatest job to date. Yet the very success of the venture, the huge amount of money involved, and the stated determination of the authorities to track down the thieves (spurred on by a reward of twenty percent of the haul) left Worth and Bullard with an obvious dilemma. To stay in New York and attempt to "work back the securities" in the traditional way was to invite trouble, since even Marm Mandelbaum would think twice about fencing such hot property. They could take the cash, abandon the securities, and head west, where the frontier states offered obscurity and where the law was, at best, partially administered. But Worth and Bullard, with their taste for expensive living and sophisticated company, were hardly the stuff of which cowboys are made, and the prospect of spending their ill-gotten gains in some dusty prairie town where they might be murdered for their money was less than appealing.

A more attractive alternative was to make for Europe, where extradition was unlikely and where wealthy Americans were welcomed with open arms and few questions were asked. Big Ike Marsh had already decided to take early retirement with his share of the loot. He returned to Ireland via Baltimore and Queenstown, and was received in Tipperary with grand ceremony, a local boy made good or, rather, bad. In the end, the Pinkertons reported, "he gambled, drank and did everything he should not have done, and eventually returned to America for more funds." Poor Ike was arrested while trying to rob another bank in Wellesborough, sentenced to twenty years' solitary confinement in eastern Pennsylvania, and ended his life "an old man, broken down in health, dependent on the charity of friends."

Worth and Bullard rightly surmised that the Pinkertons would be called in after such a large robbery. Indeed, just a week after the bank heist, the detectives had already traced the thieves and their spoil to New York, and documents in the Pinkerton archives indicate that Bullard and Worth, thanks to some loose talk in criminal circles, were the prime suspects. The news that they were wanted men rapidly reached the fugitives themselves. "Those damned detectives will get on to us in a week," Bullard warned

Worth. "I don't want to be playing the Piano in Ludlow Street [jail]."

Acting quickly, the pair dispatched the stolen securities to a New York lawyer, possibly either Howe or Hummel, with instructions to wait a few months and then sell back the bonds for a percentage of their face value and forward the proceeds in due course. At the time, this was an accepted method for recovering stolen property, winked at by the police, who often themselves helped to negotiate the return of the securities, to the advantage of both the owners and the thieves. "All [the robbers] need do is to make 'terms' which means give up part of their booty, and then devote their leisure hours to plan new rascalities," noted *The Boston Sunday Times,* one of the few organs to raise objections to this morally dubious collusion. "There must be something radically wrong in the police system of the country when such transactions of [sic] these can repeatedly take place."

Worth and Bullard then hurriedly packed the remaining cash into false-bottom trunks, bid farewell to Marm Mandelbaum, Sophie Lyons, and New York, and took the train to Philadelphia, where the S.S. *Indiana,* bound for England, was waiting to take them, in style, to Europe and a new life. For this they would need new names, and in high spirits in their first-class cabin the pair discussed how they would reinvent themselves. Bullard elected to call himself Charles H. Wells and adopt a new persona as a wealthy Texan businessman. Worth's choice of alias was inspired.

That year had seen the untimely and much-lamented demise, on June 18, of Henry Jarvis Raymond, the founder-editor of *The New York Times.* Senator, congressman, political conscience, and stalwart moral voice of the age, Raymond had succumbed to "an attack of apoplexy" at the age of forty-nine and his passing was the occasion for some of the most solemn adulation ever printed. A single obituary of the great man described him as patriotic, wise, moderate, honorable, candid, generous-hearted, hard-working, frugal, conscientious, masterly, modest, courageous, noble, consistent, principled, cultivated, distinguished, lucid, kind, just, forbearing, even-tempered, sincere, moral, lenient, vivacious, enterprising, temperate, self-possessed, clear-headed, sagacious, eloquent, staunch, sympathetic, kindly, generous, just, suave, amiable, and upright. *The New York Times* ended its adjective-sodden paean to its founder by declaring that Raymond was "always the true gentleman . . . in fact, we never knew a man more completely guileless or whose life and character better illustrated the virtues of a true and ingenuous manhood." The newspaper's journalistic rivals agreed. *The Evening Mail* noted: "He was always a gentleman . . . true to his own convictions." *The Telegram* called him "one of the brightest and most gentlemanly journalists the New World has ever produced," while *The Evening Post* also noted "he was a gentleman in his manners and language." The grave in exclusive Green-Wood Cemetery of this man of integrity, this ethical colossus, was marked with a forty-foot obelisk in honor of his achievements and virtue. "Contemporary opinion has rarely pronounced a more unanimous, more cordial or more emphatic judgment than in the case of the departed chief of *The New York Times,*" that paper declared.

Worth, already hankering after respectability to go with his new wealth, had read these breathless accolades (few could avoid them), and the repeated references to the late Mr. Raymond's "gentlemanliness" had lodged in his mind. Appropriating the name of such a man would be a rich and satisfying irony, not least because Worth, an avid collector of underworld gossip, may have known that the great moral arbiter of the age had himself led a double life of which his readers and admirers possessed not an inkling. Officially, on the night of his death, the worthy editor had "sat with his family and some friends until 10 o'clock, when he left them to attend a political consultation; and his family saw no more of him until he was discovered, about 2:30 the next morning, lying in the hallway unconscious and apparently dying." The truth was rather more dubious, for in reality Henry Jarvis Raymond, man of virtue, had died of a sudden coronary while "paying a visit to a young actress."

Adam Worth now decided that, whether Henry J. Raymond resided in the heaven reserved for great men or in the purgatory of the adulterer, he did not need his name anymore. On the voyage to England he adopted this impressive alias (replacing Jarvis with Judson, in memory of the name he used for the Boston robbery) and kept it for the rest of his life. It was one of Worth's wittiest and least recognized thefts.

Early the next year, two wealthy Americans swaggered into the Washington Hotel in Liverpool and announced they would be occupying the best rooms in the house indefinitely, since they were on an extended business trip. The pair were dressed in the height of fashion, with frock coats, silk cravats, and canes. Two Yankee swells fresh off the boat and keen for entertainment, Mr. Henry J. Raymond, merchant banker, and Mr. Charles H. Wells, Texan businessman, headed for the hotel bar to toast their arrival in the Old World. Mr. Raymond drank to the future; Mr. Wells, as usual, drank to excess.

Behind the bar of the Washington Hotel, as it happened, their future was already waiting in the highly desirable shape of Miss Katherine Louise Flynn, a seventeen-year-old Irish colleen with thick blond hair, enticing dimples in all the right places, and a gleam in her eye that might have been mistaken for availability but was probably rather closer to raw ambition. This remarkable woman had been born into Dublin poverty and had fled her humble origins at fifteen, determined even at that early age that hers would be a very different lot. Hot-tempered, vivacious, and sharp as a tack, Kitty craved excitement and longed for travel, cultured company, and beautiful things. Specifically, she understood the value of money, and wanted lots of it.

Mercenary is an unkind word. Kitty Flynn was simply practical. The squalor and deprivation of her early years had left her with a healthy respect for the advantages of wealth and a determination to do whatever was necessary, within reason, to obtain them. In her present situation this involved enduring, and blowing back, the good-natured and flirtatious chaff of the hotel's regular drinkers. But when these same patrons overstepped the mark and were foolhardy enough to suggest that Kitty might like to consider some more intimate after-hours entertainment, they were left in no doubt, by way of a stream of vivid Irish invective, that the barmaid considered herself destined for rather greater delights than they could offer. The steamer from Dublin to Liverpool had been the first stage in Kitty's planned journey to fortune and respectability; her current job as a hotel barmaid was but a way station along the route. The arrival of Messrs. Raymond and Wells opened up new and enticing vistas. Knights in shining armor were few and far between in Liverpool, and two wealthy Americans with money to burn were clearly the next best thing.

"She was an unusually beautiful girl—a plump, dashing blond of much the same type [as the actress] Lillian Russell was years ago," recounted Sophie Lyons. She was, like all the best barmaids, buxom. Her blond hair curled into ringlets reaching to the middle of her back and were arranged in such a way that they appeared to have exploded from the back of her head. Her features were delicate, her nose snubbed, her lips full, but it was her eyes, startlingly blue and slightly distended, that tended to reduce her admirers to putty. In certain lights she looked like nothing so much as an exceptionally attractive frog—which was only appropriate, since Kitty would shortly embark on a career in which, as in the fairy tale, she would be kissed by a variety of princes, charming and otherwise. In the best surviving portrait of her (a colored version of a picture by the French photographer Félix Nadar), Kitty Flynn is wearing an expression that hovers between flirtatious and simply wicked.

That expression had an electric effect on the newest arrivals to the Washington Hotel in January 1870. It was never clear which of the two felons first lost his heart to Kitty, but that both did so, and deeply, was accepted as fact by all their contemporaries. Sophie Lyons is characteristically blunt on the matter: "Bullard and Raymond [she uses Worth's real name and his alias interchangeably] both fell madly in love with her."

For the next month Kitty was besieged by these two very different suitors—the one small, dapper, almost teetotal, and intense; the other tall, lugubrious, and, as the Pinkertons put it, "inclined to live fast and dissipate." Suddenly Kitty found herself being wined and dined on a scale that was lavish beyond her most extravagant dreams and that stretched Liverpool's resources to the limit. In spite of their amorous rivalry, the two crooks remained the closest of friends as they swept Kitty from one expensive candlelit dinner to another, as Bullard serenaded her and Worth did his best to persuade her that he, rather than his exotic partner, represented the more solid investment. "The race for her favor was a close one," records the inquisitive Lyons, "despite the fact that Bullard was an accomplished musician [and] spoke several languages fluently." Finally Kitty gave in to Piano Charley's entreaties and agreed to marry him. Yet for Worth she always reserved a place in her heart and, for that matter, her bed.

Kitty Flynn became Mrs. Charles H. Wells one spring Sunday. The ceremony was performed at the Washington Hotel and a large and curious crowd of Liverpudlians turned out to watch the toast of the city being driven away in a coach and four by her handsome American husband. Adam Worth was the best man and, Lyons reports, "to his credit it should be said that the bridal couple had no sincerer well-wisher than he." Worth had good reason for his equanimity, since, although Kitty had agreed to marry Bullard, she seems to have been only too happy to share her favors with both men. If Bullard objected to this arrangement, he did not say so. Indeed, he was hardly in a strong moral position to do so, for, unbeknown to Kitty, he was married already. It was not until some time later that Kitty discovered Bullard had a wife and two children in America. Conceivably, Worth used this information to blackmail Bullard into sharing his wife. But that was hardly his style, and as the relationship between the two crooks remained entirely amicable, it seems more likely that the accommodating Kitty Flynn, the broad-minded Bullard, and Worth, who never let convention get in the way of his desires, simply found a *ménage à trois* to be the most convenient arrangement for all parties.

While Kitty and Charley enjoyed a short honeymoon, Worth passed his time profitably by robbing the largest pawnshop in Liverpool of some £25,000 worth of jewelry. The Pinkertons later gave a full account of the theft:

> He looked around for something in his line, and found a large pawnshop in that city which he considered worth robbing . . . he saw that if he could get plaster impressions of the key to the place he could make a big haul. After working cautiously for several days he managed to get the pawnbroker off his guard long enough to enable him to get possession of the key and make a wax impression: the result was that two or three weeks later the pawnbroker came to his place one morning and found all of his valuable pieces of jewelry abstracted from his safe, the store and vaults locked, but the valuables gone.

The robbery caused a minor sensation in Liverpool, where crime was rife but large-scale burglary rare. The Pinkerton account was written many years later, but seems to be largely accurate. Most of the bonds stolen from the Boylston Bank had now been "worked back" to their owners and the bank had therefore decided to call off the costly detective agency, rightly concluding that the thieves were now beyond reach. But the Pinkertons continued to keep tabs, via a network of informers, on American criminals living abroad. In the coming years their information on Adam Worth and his activities as Henry Raymond grew increasingly detailed.

Robbing pawnbrokers was easy game, and Worth was becoming restless for more challenging sport in new pastures. Kitty was also eager to find more glamorous surroundings, and Bullard did not care much where he went so long as there was money and champagne in plentiful supply, and a piano near at hand. Worth showered Kitty with expensive gifts (including his stolen gems), bought her expensive clothes, and connived and encouraged her in her determination to leave her lowly origins behind. With his stolen money, Worth sought to shape and remake Kitty just as he was reinventing himself. But grimy Liverpool was no place for a would-be lady, and the great shared fraud required a brighter backdrop.

At the end of 1870 the trio packed up their belongings, including the still considerable remnants of the Boylston Bank haul, checked out of the Washington Hotel, and headed for Paris, where the war between France and Prussia, the siege of Paris, and now the lawlessness of the Commune had rendered the French capital a particularly enticing venue for a brace of socially ambitious crooks and their shared moll.

SIX

An American Bar
in Paris

Paris furnished stark evidence of that peculiar brand of double standards Worth would absorb and adapt: under the Second Empire of Napoleon III (1852–70), a woman could be arrested for smoking in the Tuileries Gardens, but personal immorality was almost *de rigueur*. The surface was magnificent, but corruption and libertinism were rampant. Entrepreneurs speculated, hedonists indulged, and English visitors railed about the "badness of the morals." But the great gay façade of the Second Empire came tumbling down with the crushing of the French armies by the Prussian military machine.

The crippling siege of Paris, starting in 1870, was followed by the Commune, that remarkable and violent political experiment in which an insurrectionary countergovernment seized power, imposing a form of collective leadership and such radical policies as free speech, compulsory education, and cooperative ownership of businesses. The Commune lasted just three months, from March to May 1871, when the Communards were brutally crushed by the government's forces. More than twenty thousand Parisians were killed in the ensuing repression.

Worth, Bullard, and Kitty traveled slowly south through England and then tarried in London to await the outcome of the bloody events taking place in Paris, before making their way across the Channel at the end of June 1871. They found a city exhausted and partially in ruins, disordered and vulnerable, but still glamorous in her devastation: a perfect spot from which to coordinate fresh criminal activities, with plenty to satisfy the trio's extravagant tastes. As a later historian observed, "France is an astonishingly resilient patient and now—shamefully defeated, riven by civil war, bankrupted by the German reparation demands and the costs of repairing Paris—she was to amaze the world and alarm her enemies by the speed of her recovery." Here, Worth saw, were rich pickings. His namesake Charles Frederick Worth, the great couturier, had "bought up part of the wreckage of the Tuileries to make sham ruins in his garden"; now another Worth would also make his mark in the remnants of the devastated city, where, for the time being at least, the authorities were far too busy washing blood off the streets and piecing together the capital to pay much attention to the newly arrived triumvirate.

In later years Kitty would claim, unconvincingly, that she had no idea her husband and his partner were notorious international criminals. It must have been clear from the outset that her charming spouse and his friend were hardly respectable businessmen, since they paid for everything in wads of cash, did no work whatever, and never discussed anything approaching legitimate business. Kitty's part in the next stage of the drama indicates that she was involved in their criminal activities up to her shell-like ears.

With the remains of the money from the Boston robbery, Bullard and Worth purchased a spacious building at 2, rue Scribe, a part of the Grand Hotel complex near the Opéra, under the name Charles Wells, and rented large and comfortable apartments nearby. The new premises, christened the American Bar, were refurbished, according to William Pinkerton, in "palatial splendor" at a cost of some $75,000 (the equivalent, amazingly, of more than $300,000 today) with oil paintings, mirrors, and expensive glassware. American bartenders were imported to mix exotic cocktails of a type popular in New York but "which were, at that time, almost unknown in Europe."

The American Bar was a two-pronged operation. The second floor of the building was fashioned into a sort of clubhouse for visiting Americans, complete with the latest editions of U.S. newspapers and pigeonholes where expatriates could pick up their mail. "Americans were cordially invited to use it as a meeting house," a spot where they could gather and enjoy American drinks, a quiet, sober, and entirely respectable establishment, In the upper floors of the house, however, the scene was rather different. Here Worth and Bullard set up a full-scale, well-appointed, and completely illegal gambling operation. By "importing from America roulette croupiers and experts on baccarat," they gave the den a cosmopolitan sheen, but it was Kitty who turned out to be the principal lure, for "her beauty and engaging manners attracted many American visitors."

The Pinkertons' agents in Europe began keeping a watch on the place almost from the day the American Bar opened, and declared that it was fast becoming "the headquarters of American gamblers and criminals who here planned many of their European crimes." Yet even the forces of the law were dazzled by the ample charms of the hostess. "Mrs. Wells was a beautiful woman," the detectives later reported, "a brilliant conversationalist dressed in the height of fashion: her company was sought by almost all the patrons of the house."

While gorgeous Kitty presided, a vision in silk and ringlets, the affable Bullard played the piano and Worth carefully monitored the clientele. An alarm button was discreetly installed behind the bar "which the bar-tender touched and which rung a buzzer in the gambling rooms above whenever the police or any suspicious party came in." Within seconds, Worth could render the upper stories of 2, rue Scribe as quiet and respectable as the lower ones. The Paris police "made two or three raids on the house, but never succeeded in finding anything upstairs, except a lot of men sitting around reading papers, and no gambling in sight." Worth also bribed the local police to tip him off when a raid might be expected.

The American Bar, the first American-style nightclub in Paris, was an instant success, a gaudy magnet in the ravaged and weary city, and the Parisians were "astonished by its magnificence. The place soon became a famous resort and was extensively patronized, not only by Americans, but by Englishmen: in fact, by visitors from all over Europe." Businessmen, bankers, tourists, burglars, forgers, convicts, counts, con men, and counterfeiters were all equally welcome to enjoy the products of Worth's superb chef, sip a cocktail, or, if they preferred, repair upstairs, where the delightful Kitty would help them lose their money at the gambling tables with such grace that they almost always came back for more. Word soon spread through the underworld that the American Bar was the best place in Europe to make contact with other criminals, arrange a job, or simply hide out from the authorities.

The elegant and pompous Max Shinburn became a regular patron. Like his former associates, the Baron had found it necessary to relocate to the Continent rather suddenly. Some two years earlier, to his intense embarrassment, he had been publicly arrested at an expensive hotel in Saratoga where he was "masquerading as a New York banker" and had been charged with the New Hampshire robbery committed in 1865. Police found $7,000 in stolen bonds in his pockets and, on searching his New York address, discovered "a complete workshop for the manufacture of burglar's tools and wax impressions of keys." Sentenced to ten years, the Baron had managed to escape from prison in Concord after nine months—a breakout considered "one of the most dashing and skillful planned in criminal history"—and then fled to Europe, where his safecracking skills were still in great demand. "With the money he made from his various burglaries, Shinburn is said to have left the country with nearly a million of dollars," the Pinkertons reported.

Shinburn had settled in Belgium, purchased an estate and an interest in a large silk mill, and formally declared himself to be the Baron Shindell, which "nobody cared to dispute." His cosmopolitan existence included frequent visits to Paris and the American Bar, where the Baron liked to patronize his former criminal colleagues and spend "his money with an open hand." Worth resented the intrusion of the "overbearing Dutch pig," as he called him, somewhat inaccurately, but tolerated his presence for the sake of Piano Charley, who still owed the Baron a debt for springing him from jail.

Sophie Lyons, who often traveled to Europe on business (entirely criminal in nature), was another familiar face at the American Bar, and soon a motley cluster of crooks, many of them familiars from the criminals' New York days, began to orbit around the Paris club at a time when professional American bank robbers were migrating across the Atlantic in increasing numbers. "I could name a hundred men who got a good living at it [bank robbery] and then came over to Europe to try their luck. France used to be a particularly happy hunting ground," wrote Worth's friend Eddie Guerin.

Out of the criminal flotsam eddying around Paris, an unscrupulous and unsavory bunch, Worth would eventually forge one of the most efficient and disciplined criminal gangs in history. Fresh from clearing out the First National Bank of Baltimore, for example, came Joseph Chapman and Charles the Scratch Becker.

Chapman was a habitual lawbreaker with a long beard and soulful eyes who had, according to a contemporary account, "but one vice—forgery; and one longing passion—Lydia Chapman," his wife and "one of the most beautiful women the underworld of the 1870s had ever known." Becker, alias John Blosh, was a neurotic Dutch-born forger of wide renown who was said to be able to reproduce the front page of a newspaper with such uncanny verisimilitude that when he was finished no one, including Becker, could tell the original from the fake. Pinkerton considered him "the ablest professional forger in the world."

Other patrons at the American Bar included Little Joe Elliott (alias Reilly, alias Randall), a rat-like burglar of intensely romantic inclinations ("a great fellow for running after French girls," Worth called him); Carlo Sesicovitch, a Russian-born thug with an ugly temper but an uncanny knack for disguise; his Gypsy mistress Alima; and several more criminals of note.

But by no means all the clientele at the American Bar were

rogues and miscreants. Many were simply visiting businessmen, "swell Americans who were not aware that the keepers of this saloon were American professional bank and safe burglars," and tourists keen for some nightlife and a flutter at the roulette or faro tables. Their number even included some who had fallen victim to the club's owners in earlier days.

According to one police report, the American Bar "was visited by Mr. Sanford of the Merchant's Express Co. while he was in Paris, but Mr. Sanford did not know until his return to New York that Wells was the man Bullard, who had robbed the company of $100,000" back in 1868. It was also said that visiting officials from Boston's Boylston Bank spent an enjoyable evening at the club, little suspecting how the mahogany card tables and expensive furnishings had been financed.

For three years the American Bar prospered and the peculiar *ménage à trois* of the owners continued, amazingly enough, without a hitch. Kitty Flynn, her telltale Irish brogue now quite evaporated, was becoming the gracious grande dame she had always hoped to be, even if half her admirers were thieves and con men. Bullard was happily consuming American cocktails in vast quantities, beginning his day when he opened his eyes in the late afternoon and ending it when he closed them, around dawn, usually face-down on the ivories of the club piano. "In the gay French capital he soon became a man of mark as a gambler and roué"— one pair of American detectives recorded—which was all Piano Charley had ever really wanted to be. Worth was also contented enough yet strangely restless. Serving drinks was profitable, while the gambling den was a standing invitation to show his hold over fate. But the Paris operation was hardly the grand criminal adventure he saw as his destiny. The demimonde thronging his card tables were glittering and amusing, to be sure, but he had more ambitious plans for himself and Kitty than merely the life of an upscale croupier and a club hostess.

In the winter of 1873, a most unpleasant blot suddenly appeared on the horizon of the merry trio when William Pinkerton, the scourge of American criminals, wandered nonchalantly into the American Bar and ordered a drink. No man put the wind up the criminal fraternity more effectively than William Pinkerton. The detective had become a stout and florid man, whose ponderous frame belied his astonishing energy and his unparalleled talent for hunting down criminals. Pinkerton's face was known to just about every crook in America, and so was his record as a man who had "waged a ceaseless war on train and bank holdup robbers and express thieves who infested the Middle West after the close of the Civil War." The direct precursor of the modern FBI, the Pinkerton Agency was gaining international respect as a detective force, thanks in large part to William Pinkerton's phenomenal energy. The West's most notable outlaws knew only too well the discomfort of having the Pinkertons on their trail. "It was not unusual in those bandit chasing days for William Pinkerton to be days in the saddle, accompanied by courageous law officers searching the plains and hills of the Middle West tracking these outlaws to their hideouts," one of the detective's early admirers recalled. A man of great bonhomie and charm, Pinkerton could also be utterly ruthless, as many criminals had discovered at the expense of their liberty and, in some instances, their lives. "When Bill Pinkerton went after a man he didn't let up until he had got him, if it cost him a million dollars he didn't mind," recalled Eddie Guerin.

Many years later Worth, in an interview with William Pinkerton, feigned nonchalance when recalling the detective's unexpected and unwelcome arrival at the American Bar. "We were rather troubled at what had brought you to the club," Worth said. Frantic would have been a more accurate description.

Worth recognized the burly detective at once and, opting as ever for the brazen approach, offered to buy him another drink. Pinkerton blithely accepted, knowing full well he was enjoying the hospitality of the Boylston Bank robber. It was a strange encounter between the arch-criminal and the man who had already spent five years, and would spend the next twenty-five, trying to put him in prison. They chatted awhile on the subject of mutual acquaintances, of which they had many on both sides of the law, until

Pinkerton announced that he ought to be getting along. The two men shook hands, without ever having needed to introduce themselves.

The moment Pinkerton left the premises, Worth summoned Piano Charley and a visiting ruffian known as Old Vinegar and set out into the rue Scribe to follow the American detective. "There was no intention to assault you," Worth later assured Pinkerton. "We just wanted to get a good look at you." Pinkerton was fully aware he was being tailed, and after leading the trio through the streets of Paris, he suddenly turned on them. Piano Charley, his nerves frayed with drink, "nearly dropped dead" with fright and the three bolted in the opposite direction. "Old Vinegar went into hiding for weeks," Worth later remarked with a laugh.

He might not admit it, but Pinkerton's surprise visit had rattled him. Worth was only partially reassured to discover, from a corrupt interpreter with the French police by the name of Dermunond, that the detective was not in pursuit of him and his partners but was in the pay of the Baltimore Bank and had his sights set on Joseph Chapman, Charles Becker, and Little Joe Elliott. Indeed, the informant warned, Pinkerton was already preparing extradition papers with the French authorities. Worth sent the message to his colleagues that they were in mortal danger and should on no account come to the bar. A few days later Pinkerton, accompanied by two French detectives, walked into another of the gang's favored dives, a dance hall called the Voluntino, where Worth was dining with Little Joe Elliott. Worth happened to catch sight of the brawny detective as he came through the door, and rightly assuming the "entrances were guarded well," he bundled Elliott upstairs to a private room, opened the window, and, holding Joe's hands, dropped him fifteen feet into a courtyard below. "Joe made the drop alright and got up and hobbled away," Worth recalled, but it had been another unpleasantly close escape.

The gang got a welcome, if only temporary, reprieve when Pinkerton was called away to help investigate a series of forgeries perpetrated on the Bank of England. Pinkerton accurately identified the forgeries as the work of brothers Austin and George Bidwell, "two well known American forgers and swindlers" who also happened to be two of Worth's regulars. While the Pinkertons were busy chasing the Bidwells (Austin was arrested in Cuba, George in London), Joe Chapman and the others slipped out of Paris and went into hiding.

By now Worth had concluded that the days of the American Bar were numbered. During his brief visit to the club, Pinkerton had correctly guessed that some sort of early-warning system was in place to alert the gamblers upstairs of an impending raid. On his return to the United States, he informed the Paris police of this hunch and began pestering the Sûreté to do something about the nest of foreign criminals flourishing in the rue Scribe. Even the French police, sluggish through bribery, were propelled into action when Pinkerton provided detailed case histories of Worth, Bullard, Shinburn, Chapman, Becker, Elliott, Sophie Lyons, and many of the bar's other regulars. The following May, Worth was again tipped off by Dermunond to an imminent raid and managed to remove all evidence of gambling just minutes before the police burst in. But the attentions of the Sûreté were proving bad for business, particularly among the jittery criminal clientele. "The respectable people did not patronize it, and it soon went to the dog," Pinkerton recorded triumphantly.

With profits declining, Worth decided to improve matters in his traditional way, by stealing a bag of diamonds from a traveling dealer who had carelessly left them on the floor as he stood at a roulette table. It was a spur-of-the-moment larceny—Worth cashed a check for the diamond salesman and distracted him while Little Joe Elliott crept under the table and substituted a duplicate bag for the one containing the diamonds. The theft netted some £30,000 worth of gems, and it was Worth himself "who insisted on the police being called in and the place searched from top to bottom. But he did not suggest that they look at a near-by barrel of beer, at the bottom of which reposed the precious jewels." In spite of this elaborate bluff, the diamond dealer demanded that the club manager be arraigned on a charge of robbery. At a preliminary hearing Henry Raymond, playing the part of an enraged foreign businessman whose good name was being dragged in the mud, demanded that he be allowed to cross-examine his accuser and so confused the merchant by bombarding him with angry questions that the poor man was unable to remember clearly whether he had had the bag with him in the first place. Worth was released, but the theft, while lucrative enough, sealed the fate of the American Bar.

"The robbery startled all Paris, and was the means of attracting suspicion to the house [which] lost prestige and soon went to pieces." Pinkerton had been recruiting international support in his bid to close the American Bar; most notably, Inspector John Shore of Scotland Yard in London. Shore had been receiving reports for some time of a clutch of criminals operating out of Paris, and he, too, began to demand that the Paris police shut down the establishment once and for all. Through his spies, Worth learned that the English policeman was putting pressure on the French authorities, and his alarm redoubled. It was the first time Shore and Worth had crossed swords.

"The place was finally raided by the police," Pinkerton reported, but this time the Sûreté were not going to be beaten by Worth's alarm system. "The bar-tender was seized as soon as they entered, and rushing upstairs, they found the gambling in full blast." Worth and Kitty, by lucky chance, were not in the building at the time, but "Wells [Bullard] and others [a pair of unfortunate croupiers] were arrested and charged with maintaining a gambling house, but were admitted to bail." Bullard, the nominal owner of the bar, skipped bail and fled to London, leaving Worth and Kitty to sort out what remained of the business.

Worth later told Pinkerton that he had already decided the bar would "never again be a success the way he wanted it," and the building was sold to an "English betting man or bookmaker named Jack Ballentine," who kept it going for two more years before the American Bar was finally closed.

Pinkerton later wrote, on Worth's authority, that "the ruction which I kicked up was the means of ruining Bullard in Paris, driving him out, breaking up the bar and sending, as he termed it, all of them on the bum." But rather than resenting Pinkerton's rude intrusion into his affairs, Worth seems to have admired Pinkerton's detective efforts. "Afterwards when we met in London [he said] that he had always fancied me and found that I was a man who kept his own counsel and that he had always felt a kindly feeling towards me," Pinkerton wrote. They might be on opposite sides of the law, but the thief and the detective had developed a healthy respect for each other's talents which would eventually blossom into a most unlikely friendship.

So far from being "on the bum," Worth was still a wealthy man. The breaking up of the American Bar simply closed one chapter in his life. He increasingly craved, for himself and the aspiring Kitty, if not genuine respectability, then at least its outward trappings, and at the age of just thirty-one he could afford them.

There was really only one destination for a man of social and criminal ambition, and that was London, center of the civilized world, where the gentlemanly ideal had been elevated to the status of a religion, abounding with wealth and therefore felonious opportunity.

Victorian Britain was reaching the pinnacle of its greatness, and smugness. "The history of Britain is emphatically the history of progress," declared the intensely popular writer T. B. Macaulay at the dawn of the Victorian era. "The greatest and most highly civilised people that ever the world saw, have spread their dominion over every quarter of the globe." A similar note of patriotic omnipotence was struck earlier in the century in an essay by the historian Thomas Carlyle: "We remove mountains, and make seas our smooth highway, nothing can resist us. We war with rude nature, and by our restless engines, come off always victorious, and loaded with spoils." For a crook at war with the natural order, such heady recommendations were irresistible. Huge spoils, and the social elevation they brought with them, were precisely what Worth had in mind.

Piano Charley was already across the Channel, operating under the cover of wine salesman and steadily drinking a large proportion of his supposed wares. Worth, Kitty, and the rest of the gang packed up what was left from the American Bar—the chandeliers, brass fittings, and oil paintings—and merrily headed back across the Channel to the great English metropolis.

The upper floors of what was once Worth's gambling den are now the bedrooms of the Grand Hôtel Intercontinental, one of the most expensive hotels in Paris. Still more appropriately, given the next phase of Worth's life, the door to number 2, rue Scribe now leads into "Old England," a chain of stores where one can still buy all the appurtenances, from monogrammed riding boots to top hats, of a pukka English gent.

SEVEN

The Duchess

By coincidence, or fate, in 1875 Gainsborough's portrait of Georgiana, Duchess of Devonshire, was also about to make a triumphant public reappearance in the English capital after long years in hiding.

Georgiana Spencer (pronounced George-ayna) was just seventeen in 1774 when she married William Cavendish, fifth Duke of Devonshire. The duke, one of the richest and oddest men in England, was also, by popular assent, one of the luckiest, for the eldest daughter of John, first Earl of Spencer, was considered the most beautiful and accomplished woman in the nation. Poets praised her to the heavens, the Prince of Wales fawned on her, and painters vied with one another to depict her charms. Her detractors were equally emphatic, portraying her as an aristocratic slattern whose hats were too tall and whose morals were too low. Everyone had an opinion on Georgiana.

Thomas Gainsborough began his celebrated painting of the duchess around the year 1787, and it was no easy commission, even for the great portraitist. There was something about the pucker of her lips, the hint of a smirk, playful and suggestive, that defied reproduction. Or perhaps it was simply the captivating presence of the sitter herself, "then in the bloom of youth," that baffled the master. Gainsborough's frustration mounted as he drew and redrew Georgiana's mouth, trying to catch that fleeting, flirting expression, "but her dazzling beauty, and the sense which he entertained of the charm of her looks, and her conversation, took away that readiness of hand and happiness of touch which belonged to him in ordinary moments." Finally he lost his temper. "Drawing his wet pencil across a mouth which all who saw it considered exquisitely lovely, he said, 'Her Grace is too hard for me!' "

Gainsborough painted Georgiana, as far as we know, three times: as a child in 1763, a delightful painting "giving promise even then of her remarkable charms," which now hangs in the collection of Earl Spencer at Althorp, England; and a second time in 1783, for a full-length portrait which is now in the National Gallery in Washington, D.C. In the latter painting the duchess is draped around a column in a classically demure posture, but appears a trifle seedy and "greenish," in Walpole's words, possibly after some hard nights on the town. By the time he came to paint her a third time, both artist and sitter had become yet more celebrated and Gainsborough was plainly determined to capture Georgiana's very allure. Hence his frustration with the duchess's elusive mouth.

He persevered, and the resulting portrait was a masterpiece, seeming to distill Georgiana's delectable expression. Her left eyebrow is arched and winning, a tantalizing half-smile plays across her lips, and beneath the huge cocked hat her glance is slyly mischievous. In one hand she grasps a blooming rose and in the other, pinched suggestively between thumb and forefinger, a ripe pink rosebud. Georgiana had not proved too hard for him after all, and the finished product was devastating, frankly sexual yet strangely coy.

She had been painted many times before and would be painted again, by the greatest artists in the land, including Reynolds, Romney, and Rowlandson. As one critic noted in 1901: "More portraits exist of Georgiana than of any other English lady of the eighteenth century." Yet, for grandeur and impudence, personality and piquancy, none matched Gainsborough's painting of the duchess in full bloom.

There is no evidence that the portrait ever hung in the ducal home of the Devonshires at Chatsworth, but at around the time that Georgiana became pregnant by her lover, the future Prime Minister Charles Grey, the lovely Gainsborough painting abruptly and inexplicably vanished. Perhaps the duke, although himself a serial adulterer, found the portrait of his wife with her coquettish smile and arched brow too powerful a reminder of her affair, and banished it from his presence.

In the autumn of 1841, three years before Adam Worth came into the world, the London art dealer John Bentley was making one of his annual forays through England's Home Counties in search of rare paintings. An astute art connoisseur, Bentley owned a thriving dealership in the metropolis and was much in demand as a valuer of Old Masters. Over the course of his career, for pleasure and profit, he had made it a rule to spend a few weeks every year wandering through the small villages and towns of England, making inquiries as to whether any of the local residents had works of art or other antiques they wished to value or sell. Many a bargain was to be found in this way, and the practice enabled Bentley to shed, for a while, the cares and strains of metropolitan life in a bucolic and nomadic quest for art.

In this particular year, Bentley's enjoyment of his annual outing had been sharply diminished by a stinking cold which had settled both on his chest, making him cough and sneeze, and on his mind, making him grumpy. On the morning of September 17, Bentley's ill humor and streaming nose were suddenly forgotten when his researches brought him to the small sitting room of one Anne Maginnis, an elderly English schoolmistress long retired. For there, above Mrs. Maginnis's fireplace, grimy but unmistakable, was the portrait of Georgiana, Duchess of Devonshire, by Thomas Gainsborough. How the widow Maginnis, who had little money and even less interest in fine art, managed to get her hands on Gainsborough's famous missing portrait has never been adequately explained. According to one account, the old lady "spoke of it as the portrait of a relative of hers, and that it was bought, not as the picture of the beautiful Duchess, but merely as 'a Gainsborough.' " Bentley never inquired too closely into how she had obtained the great picture, partly out of tact, but largely because he had immediately identified the missing duchess, knew a sucker when he saw one, and wanted to buy it cheap.

No one can be sure what had happened to the painting in the intervening years. One biographer quotes the Reverend Henry Bate as referring to two Gainsborough portraits of the duchess, "one of which Lady Spencer has, the other, we think, is in Mr Boothby's possession." One possibility is Charles Boothby-Skrymshire, also known as Prince Boothby, a man of fashion so named on account of his egregious social climbing and his tendency to "abandon friends as soon as he met people of higher social position or rank." He was believed to be a close friend of the Devonshires and may have obtained the picture when the duke decided he no longer wanted it. Prince Boothby committed suicide on July 27, 1800, whereupon his "effects were dispersed." Another candidate for the elusive "Mr Boothby" is Sir Brooke Boothby of Ashbourne Hall, just twenty miles from Chatsworth, a scholar, poet, friend of Rousseau and Charles James Fox, satirist and art collector who owned at least one other portrait of the duchess as well as a crayon drawing and was acquainted with his ducal neighbors. Sir Brooke may have sold the Gainsborough in 1792 when he suddenly ran out of money. Whichever Boothby had briefly owned the *Duchess*, the portrait had vanished until it cropped up again in Mrs. Maginnis's tiny cottage under Bentley's knowing and excited gaze. The elderly woman plainly had no idea what the painting was, or what it was worth, for in a singular act of vandalism some years earlier she had cut off the Duchess's legs just above the knee, shortening the painting to three-quarters of its original size and consigning Georgiana's feet to the fire. Henry James would criticize the "very wooden legs" in Gainsborough's portraits, but that was hardly a reason for burning them and Mrs. Maginnis's brainless surgery left the portrait out of balance: Georgiana seems almost overpowered by her vast hat. But even in these sadly reduced circumstances, Bentley recognized Gainsborough's *Duchess*, admired her still-saucy smile, and scented a bargain.

Many years later Bentley's grandson, one Sigismund Goelze, explained what had happened, recalling his grandfather's discovery in a letter to *The Times*: "It was then hanging in her sitting-room, over the chimney piece, and, knowing that originally the picture was painted full-length, he asked her how it was that it only showed to the knees. The old lady told him that she had cut it down to fit the position it then occupied, and added that she had burnt the piece which she had cut off."

Although Bentley could not be certain that this was indeed the *Duchess*, his expert's hunch told him to take a gamble. The widow Maginnis, while no expert in matters artistic, knew the value of money and was, moreover, an experienced haggler. After some lively negotiations lasting several hours, the old lady agreed to let the art dealer take the painting away on the basis that he knew a man who might pay as much as £70 for it. Bentley was careful not to mention whom the picture portrayed, for even thirty-five years after her death Georgiana's name could only increase the expectations of an impoverished English schoolmistress.

On October 6, Mrs. Maginnis wrote:

> Sir, I am obliged by your prompt attention to the disposal of the picture, and will take 70 for it, ready money, if the gentleman will give it, as I feel assured you will make the most you can of it.
>
> Hoping you are in better health than when I last saw you,
> I remain, Sir, your obedient servant,
> Anne Maginnis

In the end, Bentley managed to persuade Mrs. Maginnis to let him keep the portrait for the sum of £56, one of the most advantageous deals he ever made. According to his grandson, Bentley "never had the slightest doubt as to the genuineness of the picture; and to an artist it is obviously impossible for any copyist to success fully reproduce the swift, spontaneous touch of the greatest master of female portraiture." The dealer carried the painting to London, where he cleaned it up and proudly displayed the *Duchess* to his admiring friends. "The picture remained in my grandfather's possession for some time, and my mother still remembers it hanging in the dining room of her old home in Sloane Street," Goelze wrote.

Bentley subsequently agreed to sell the *Duchess* to his friend and fellow connoisseur, a silk merchant named Wynn Ellis— "characteristically declining to take any profit, so I have been told," Goelze reported. "Mr Bentley was the intimate friend and adviser of most of the great collectors during the early years of the late reign; but he made it a rule never to receive any remuneration for his services in assisting to form collections of pictures, a habit which I fear must in these days seem curiously Quixotic. The reason he gave was that in this way only could he prove his advice to be absolutely disinterested."

Wynn Ellis (probably the painting's fifth owner) started out in business in 1812 as a "haberdasher, hosier and mercer" and ended up as owner of the largest silk business in London and a man of immense wealth, excellent taste, and profound views. As a Member of Parliament for Leicester and a Justice of the Peace in Hertfordshire, where in 1830 he purchased a large estate called Ponsborne Park, Ellis advocated the repeal of the Corn Laws and considered himself an advanced liberal. But his most trenchant views happened to address a pastime dear to Adam Worth's heart, for Wynn Ellis "had an intense dislike of betting, horse-racing and gambling." Ellis did not gamble on anything, and least of all on the great paintings which he purchased with his grand fortune. John Bentley, on the other hand, was a most canny art dealer who did not scruple to extract a tough bargain from an elderly schoolmistress. So, whatever his grandson's claims and the demands of friendship, it would have been far more characteristic of the man had Bentley charged Ellis a small fortune for the painting. Sadly, we will never know how much profit Bentley made on his investment of £56, for the silk manufacturer—like other, later owners of the portrait—flatly declined to say what he had paid for it and allowed the rumor to circulate uncontradicted that he spent just 60 guineas on the purchase. Ellis sent the painting to be engraved by Robert Graves of Henry Graves & Co., and the result, simply identified as Gainsborough's *Duchess of Devonshire,* was published on February 24, 1870.

Ellis owned one of the finest art collections in England, and the great Gainsborough now took a prominent place in it. Did Wynn Ellis know for sure that "the painting which had been mutilated to hang above a foolish old woman's smoke-grimed mantel shelf was . . . a pearl of rarest price"? Some, subsequently, had their doubts. "There was . . . a very general belief among those interested in art matters, that not a few of the pictures [in the Wynn Ellis collection] bearing the names of distinguished English painters were copies or imitations." Had Wynn Ellis been too hasty in declaring the painting to be Gainsborough's Duchess of Devonshire? "Though a great lover of art he was not an infallible judge," one critic observed, "and it is recorded that his discovery that three imitation Turners had been foisted upon him at great prices led directly to his death"—an event which took place on January 8, 1875. Ellis was eighty-six years old and had amassed a fortune, it was estimated, little short of £600,000. His 402 paintings, along with "watercolour drawings, porcelain, decorative furniture, marbles &c.," were left to the nation. The trustees of the National Gallery selected some forty-four Old Masters, as directed in Ellis's will, and the rest of the vast collection was put up for auction. Gainsborough was then considered a modern artist and so the painting, too, was offered for sale by the auction house of Messrs. Christie, Manson & Woods.

After years in mysterious obscurity, Gainsborough's *Duchess* was about to make her first public appearance in nearly a century, and tales of the charming Georgiana and her piquant history began to circulate once more in London's salons. The auction was set for May 6, 1876, and suddenly the duchess was all the rage again: where the Georgians had fallen in love with the rumbustious woman herself, the Victorians were about to be smitten by Georgiana's portrait.

EIGHT

Dr. Jekyll and
Mr. Worth

To mark the first stage of his transformation from the raffish boulevardier of the rue Scribe to the worthy gentleman of London, Adam Worth established himself, Kitty, and Bullard in new and commodious headquarters south of the Thames, using the remaining profits from the sale of the American Bar and the stolen diamonds. Alerted by the Pinkertons and the Sûreté, Scotland Yard was already on guard and soon sent word to Robert Pinkerton, brother of William and head of the Pinkerton office in New York, that the resourceful Worth "now delights in the more aristocratic name of Henry Raymond [and] occupies a commodious mansion standing well back on its own grounds out of the view of the too curious at the west corner of Clapham Common and known as the West Lodge."

Bow-fronted and imposing, the West, or Western Lodge was built around 1800 and had previously been home to such notables as Richard Thornton, a millionaire who made his fortune by speculating in tallow on the Baltic Exchange, and more recently, in 1843, to Sir Charles Trevelyan: precisely the sort of social connections Worth coveted. The rest of the gang, including Becker, Elliott, and Sesicovitch, lived in another large building leased by Joe and Lydia Chapman at 103, Neville Road, which Worth helped to furnish with thick red carpets and chandeliers.

Worth almost certainly knew that Scotland Yard was watching him, but since he entertained a low opinion of the British police in general and Inspector John Shore in particular, the knowledge seems to have worried him not a bit. With a high-mindedness that was becoming characteristic, Worth made no secret of his opinion that Shore was a drunken, womanizing idiot and declared him to be "a big lunk head and laughing stock for everybody in England [who] knew nobody but a lot of three card monte men and cheap pickpockets." He had come a long way in his own estimation since he, too, had been a lowly pickpocket on the streets of New York.

But while Worth was beginning to take on airs, styling himself as an elegant man about town, and while he set about laying the foundations for a variety of criminal activities, the original threesome was beginning to fall apart. Back in October 1870, Kitty had given birth to a daughter, Lucy Adeleine, who would be followed, seven years later, by another, named Katherine Louise, after her mother. The precise paternity of Kitty's daughters has remained rather cloudy, for obvious reasons. Kitty herself may not have known for sure whether Bullard or Worth was the real father of her girls—they may have shared them, one each, as they did everything else—but most of their criminal associates simply assumed that the children were Worth's, as he seems to have done himself. William Pinkerton believed that Worth had simply taken over his partner's conjugal rights when Bullard became too alcoholic to oblige. "Bullard, alias Wells, became very dissipated; his wife, in the meantime, had given birth to two children, daughters, who were in reality the children of Adam Worth," the detective stated.

More irascible and introverted with every drink, Bullard was no longer the carefree, dashing figure Kitty had fallen for at the Washington Hotel in Liverpool. He would vanish for long periods in London's seamier quarters and then return, crippled with guilt and hangover, and play morosely on the piano for hours. To make matters worse, Kitty had learned of Bullard's preexisting marriage and his children by another woman. Though she had few qualms about sharing her favors with two men, Kitty was furious when she discovered Bullard was not only a depressing drunk but also a bigamist.

Aware of Kitty's restlessness yet hoping to keep her by dint of greater riches, Worth was now laying the groundwork for the most grandiose phase of his criminal career. In addition to the Clapham mansion, with its "tennis courts, a shooting gallery, and a bowling green," he also took apartments in the still more fashionable district of Mayfair, renting a large, well-appointed flat at 198, Piccadilly for £600 a year. The apartment was just a few hundred yards up the street from Devonshire House at number 74, where the duchess once entertained on a lavish scale, and is now the Bradford & Bingley Building Society—precisely the sort of business Worth would once have had no hesitation in robbing. From here, with infinite care, Worth began masterminding a series of thefts, forgeries, and other crimes.

Using his most trusted associates, he would farm out criminal work, usually on a contract basis and through other intermediaries, to selected men (and women) in the London underworld. The crooks who carried out these commissions knew only that the orders were passed down from above, that the pickings were good, the planning impeccable, and the targets—banks, railway cashiers, private homes of rich individuals, post offices, warehouses—had been selected by a master organizer. What they never knew was the name of the man at the top, or even of those in the middle of Worth's pyramidal command structure. Thus, on the rare but unavoidable occasions when a robbery went awry, Worth was all but immune, particularly when the judicious filtering of hush money down through the ranks of the organization ensured additional discretion at every level. Ever the control fanatic, Worth established his own form of "omertà" by the force of his personality, rigid attention to detail, strict but always anonymous oversight of every operation, and the expenditure of a portion of the profits to ensure, if not loyalty, then at least silence. He was happy to entertain senior underworld figures, knowing, like a mafia godfather, that their survival depended on discretion as much as his, but the lesser felons who were his main source of income never knowingly saw his face. Before long, the Piccadilly pad became an "international clearing house of crime."

Worth's phenomenal success in these years is perhaps best described by the frankly admiring assessment of the Pinkertons, who considered him "the most remarkable, most successful and most dangerous professional criminal known to modern times." In an official history published many years later, the detectives recalled that "for years he perpetrated every form of theft—check forging, swindling, larceny, safe cracking, diamond robbery, mail robbery, burglary of every degree, 'hold ups' on the road and bank robbery—with complete immunity . . . His luxurious apartment at 198 Piccadilly, where he received in lavish style . . . became the meeting place of leading thieves of Europe and America. His home became the rendezvous for noted crooks all over the world, especially Americans, and he became a clearing house or 'receiver' for most of the big robberies perpetrated in Europe. In the latter 70's and all through the 80's, one big robbery followed after another; the fine 'Italian hand' of Adam Worth could be traced, but not proven, to almost every one of them."

As another contemporary recorded: "Crimes in every corner of the globe were planned in his luxurious home—and there, often, the final division of booty was made." A particular specialty of Worth's gang was stealing registered mail from the strongboxes carried by train and in the cross-Channel steamers. "One robbery followed another in quick succession . . . from two to five million francs were abstracted from the mails in this way." To initiate these robberies, Worth relied on his trusted compatriots, preferring reliable American crooks to the more fickle British variety. Finding recruits was not hard, for, as one recorded, "the West End was full of Americans, bank robbers, safe smashers, forgers, con men and receivers." Many years later Worth offered this opinion of the British criminal classes: "There were some men among the Englishmen who were really staunch, loyal fellows and could do good work and take a chance, but the majority of them were a lot of sticks."

The key figures of the Worth gang included the forgers Joe Chapman and Charles "the Scratch" Becker, Carlo Sesicovitch, the bad-tempered Russian, and Little Joe Elliott, whenever he could be persuaded to stop chasing chorus girls. To their number was added the imposing figure of Jack Junka Phillips, a vast and vastly stupid burglar, so named on account of his habit of carrying quantities of junk in his coat pockets. He was the only English crook to be admitted to the inner circle, a decision Worth would live to regret. Combining ignorance and treachery in almost equal degrees, Junka was a terrifying figure with a prognathous chin, long mutton-chop whiskers, and a face that might have been carved out of Parmesan cheese. A former wrestler, he was well over six feet, with a ferocious visage and colossal strength. Junka could carry even the largest safe on his back, and the safe could then be broken open at leisure. His daunting appearance made an excellent deterrent to the overinquisitive. There is a hilarious photograph in the Pinkerton archives of Junka, under arrest some years later, in full evening dress, tied to a post. Like a criminal Samson, Junka is straining at his bonds, his eyes screwed up in fury. The Pinkertons, with rare understatement, labeled the image "An unwilling photograph."

The scope of Worth's operations was increased considerably by the purchase of a 110-foot yacht, requiring, it was later said, "a crew of twenty-five," which he equipped lavishly and then used to ferry his criminal cohorts on a series of foreign expeditions. He named the vessel *The Shamrock,* in honor of his Irish love.

In 1874 the gang set off for South America and the West Indies and in a single operation they looted $10,000 from a safe in a warehouse in Kingston, Jamaica, before slipping back out to sea. "This last exploit would have ended in his capture by a British gunboat which pursued him for twenty miles had his yacht not been a remarkably speedy craft," said Lyons, who was apparently aboard at the time. The Colonial police in Kingston sent a report of the robbery to the Pinkertons and Scotland Yard. "Inspector Shore agrees with me this must be Adam Worth," William Pinkerton wrote to his brother in New York. The hunch was accurate enough, but without proof they were powerless to pin him down.

The yearning for respectability, for gentlemanly rank, was arguably the single strongest motivation in Victorian society; stronger, even, than the lust to acquire money, which was, for many Victorians and certainly for Worth, simply a means to that end. As the philosopher Herbert Spencer noted: "To be respectable means to be rich." It was an age of immense snobbery at every level, of intense social consciousness, but also upward (and downward) mobility. A man could raise his position in the hierarchy, through work, wealth, or good fortune, and by the governing precepts of the day, he should. "Now that a man may make money, and rise in the world, and associate himself, unreproached, with people once far above him," wrote John Ruskin some years earlier, "it becomes a veritable shame to him to remain in the state he was born in and everybody thinks it is his DUTY to try to be a 'gentleman.'"

Defining what it took to be a gentleman at the various levels of society was trickier, since, as Anthony Trollope observed in his *Autobiography,* any attempt to do so was doomed to failure, even though everyone would know what was meant by the term. One historian has written that a Victorian gentleman was "expected to be honest, dignified, courteous, considerate and socially at ease; to be disdainful of trade and . . . to uphold the tenets of 'noblesse oblige.' A gentleman paid his gambling debts, did not cheat at cards and was honourable towards ladies"—all of which qualities Worth displayed to the full, with the sole exception of the first: honesty. Added to this was the general perception that the less obvious industry a man expended and the greater his expenditure, the higher his rank on the social scale. As far as his neighbors and noncriminal associates could tell, Henry Raymond did not a hand's turn of work and spent money at a rate that might have been suspicious had it not been so thoroughly satisfying to the Victorian sense of priorities. As Oscar Wilde remarked: "It is only shallow people who do not judge by appearances." Worth built himself a shell of glittering wealth and possessions to hide his humble beginnings and crimes, and he remained a sober, even punctilious figure, laying on a lavish dance but watching his creation from one remove, forever an outsider, a prototype for Fitzgerald's Jay Gatsby.

With extraordinary ease he slipped into the life of an English gentleman, hosting grand dinner parties in the Mandelbaum tradition in his Piccadilly apartment and his Clapham mansion, both of which were now equipped with "costly furniture, bric-a-brac and paintings," as well as rare books and expensive china. He mixed as easily with men and women of wealth and fashion as he did with the denizens of London's underworld, for, as the head of Scotland Yard's Criminal Investigation Department, Sir Robert Anderson, later acknowledged, "he was a man who could make his way in any company," effortlessly switching roles from the rich man of leisure to the criminal mastermind. While he "lived like a prince," Worth also seems to have sought to improve his mind and knowledge of culture. "He became a student of art and literature," Lyons notes, the better to play his role of man about town, but also out of a genuine interest in the finer things that could be obtained with others' money.

Like any wealthy chap of a sporting disposition, Worth took an interest in the turf and purchased a string of "ten racehorses, and drove a pair of horses which fetched under the hammer £750." To his Piccadilly neighbors Worth was a polite and evidently prosperous American, who entertained often and well, and had his suits made in Savile Row. To the frustrated Inspector Shore he was a permanent gall, for Worth always managed to stay a jump ahead by covering his tracks with infinite care and bribing sources within Scotland Yard to keep him abreast of Shore's doings. One account even claims "he employed a staff of detectives and a solicitor, and his private secretary was a barrister."

To his criminal colleagues Worth was a source of wonder, and regular income, whose largess was legendary. "When he had money, he was generous to a fault, never let a friend come to him a second time, and held out a helping hand to everybody in distress, whether in his mode of life or no," one associate later wrote, a view confirmed by the Pinkertons. "Anybody with whom he had a speaking acquaintance could always come to him and receive assistance, when he had it in his power to give." In an oblique recognition of his own humble, and now wholly concealed, beginnings, he only ever stole from those who had money to spare and remained adamant that crime need not involve thuggery: the Pinkertons found it astonishing that "throughout his career he never used a revolver or jeopardized the life of a victim."

Perfectly confident in his own abilities to avoid detection, Worth began to take ever greater risks and reap ever larger rewards. As he told his followers, "It's just as easy to steal a hundred thousand dollars as a tenth of that sum . . . the risk is just as great. We'll, therefore, go out for the big money always." Many years later the forger Charles Becker was interrogated by the Pinkertons and gave this account of the gang's philosophy. It is worth quoting in full, for it provides important clues to the strange double life of Adam Worth:

> If you want to get on quickly you must be rich or you must make believe to be so. To grow rich you must play a strong game—not a trumpery, cautious one. No. No. If in the hundred professions a man can choose from and he makes a rapid fortune, he is denounced as a thief. Draw your own conclusions. Such is life. Moralists will make no radical changes, depend on that, in the morality of the world. Human nature is imperfect. Man is the same at the top, the middle or the bottom of society. You'll find ten bold fellows in every million of such cattle who dare to step out and do things, who dare to defy all things, even your laws. Do you want to know how to wind up in first place in every struggle? I will tell you. I have traveled both roads and know. Either by the highest genius or the lowest corruption. You must either rush a way through the crowd like a cannon ball or creep through it like a pestilence. I use the cannon ball method.

In its way, this was a peculiarly Victorian philosophy. Worth was (or considered himself to be) a superior being, equipped with greater resources for the Darwinian struggle for survival, which is, after all, a struggle without morals. Like many Victorians he considered the acquisition of wealth, and the respectability that went with it, to be a worthy goal in itself, but how the money was accumulated was, to Worth, a matter of the most profound indifference. The mere fact that he could dance one step ahead of the Pinkertons and Scotland Yard was proof that he ought to. None knew better than Worth that man is the same at the top, the middle, and the bottom of society, for he had visited all three. The morality of the time was a strange, malleable thing. "They pretended to be better than they were," as one historian noted. "They passed themselves off as incredibly pious and moral; they talked noble sentiments and lived—quite otherwise."

Victorians strove to live outwardly "good" lives, and made much of the fact, yet they enjoyed behaving "badly" as much as any other society in any other period of human history.

The contrast between outward protestations and actual behavior was particularly acute in the area of sexual morality, for while the prudish "official" line taken by most ethical commentators stressed home, hearth, and sex within marriage, or preferably not at all, the populace casually ignored most of these rules and appears to have enjoyed an interest in sex that was, if anything, even more obsessive than our own, precisely because it was so secretive. The Victorians, it should be remembered, were the first to publish pornography on an industrial scale. Worth's own code of morality was a stern one, genuinely adhered to. He prided himself on a strict personal regime, abstained from strong drink, rose early, worked hard at his chosen profession, gave to charity, and may even have attended church, while he broke every law he could find and enriched himself with the wealth of others. If Worth held to a set of high-minded convictions that were utterly at variance with his actions, he was by no means alone. He would have enjoyed Wilde's ironic quip in *The Importance of Being Earnest*: "I hope you have not been leading a double life, pretending to be wicked and being really good all the time. That would be hypocrisy."

Sober, industrious, loyal, Worth was a criminal of principle, which he imposed on his gang with rigid discipline. With the exception of Piano Charley, drunks were excluded and violence was specifically forbidden. "A man with brains has no right to carry firearms," he insisted, since "there was always a way and a better way, by the quick exercise of the brain"; robberies were to be inflicted only on those who could afford them, and the division of spoils was to be fair. Myriad crooks and hangers-on owed him their livelihoods, yet Worth was no Robin Hood, robbing from the rich to give to the poor. Then again, neither was Robin Hood.

"It was his almost unbroken record of success in getting large amounts of plunder and escaping punishment for crimes that gave the underworld such confidence in him and made all the cleverest criminals his accomplices," Sophie Lyons concluded.

Worth delighted in his newfound position, elevated in both respectable society and the underworld. Slowly his confidence expanded into hubris. In the mid-1870s he met William Pinkerton again, on this occasion in the Criterion Bar in Piccadilly, a noted meeting place for *flâneurs* and sporting men, but this time Worth felt so secure at the center of his criminal network that he could offer the American detective a compliment, while damning his English counterpart, Inspector Shore. The Scotland Yard detective, he said, "could thank God Almighty the Pinkertons were his friends or he would never have gotten above an ordinary street pickpocket detective." Secretly William Pinkerton was inclined to agree, for the Agency had by now built up an extensive file on Worth and his doings, and without the regular flow of information from the United States, the British authorities would know even less than they did about the criminal network radiating out of London. "What he says is true," Pinkerton reflected, "outside of our agency Shore would never have amounted to anything."

"How much flattery there was in all this I am not prepared to say, but will say for him he always treated me well in London. He tried to make me various presents," William reported, adding quickly, "all of which I refused."

William had good reason to emphasize his incorruptibility.

For all his growing prestige as a hard-minded and unbending up-
holder of the law, he was a complex man and in some ways an
unlikely detective. Pinkerton projected a callous image. His job,
he declared, was "to relentlessly hunt down train robbers if it
means travelling the country 20 times," and he claimed to loathe
outlaws "with an unyielding passion." His methods, and those of
his detectives, were necessarily fairly brutal when he was dealing
with such trigger-happy bandits as the Renos, the James brothers,
and the "Wild Bunch"; if he was sometimes forced to shoot first
and ask questions later, that was because he was dealing with men
who tended to shoot without asking any questions at all. William
was believed by many to have led the Pinkerton posse during the
notorious raid on the James brothers' cabin in January 1875,
which ended in a tragic fiasco when a "bomb" was hurled into the
building, resulting in the death of Jesse's eight-year-old half-
brother and the maiming of the outlaws' mother. Jesse James—
who was, needless to say, elsewhere—vowed to kill the Pinkertons
at the first opportunity.

Such incidents added to William's mystique, but his forbid-
ding reputation was only partly deserved. Pinkerton protected the
Establishment (such as it was), but the big detective always preferred underworld company to the marshals, railroad owners,
mining magnates, and sheriffs that were his colleagues and em-
ployers on the right side of the law. "Uppermost in their mind is
how they can kill you and go free," William declared of the outlaw
breed, but one of the more intriguing aspects of William's character is that he got on so well with many of the criminals he hunted,
jailed and, not infrequently, sent to the gallows. In Chicago he was
often to be found at Mike McDonald's saloon, The Store, a notorious hangout for villains. He was there to gather gossip and memo-
rize the names and faces of the city's criminal and sporting frater-
nities, but he also found such people more congenial than the
straitlaced men of importance with whom his father and more
conventional brother consorted. Many of his closest friends were
gamblers, dubious exotics such as John Ringling of circus fame,
and politicians of uncertain honesty.

Pinkerton was, Shinburn declared, "a good mixer." Too good for the tastes of his puritanical father, who reckoned that William was overfriendly with people of suspicious character. Allan Pinkerton watched his older son's fraternizing, his drinking, his traveling, and his tendency to spend lavishly, with a hard Scottish eye. The stern patriarch talked of sending William on a "water cure" to improve his liver and morals, and instructed the agency accountant that if his son did not rein in his spending he was to be put on an allowance "and nothing more." William ignored the remonstrances, and the rows were furious.

So while Worth was making his way up in the world, Pinkerton was, in a sense, making his way down.

In some ways Worth was an archetypical product of his time: determined to better himself, caring little what moral compromises were made along the way, at once utterly upright and utterly corrupt. But while he was clearly in thrall to society and its rules, he was at the same time bitterly, implacably at war with them. He aped his bourgeois contemporaries, and stole from them, and all the time he despised them.

The view taken by Friedrich Engels that the most courageous people on society's lowest economic rung become thieves in order to wage "open war against the middle classes" has some truth in respect to Worth, for his imposture was an act of angry rebellion and disdain for the society from which he would be, whatever his strivings, a permanent outcast. It seems unlikely that Worth ever considered himself a social revolutionary, but the subversive implications of his actions were wholly intentional. If the quest for gentlemanly position was a central commandment of Victorian life, to claim that status fraudulently was social blasphemy, undermining the very hierarchy on which the elaborate Victorian sense of worldly order was built.

Indeed, 1874 saw the culmination of one of the most notorious cases of social imposture in British history, known as the "Tichborne Saga." In April 1854, fully twenty years earlier, a steamer sailing from Rio de Janeiro to Liverpool vanished without a trace, taking with it Roger Charles Tichborne, heir to a baronetcy and extensive estates in Hampshire. Lady Tichborne, his mother, refused to believe her son had perished, and when in 1866 a man presented himself as her missing heir, she immediately clasped him to her breast. This was no easy task, because the original Roger Tichborne had been slim, dark, and well educated, whereas the pretender to his name was freckled, semi-literate, and weighed 340 pounds. "I think my poor Roger confuses everything in his head, just as in a dream and I believe him to be my son," Lady Tichborne maintained. And so, until her death, he remained, enjoying all the benefits of a prodigal son. In 1870, however, with the dowager Lady Tichborne out of the way, her relations filed a lawsuit for criminal impersonation against the bulky and, as matters turned out, entirely bogus baronet. The case caused a sensation and dragged on for years. One speech by the defense lasted fully two months. But finally in 1874, at the precise moment that Adam Worth was beginning to build his counterfeit life in London, the Claimant was exposed as Arthur Orton, a butcher from Wapping, and sentenced to fourteen years' penal servitude. In the meantime, however, the vast impostor had become a focus for the popular resentment that bubbled just beneath the smooth surface of Victorian society. Seen as a "victim of the richer classes, and of Queen Victoria" herself, Orton-Tichborne was a potent symbol of revolt. Thousands subscribed to a magazine in his defense, for "by support of The Claimant the Tichbornites were expressing their opposition to the Establishment and their approval of a champion who appeared to challenge its codes and practices." The magazine *Punch* characterized the attitudes of the Claimant's supporters thus: "I don't care whether he is Roger Tichborne or Arthur Orton, I don't like to see a poor man done out of his rights."

The Tichborne case, which continued to arouse heated debate throughout the 1880s, vividly illustrated how the criminal appropriation of a superior station in this stratified society struck at the very core of comfortable Victorian assumptions. But it also showed how empowerment through fraud struck a chord with the thousands outside (i.e., beneath) the genteel upper stratum.

Worth's spurious claims were all the more seditious for being as yet undetected, and he reveled in his double life, "maintaining his guise of a well-heeled American and going nightly to a thieves hangout in the East End of London." According to one account, "he would change his fine clothes for humbler garb to confer with his criminal colleagues, then seek a railroad washroom to change back into his 'gentleman's clothes' before stealing back to [his] bedroom as dawn was breaking."

As he grew richer and more respectable, Worth was slowly evolving into that most familiar and feared of figures from Victorian literature: the double man, a Jekyll and Hyde who concealed his darker personality from the world, glorying equally in his real wickedness and his apparent probity. He had long ago buried the distinction between a life based in reality and the one of his own crooked invention. He had stolen the name of the most worthy gentleman he could find; he had robbed and forged himself a gleaming carapace of respectability, an exemplary existence that was in truth a dazzling counterfeit. The Victorians read Robert Louis Stevenson's masterwork with delicious terror, for Dr. Jekyll and Mr. Hyde—like Henry Raymond and Adam Worth—were the dark and light sides of man himself, shackled together in febrile contrast, and a chilling glimpse into the dark and daunting depths of their own natures.

By the year 1875, Adam Worth had settled comfortably into the personality of Henry Raymond, wealthier and further from the law's clutches than he had ever been in his life. Then three blows fell in quick succession: Piano Charley Bullard, his partner in crime, who had been heading off the rails at considerable speed for years, wound up in an American jail; the core members of his gang—Elliott, Becker, Sesicovitch, and Chapman—were arrested and flung into a foreign prison; and finally, most devastatingly, Kitty Flynn, the woman he had helped to invent from nothing, developed a mind of her own.

NINE

Cold Turkey

For two years the Worth gang had been running a highly profitable forgery ring throughout Europe. The forgeries, usually circular letters of credit, were the work of the talented but unstable Charles Becker. Worth had high regard for the Scratch's artistry and a commensurately low opinion of his dependability, considering him "the biggest coward in the world." As Worth once remarked: "How he kept his nerve and kept from squealing as long as he did was a mystery." But despite his questionable temperament, Becker was one of the lynchpins of Worth's organization, a forger of such brilliance that even Pinkerton admitted his reproductions of currency, bank drafts, and securities could withstand the most "microscopic scrutiny."

Passing off the counterfeits, or "passing the queer," as it was known in underworld cant, was principally the work of Little Joe Elliott, a plausible, dandified rogue with "a small black moustache and short bushy black hair" who never failed to convince bank clerks of his "bona fides," despite seemingly in a state of permanent and chronic agitation. "He has a very nervous manner and cannot sit still for a moment," one contemporary noted. "His eyes are everywhere—continually jerking his arms and twitching movements generally." The Russian Sesicovitch and the lugubrious Joe Chapman completed the four-man forgery gang as lookouts and backup men. "Chapman had been trained as a bank clerk in Chicago, and his familiarity with banking customs was of essential service to his confederates."

Late in 1874, Worth hit on a plan to pass off some forged letters of credit in Turkey, blithely assuming that the Turkish authorities would not recognize the fakes until the gang was safely back in London. Becker turned out some exquisite replicas of the credit letters of Coutts & Co., the London bankers, and Worth dispatched the team to Smyrna. Worth remained with Kitty in London. Bullard, characteristically, had vanished, having lost his remaining money at the card table. As Pinkerton later observed, "Bullard was, like all thieves, a lavish scatterer of his wealth."

The ruse got off to a good start, and the gang headed "through the principal cities of France and Germany, leaving a trail of forged paper behind all the way to Smyrna." Some $400,000 had been collected in various cities and "the bulk of the money had been sent to London," before disaster struck. The foursome was arrested while trying to pass off a particularly large credit letter. They were tried in the British consular court, convicted of forgery, and sentenced to seven years' hard labor in a Constantinople jail. John Shore of Scotland Yard was notified of the arrests and sent the Turkish police complete dossiers on each man; the Pinkertons announced that they planned to extradite the gang to the United States.

At first the gang was nonchalant in captivity, confident that the resourceful Worth would somehow get them out. "Jail meant nothing to us as men of experience," Becker insisted. "It was the country, not the jail that held us. We couldn't get out of the country." But gradually, as the weeks turned to months and the Turkish authorities simply ignored every entreaty—from Lydia Chapman, from Worth, and even from the American consul, who had been persuaded that the foursome had not had a fair trial— the seriousness of their plight began to sink in. Even Carlo Sesicovitch, a man of granite resilience by any standards, started to crumble. He wrote to his Gypsy mistress, "My Dearest Alima," describing the unspeakable conditions in the jail, compared to which the toughest American prison appeared almost luxurious: "I have had but bread once every twenty-four hours, no bed to sleep on but the bare plank floor, packed to the number of thirty-five or forty in a room not large enough for twenty. You can imagine the amount of filth and vermin there must exist. Actually the bread I eat would not suffice to feed the hungry bugs, fleas and lice which constantly gnaw at my naked flesh . . . There is little hope, so little hope."

Back in London, Worth was beside himself with anxiety. Sophie Lyons thought the "reason for his leadership was his unwavering loyalty to his friends. Raymond [Worth] never 'squealed'— he never deserted a friend. When one of his associates ran afoul of the law he would give as freely of his brains and money as if his own liberty was at stake." Whatever the mythologizing of his contemporaries, it does seem that Worth felt a moral obligation to protect and defend the rascals and louts who were his minions. The Pinkertons regarded the fact that he "never forsook a friend or accomplice" as his principal redeeming trait.

After the men had endured several months of incarceration, Worth made his move. Accompanied by Lydia Chapman, he sailed on *The Shamrock* to Constantinople, "in the guise of an American millionaire taking a grand tour," and set about engineering the release of his underlings. As a plan it was hardly sophisticated, simply employing the oldest but most reliable form of criminal persuasion: bribery, on a vast scale. Worth never admitted how much money he handed over to the Turkish jailers, officials, and judges, but finally he told Lydia that he had done all he could, and the dejected pair returned to London. Worth kept up a steady flow to various venal Turkish officials, and eventually, one January morning, Becker, Elliott, and Sesicovitch were ejected from prison as suddenly and violently as they entered it, and found themselves on the streets of Constantinople penniless, filthy, and free. Years later Worth told Pinkerton "that it was he who took the money to Constantinople which effected the release of Little Joe

Reilly [Elliott], Becker and Sesicovitch from the prison; that he arranged all the details of the work."

Chapman, however, was not so lucky. Some days earlier the bearded forger had fallen out with Elliott, whom he unfairly accused of trying to cut a deal with Scotland Yard. A fight had ensued, and Chapman was isolated in another wing of the prison at the critical moment when the jail doors, oiled by bribery, opened. Worth and the increasingly hysterical Lydia did everything they could to liberate the last member of the gang. He employed an expensive lawyer, sent letters to the American consul, George Baker, and bombarded Chapman's jailers with enough money to make them rich men, but to no avail. Chapman finally told Lydia to forget him and return to America, advice she ignored, pining away in her house in Neville Road and making futile trips to Constantinople to plead with her husband's jailers.

Unwilling to linger a moment longer than necessary in Turkey, the three other members of the gang had set off overland for London but had to run yet another horrifying gauntlet before they made it home. According to the Pinkerton files, "while passing through Asia Minor they were captured by Greek bandits, who, in spite of the fact that their captives were fugitives from prison, held them for ransom." The bandits finally allowed Little Joe to head for London; his companions would not be released until he returned with more money. But they omitted to provide Elliott with traveling expenses. "The only thing that Reilly [Elliott] had to pawn were his gold teeth," Worth later recalled. "He pawned these and with the money which he got for them he bought a cheap ticket and worked his way over to London." Worth raised another two thousand pounds, "which money Little Joe took back and delivered to the bandits, and effected the liberation of his comrades."

If the Turkish escapade was an impressive example of honor among thieves, its final episode revealed quite another side of criminal life. Back in London, the volatile Sesicovitch and his Gypsy mistress, using the names William and Louise Wallace, moved in with Lydia Chapman in her new home at 46, Maude Grove, Chelsea. Before long, Sesicovitch was dunning Lydia for money, claiming her husband had diddled him out of his share of the profits from the original forgery. Sesicovitch told Lydia he "needed money from her with which to defray . . . expenses on a trip to Australia for the purpose of committing forgeries there." He was apparently under the mistaken belief that Chapman's wife "was possessed of considerable money and jewelry," and his demands became increasingly threatening. Lydia Chapman, who now went by the name of Mrs. Porter, in turn tried to persuade Sesicovitch to return once again to Constantinople to try to free her husband.

A few months later the body of Lydia Chapman, apparently dead from poison, was found in her elegant home. Perhaps she had committed suicide, but Scotland Yard, and for that matter Adam Worth, was convinced that the sinister Sesicovitch had had a hand in her death. The Yard even named Sesicovitch and his mistress as the murderers, alleging that, because Lydia had refused to part with the money for the Australian caper, "a scheme had been concocted for the purpose of robbing her [and] that in order to rob her they had dosed her with some narcotic, her death resulting therefrom." William Pinkerton was still more specific, insisting that "her death at the hands of Carlos Sescovitch was brought about by her having heart disease, and the shock which she got when Sescovitch tried to chloroform her and steal her jewelry."

The crime was never solved, but Worth refused to have anything more to do with the Russian, whom he had long mistrusted. Sesicovitch returned to America and opened a drinking parlor beneath Booth's Theatre in New York. Two years later, in April 1878, under the alias Dugan, Sesicovitch was arrested for forgery in Cincinnati. He was identified by Robert Pinkerton when Pinkerton was informed that "the first and second fingers of [his] left hand are off at the second joint, and that a little piece of the thumb of the left hand is missing," the consequence of an earlier accident. "I have no doubt that [Dugan] and Carlo Sesicovitch, alias 'Charles Gandy,' alias 'William Wallace,' alias 'Howard Adams,' alias 'John Hoare' are identical.'' The man who probably killed Lydia Chapman eventually died in prison, but that was little comfort to her husband. It was not until 1881 that Chapman, still mourning his lovely moll, was finally released from the Turkish jail, having "served his full sentence," a man broken in health and spirit.

The drawn-out Turkish saga and Lydia's death had exhausted Worth and seriously reduced his finances. To make matters worse, the original partnership of Little Adam, Piano Charley, and pretty Kitty had finally disintegrated for good. Worth had never forsaken Charley Bullard or declined to provide the "loans" he demanded with ever increasing frequency, but the pianist's temper had soured and his taste for unnecessary risk-taking had grown. To Worth's further annoyance, Bullard was still on friendly terms with Max Shinburn, the haughty safecracker. Some said Worth's fury had been ignited by the Baron's attentions to his beloved Kitty. Shinburn's advances got nowhere, but anyone who looked at her, indeed anything that disturbed Worth's regulated universe, provoked his ire.

While Worth was still trying to sort out the Turkish affair, Bullard went on one of his boozy jaunts and idiotically wound up in New York. "With Raymond's cool, calculating brain no longer there to guide him, Bullard became reckless and fell into the hands of the police," wrote Sophie Lyons. Piano Charley was promptly identified, arrested, tried for the Boylston Bank robbery of 1869, and sentenced to twenty years' imprisonment at the state penitentiary in Concord, Massachusetts.

Kitty, already estranged from her rapscallion, bigamous husband, bored with life in London, promptly headed to New York herself, despite Worth's entreaties, taking both daughters and, for old times' sake, the paintings, mirrors, mahogany tables, and crystal ware that had once adorned the American Bar in Paris. In New York she pawned some of the jewelry lavished on her by Worth, sent the girls to expensive schools, and opened a boarding house for fashionable gentlemen, where her social talents and striking looks soon attracted an appreciative clientele. Like many gentlewomen in reduced circumstances, she hired herself out as a ladies' companion, while waiting for an opportunity to scale the next rung up the ladder to fortune and fame.

Worth was devastated by Kitty's defection. So far, he had managed to keep an iron control on every aspect of his life, but the one thing he desired most had now slipped from his grasp. He remained obsessed with Kitty, not least because her two daughters were almost certainly his. In her memoirs the indefatigable Sophie Lyons, who was plainly a little jealous of Kitty, is as categorical on this point as she is on most matters pertaining to Worth's emotional state. " 'How's Kate?' would be his first question whenever we met in London. He would eagerly ask about her health, how she looked, and how were the two children, which we all knew were Raymond's." The elderly burglar Eddie Guerin agreed, describing how Worth talked constantly of "an old sweetheart of whom he remained passionately fond to the end of his days," and whose loss was "a canker continually eating at his heart."

Worth begged Kitty to return to London and marry him, but she declined. "Had this woman become Raymond's wife I am confident that the whole course of his life would have been changed, and that the world would have something to remember him for besides an unbroken record of crime," Lyons opined, with a hypocritical piety characteristic of the age. This was probably nonsense, since Kitty surely knew all about Worth's criminal enterprises, and while she never actively took part, she seems to have made no effort to reform him. But on one aspect of the strange relationship between Adam Worth and Kitty Flynn, Lyons was surely right: "He never forgot the winsome Irish barmaid who had won his heart." She had loved him, too, but she had chafed under his control, refusing to ornament the gilded frame he had fashioned for her. As blithe and reckless as Worth was intense and calculating, Kitty had provided a vital counterpoint in his life, yet she fluttered out of it as gaily as she had wandered in.

They corresponded amicably and met often in the ensuing years. In time Kitty would repay him for helping to set her on the crooked path to upward mobility, but the love affair between Adam Worth and Kitty Flynn was over, at least in fact.

TEN

A Great Lady
Holds a Reception

In the spring of 1876 Worth, like anyone else who bothered to open a newspaper, read of the mounting excitement surrounding the auction of Gainsborough's celebrated portrait of the Duchess of Devonshire.

The painting had a galvanic effect on the English public, providing a small historiçal window into the Victorian soul. Gainsborough was all the rage, following an exhibition of his work at the Royal Academy earlier in the year which had drawn thousands of visitors, including Henry James, who lauded the painter's "natural refinement," "charm of facility," and "softness of style." Just as the Georgians had once expatiated, breathlessly, on Georgiana's looks and character, so the Victorians now lavished praise on the Gainsborough portrait that had so perfectly encapsulated those qualities, while they looked back on the details of her extraordinary life. Georgiana was a towering figure of her time; her charms, her behavior, and even her failings might have been tailor-made for Victorian tastes. Considerable energy was expended on a discussion of whether the duchess was, or was not, the most perfect of the Georgian belles, and numerous worthy judges from the past were cited one way or the other.

Exactly one century earlier, in 1776, *The Morning Post* had held a competition to find the most attractive female of the age: Georgiana was awarded "15/20 for Beauty, 17/20 for Figure, 13/20 for Elegance, 11/20 for Wit, 5/20 for Grace, 3/20 for Expression, 10/20 for Sense, 9/20 for Sensibility and 16/20 for Principles." Fanny Burney thought her "very handsome"; Horace Walpole celebrated "her youth, figure, flowing good nature, sense and lively modesty." The actress and royal mistress Mary Robinson, being an expert in such matters, noted her "early disposition to coquetry." Georgiana's mother called her "one of the most showy girls I ever saw."

The usually mordant satirist Peter Pindar was positively sweaty when offering his "Petition to Time in Favour of the Duchess of Devonshire," possibly the worst of many very bad poems dedicated to the fair duchess:

> *Hurt not the form that all admire—*
> *Oh, never with white hairs her temple sprinkle—*
> *Oh, sacred be her cheek, her lip, her bloom*
> *And do not, in a lovely dimple's room,*
> *Place a hard mortifying wrinkle.*

This goes on for several more ghastly verses.

Her allure is more pithily described by an Irish drunk who, after an encounter with the duchess, remarked wistfully, "I could light my pipe at her eyes."

Some Victorian commentators recalled the more scandalous aspects of Georgiana's reputation, for which there was equally ample evidence. Like her great-great-great-grandniece, Diana, Princess of Wales, the duchess had been idolized into an emblem of her time, a symbol of fashion, beauty, and sexuality.

Like Princess Diana's, Georgiana's sartorial tastes had set the trend for her peers. Enormous hats festooned with ostrich feathers were in, for example, and her every characteristic, whether intended or otherwise, was aped or criticized by society. She could hardly blow her nose before it was turned into a fashion statement. "The slaves of fashion, rather than not resemble her in something, would gnaw their fans and imitate tricks for which a boarding school girl would have been reproved, stick out their chins and affect to be short-breathed," an observer from the older generation noted. To add to her accomplishments, the duchess wrote reasonable fiction, better letters, and poetry that was translated into several languages. No less a judge than Samuel Taylor Coleridge admired her verses, rather to his own surprise:

> *Oh Lady, nursed in pomp and pleasure,*
> *Whence learned you this heroic measure?*

Even by the louche standards of the day, Georgiana's social life was raunchy in the extreme. The hard-living duchess, a determined but hopelessly inexpert gambler, was addicted to the card game faro (at which she lost several fortunes) and thought nothing of drinking and carousing with her companions until dawn, night after night. The playwright Richard Brinsley Sheridan, who captured the antics of the Devonshire House set in his *School for Scandal*, recalled one particularly unsuccessful evening at the card table when "he had handed the Duchess into her carriage when she was literally sobbing at her losses." Her "early disposition to coquetry," meanwhile, gradually developed into a full-fledged, if only partially deserved, reputation for sexual immorality.

The whiff of scandal sprang from two sources. The first was Georgiana's somewhat overenergetic canvassing on behalf of her friend, the Whig politician Charles James Fox, during the bitterly contested Westminster election of 1784. She at once became infamous for trading kisses for votes among the London electorate, behavior which outraged her more straitlaced contemporaries, who regarded kissing common butchers as clear evidence of nymphomania. "When people of rank descend below themselves and mingle with the vulgar for mean and dirty purposes, they give up their claim to respect," sniffed one critic. Another account ¹aimed she was spending up to £600 a day in the Whig interest ⁻ⁱng fairly plastered in the process by "drinking daily since the poll commenced, two pots of purl, a pint of Geneva and a gallon of porter."

Georgiana's sex life was a matter of consuming public interest and avid speculation. She was the "irresistible queen of ton" and "the most brilliant of the gay throng." The Duke of Devonshire, however, seems to have been one of the few people not wholly smitten by his wife's charms, and his philandering was legendary. His mistress, Lady Elizabeth Foster, eventually moved in with the duke and duchess at Chatsworth, the vast ducal seat in Derbyshire. In an odd foreshadowing of Adam Worth's unorthodox domestic arrangements with Kitty Flynn and Piano Charley, Georgiana and the woman who shared her husband's bed remained the best of friends.

The Devonshires' *ménage à trois* with Lady Elizabeth Foster was a notorious scandal. The women took turns bearing the duke's children: Georgiana had three, including an heir, while Lady Elizabeth produced two and, after Georgiana's death, became Duchess of Devonshire. Perhaps to show that adultery was a two-way street, but more likely out of boredom and depression, Georgiana also took a lover, the prickly Charles Grey, later Prime Minister. She seems to have felt a deep passion for Grey, but the affair ended in disaster. She became pregnant and the duke, in a towering, hypocritical rage, banished her from Chatsworth. She gave birth to Grey's son in Europe, at about the same time that Gainsborough's great portrait of her vanished, to reappear decades later, as legless as she had often been in life, above Mrs. Maginnis's fireplace.

By the end of her remarkable life, Georgiana had lost most of her hair, all her money, her girlish figure, and the sight of one eye, but her pride was intact. In a sharp note she warned posterity: "Before you condemn me, remember that at seventeen I was a toast, a beauty and a Duchess." She died of an abscess on the liver on March 30, 1806, at the age of forty-eight, in Devonshire House, Piccadilly, the scene of her greatest social and political triumphs. When the Prince of Wales heard of her death, he observed sadly: "Then the best-natured and best-bred woman in England is gone." The "empress of fashion," who had electrified every red-blooded man in Georgian England, and sent the scuttlebutt hurtling around the nation like no other, now had a similar effect on their Victorian descendants thanks to the reappearance of the Gainsborough portrait which came nearest to capturing her singular élan.

The Victorians' rediscovered enthusiasm for Georgiana was principally, if covertly, sexual: the chocolate-box coquetry of Gainsborough's portrait, when considered in conjunction with her racy reputation, was just the thing to send a delicious testosterone jolt through the average buttoned-down Victorian male. While they might appear repressed in sexual matters, a function of the fashion for strict outward probity, the Victorians were anything but frigid and knew a sex goddess when they saw one. "The beauty of the subject created a furor," reported one observer, and in several instances the *Duchess* provided an opportunity for some distinctly torrid praise, neatly disguised as art criticism. "Her protean beauty becomes a reality to us," one wrote. "We see the mercurial temperament that made her, in truth, the beauty of a hundred moods." Over the next half century, Gainsborough's *Duchess* would become an icon of femininity, a sex symbol, a fashion statement, and one of the most instantly recognizable images in the world. Reproduced time after time on cheap biscuit tins and expensive china, in parlor prints, cigarette cards, books, and marble busts, she could be admired, read, smoked, nibbled, or simply swallowed whole.

When Gainsborough's *Duchess of Devonshire* was displayed at Christie's early in May 1876, it prompted, in almost equal measure, genuinely artistic admiration, titillation, and blistering controversy. Some claimed it was a fake. The painter John Millais insisted that Gainsborough had never laid eyes on it, let alone painted it. "Artists and connoisseurs who should be entitled to a hearing, boldly impugned its genuineness." Some argued that "the handling appeared to be less light and airy than is usual with painter." Others found that "in the voluptuousness of the ∼d the extreme redness of the lips Gainsborough's characteristic refinement seemed to be wanting." Another critic suggested that it was "originally a sketch by Romney . . . made into a finished picture by a man whom Wynn Ellis kept to look after his pictures"—possibly a veiled reference to Bentley, who was also a restorer and minor artist. Yet another faction insisted that "the head was painted by [Sir Thomas] Lawrence, and the accessories of dress etc. filled in by an artist of forgotten name."

The identity of the sitter was disputed as vehemently as the question of who had painted it; some contended that this was indeed a Duchess of Devonshire, but not *that* Duchess of Devonshire. One Mrs. Ramsden, "who had known both of these ladies personally, expressed her opinion most strongly . . . that the portrait was not that of Georgiana, Duchess of Devonshire, but of Elizabeth Foster, who afterwards became Duchess of Devonshire." The painted *Duchess,* in other words, was the other corner of that strange aristocratic love triangle.

"There thus arose constantly the most lively discussions before the picture," *The Times* reported. When the auction house put it on display in the weeks before the sale, "to convince those who were disposed to be sceptical as to the right naming of the portrait, there were placed in the room two small engravings from portraits of the same personage, one of which bore the name plainly engraved on it, and was taken from a small whole-length sketch or study in grisaille by Gainsborough which had been in the possession of Lady Clifden for a great length of time. This corresponded precisely with the picture."

The grisaille in question, now in the National Gallery of Art in Washington, D.C., has been convincingly attributed to Dupont, Gainsborough's son-in-law. Measuring some two feet by just under sixteen inches, the monochrome shows the Gainsborough portrait before it was cut down and gives a tantalizing glimpse of the full, balanced portrait before the vandal Mrs. Maginnis got to work with her scissors. It belonged to the First Baron Dover, who was married to Lady Georgiana Howard, granddaughter of our own Georgiana, Duchess of Devonshire. Perhaps the most convincing proof that it does, indeed, depict Georgiana is the fact that the family in whose possession it remained until 1922 (when it was sold to the great collector Andrew Mellon) were never in any doubt that it represented their famous ancestor.

In a magisterial vein, *The Times* summed up the dispute: "So much interest has arisen over this remarkable picture that we may endeavour to state something of the various opinions that have been expressed upon it during its exhibition. There were the two opposite opinions which divided the numerous admirers of the picture, and in which more than one distinguished academician agreed, either that it is the work of Gainsborough's highest quality, and entirely authentic, or that it is not by his hand at all." The debate over the painting's authenticity continued for many years, and it continues still. Some rightly insist that the face in this painting is rather different from other portraits of Georgiana, not merely by other artists, but by Gainsborough himself. Those who disliked the painting claimed it lacked the artist's characteristic subtlety of expression, and maintained that "the solid surface of flesh could not have been painted by the master." Defenders of the portrait, however, have responded that "this is simply one of the many instances in which two portraits of one individual, painted by the same artist after a lapse of a decade, may be made, quite unconsciously, to appear as two totally distinct personages. The change is not so much in the sitter, as in the artist, who may have effected a revolution in his style, or whose views may have undergone a very considerable change." Certainly it is true that in the years between the first full-length portrait executed by Gainsborough and the second, the duchess's reputation had evolved from dutiful ducal wife to society's premier coquette. Perhaps Gainsborough was merely reflecting this, by painting Georgiana as the sex symbol she had become.

One writer claimed: "The answer is that it is an experiment in solid painting: but look 1) at the delicate cracks; 2) at the eyes; 3) at the marks of the sable brush (not hog's bristle) at the end of the nose and at the turn of the chin, and you see the unmistak-
ble handling of Gainsborough." *The Times*, after discussing the
cons, hedged. "The Doctors, though they differ as to

authorship, agree as to the high merits of the picture." That was probably the view taken by all but the most adamant nay-sayers; even if the portrait was not by Gainsborough, or had been completed by another hand, or even if it depicted not the famous duchess but someone else entirely, it was still a very remarkable painting. "The majority," in any event, "were captivated by its beauty," and the Duchess "well nigh monopolized the conversation of the day."

The auction began to take on the appearance of a public courtship, and as the day of the sale dawned amid intense speculation, at least three very wealthy men had decided that, authentic or no, they wanted the *Duchess*; these were the Earl of Dudley, Baron Ferdinand de Rothschild, and William Agnew, art dealer, who thought that Georgiana would be just the personage to grace his new gallery at 39, Old Bond Street.

The sale itself, on Saturday, May 6, 1876, "created such a sensation as has never been experienced in the picture world of London," *The Times* reported.

> Throughout the week the pictures had attracted considerable numbers of visitors, but on the day preceding the sale the interest came to a climax, and crowds filled the rooms of Messrs Christie, Manson and Woods all day.

By the standards of the day, the newspaper's account of the occasion verges on the hysterical:

> Any one passing the neighbourhood of St James's Square might well have supposed that some great lady was holding a reception, and this, in fact, was pretty much what was going on within the gallery in King Street. All the world had come to see the beautiful Duchess, created by Gainsborough, and, so far as we could observe, they all came, saw and were conquered by her fascinating beauty.

The sale was a public spectacle, the social event of the season, attended by every follower of fashion, including various doyennes of the chattering classes clad in replica Duchess of Devonshire outfits.

When the portrait was placed before the crowded audience, a burst of applause showed the universal admiration of the picture.

Like a master of ceremonies introducing his leading lady, the auctioneer, Mr. Woods, offered a short history of the painting, and the battle was joined.

The biddings then commenced at 1,000 guineas, which was immediately met with one of 3,000 guineas from Mr Agnew and, amid a silence of quite breathless anticipation, the bids flowed in quick succession, at first by defiant shots across the room of a thousand guineas then, as if the pace was too severe, the bids were only 500 up to 6,000 guineas, when again another thousand-pounder was fired by Mr Agnew, making it 7,000 guineas. Still the fight went on briskly with 500's, till there was a shout of applause at 10,000 guineas, and then a serious pause for breath between the combatants, when Mr Agnew was the first to challenge "any further advance" with his 10,000 guineas and won the battle in this extraordinary contest. The whole affair was, of its kind, one of the most exciting ever witnessed; the audience, densely packed on raised seats around the room and on the "floor of the house," stamped, clapped and bravoed.

Uncertainties about the painting's authenticity would linger on, but for the time being, with such a vast price-tag attached to the portrait, "the doubters were put to the rout."

The Wynn Ellis collection was sold for a total of £56,098 2 shillings, and eightpence, but the price of the Gainsborough alone—the equivalent of some $600,000 at today's prices—set a record that would stand unchallenged until 1893. The underbidder was Lord Dudley, who was traveling abroad at the time of the sale and had left an agent with orders to bid up to 10,000 guineas. Dudley had assumed that such a massive sum would be more than sufficient to see off any rivals, and went into a three-day rage when informed otherwise.

Exhausted by his own eloquence, the *Times* writer concluded:

> The sale will long be remembered as much for the extraor-
> dinary price of the Gainsborough portrait . . . as for the very
> interesting questions [of authenticity] which have arisen in con-
> nexion with it, and which we imagine must for some time afford
> matter for discussion.

These were prophetic words. As William Agnew bore the painting back to his gallery in triumph, the duchess's travels were about to begin again, this time in the company of a man who knew more about counterfeiting than any other in London.

ELEVEN

A Courtship
and a Kidnapping

Worth read about the sale but did not attend it. When not moping around London lamenting the departure of his beloved Kitty, he was preoccupied by a series of pressing considerations. With an expensive life-style to maintain and a gang of crooks dependent on him, Worth was rapidly running out of money. According to one account, he "lived at the rate of £20,000 a year for many years," and since the Turkish debacle, precious little money had been coming into the crook's coffers but a great deal had been going out.

To make matters worse, early in 1876 Worth's younger brother John, who had participated in Worth's first, botched heist back in New York, arrived in London without a penny to his name. John Worth was a notably ineffectual criminal, "a damn fool for a crook," in Worth's words. A credulous, weak fellow, John was liable to brag and easy to manipulate. Worth saw him as a serious menace, but since both their parents were dead, he seems to have felt a strong, almost paternal bond with his siblings. His sister Harriet had married in America, and Worth had sent his brother-in-law enough money to launch his own corrupt legal business in Buffalo. John Worth would have to be added to the payroll.

Charles Becker and Little Joe Elliott were anxious to go on another forgery spree. Since his escape from the Turkish jail, Little Joe had returned to the United States and fallen hopelessly in love with Kate Castleton, an English comic star of the American stage. He had become a theatrical groupie and spent most of his ill-gotten gains financing disastrous American productions. "He has generally followed in the wake" of Castleton's touring theatrical company, the police noted, "and under its cover, beaten banks, and taken a trick on the sneak, when opportunity offered." Why Kate Castleton, this "rose cheeked girl," as William Pinkerton remembered her, should have had anything to do with the reptilian robber is a mystery, but Elliott pursued her with astonishing energy and lavish expense and she finally agreed to marry him. "Joe courted the lady with lightning speed and married her within three days," according to Eddie Guerin. Little Joe persuaded Kate to leave the stage, and for a while "they settled down in elegantly furnished apartments on 21st Street," in New York. But by 1876 Elliott had tired of domesticity and was reunited with his bent buddies in London, having abandoned Kate in New York.

All of which left Worth in a bind: money was short, but his lifestyle was increasingly lavish; the gang was clamoring for work, but Inspector Shore of Scotland Yard was itching for him to make a false move. The policeman knew he was being made to look foolish in the eyes of the underworld, and his determination to catch and jail Worth had become a personal vendetta. Worth complained bitterly that Inspector Shore "persecuted him like a human tiger"—a bizarre and peevish grievance (Shore would hardly be expected to do otherwise), but he was so wrapped up in his own grand invented world that he took personal offense when the forces representing the law tried to stop him from breaking it. On one occasion when Worth noticed he was being tailed by John Shore himself, he suddenly "turned on him in the streets and denounced him."

William Pinkerton was also back in London and had warned Shore, his police colleagues, and the country's banks and brokerage houses to be on the lookout for another wave of forgeries. By now the authorities were acutely aware of Worth's methods. Pink-erton warned: "To prevent detection and avoid arrest, after ob-taining money on the forged paper, the thieves would at once flee to the Continent and get the money changed at broker's offices, banks or exchange offices for notes of other numbers before the numbers of the stolen notes were published."

Worth began his new counterfeiting campaign cautiously, tell-ing Becker to forge checks for small sums only. But over the months, as the gang got into gear, the forgeries grew larger and more audacious. Worth's coffers were again becoming pleasantly full when, in April 1876, the Scratch made up a counterfeit check for £3,500 which Little Joe, as insouciant as ever, promptly cashed at the London and Westminster Bank. It was now necessary to get the money to France and change it fast before the bank realized what had happened and the police sent word for cashiers to be on the lookout for notes with certain numbers.

Instead of relying on one of his minions at the bottom of his pyramidal organization, on this occasion Worth dispatched his brother to Paris with instructions to change the money at a busy currency-exchange office on the Grand Boulevard and return by the next boat to London. The inept John Worth proved unequal even to this simple task. He did not go to the *bureau de change* as directed, but for reasons that remain obscure went instead to the Paris office of Meyer & Co. on the rue St.-Honoré. Meyer had already fallen victim to one of Becker's scams and had been alerted by John Shore to watch for English notes of large denomi-nation. An eagle-eyed clerk spotted one of the notes and John Worth was arrested.

Back at Scotland Yard, Inspector Shore was ecstatic when a telegram arrived announcing the arrest. Although the bovine John Worth looked quite different from the rat-like Little Joe El-liott, John himself was charged with carrying out the forgery. John Worth was extradited to England after a brief but fierce legal tus-sle, and lodged in Newgate jail. Whatever the imprisoned man might call himself (John had had the wits to give a false name), Shore was convinced that the forgery had to be the work of Adam

Worth, alias Henry Raymond, or his associates. Worth threw one of his rare tantrums when informed of his brother's arrest and pledged to get even, not just with Shore but also with Monsieur Meyer, the director of Meyer & Co., who would eventually feel the full force of Worth's wrath. But first Worth had to get John out of prison, preferably on bail, and send him back to America, where he could do no more damage. This was no easy task.

Although Worth had money enough to furnish bail, English law at that time required anyone posting bail to be a freeholder and "a man of good position, character and property." His elaborate smokescreen of wealth, his smart London properties, his expensive possessions, his racehorses, and his yacht might convince any judge that Henry Raymond was a gentleman of substance, but that would only confirm suspicions at Scotland Yard that he was implicated in, if not the mastermind behind, the entire operation. The police were watching closely, and Worth knew that "the application for bail would be bitterly opposed by the prosecution, backed by the Bankers' Protection Association, it being the fourth of a series of forgeries done in an identical manner, and aggregating to some £12,000." Bail for John Worth was finally set at £3,000.

Worth needed someone who would not be linked to Henry Raymond. This person would post bail for John and then profess absolute astonishment when the felon absconded. With John's trial just weeks away, Worth needed such a person fast.

On the afternoon of May 27, 1876, Worth was walking down Old Bond Street with Jack Junka Phillips, the giant English thug with the drooping mustaches and barrel chest, a terrifying sight. Junka had a reputation in the London underworld for extreme and gratuitous violence, which suited Worth's purpose. Worth's activities had earned him enough enemies to make a bodyguard an essential part of his entourage; his principled opposition to violence did not include self-defense. With Junka lumbering along at his side, clad in the somber outfit of a gentleman's gentleman, even the boldest antagonist or bravest Scotland Yard detective would think twice about accosting Worth. If Worth's respectable neighbors in Piccadilly had given it any thought, they might have paused to wonder why the rich American had employed a gorilla for a manservant. But although some of the elegant passersby browsing the art galleries of Bond Street may have been startled at the ferocious-looking mastodon who trundled along behind the dapper little gent, most did not give the pair a second glance: Worth was just another rich man enjoying the art galleries with a chunky butler in tow. Quite apart from his protective role, Junka was a useful companion in other ways: his almost total ignorance on every subject meant that, apart from the odd primal grunt, he was silent, offering no interruption to his leader's train of thought.

A large crowd was milling outside Agnew's art gallery, where the celebrated Gainsborough portrait of the Duchess of Devonshire, sold just two weeks earlier, had been placed on display in an upper gallery. The *Duchess,* now valued at some £20,000, was the focus of London gossip and the source of countless rumors. According to one such, the extraordinary auction was the result of a feud between Sir William Agnew and Lord Dudley, who "was at this time buying pictures largely, and had employed Agnew to buy for him." Dudley had fallen in love with the painting but "employed another agent to bid for him at the sale . . . Agnew, hearing of this, bid 10,100 guineas [and] then wrote to Earl Dudley and offered him the picture at the price he had paid for it plus his commission." If that was indeed Agnew's ruse, prompted by pique at not being asked to bid for Lord Dudley, it did not work. Immediately after the sale, none other than the Duke of Devonshire whipped up fresh controversy by claiming, in a letter to *The Times,* that the only "portrait of the Duchess of Devonshire by Gainsborough was in his possession and had been in the possession of his father and grandfather, and therefore [the one sold to Agnew] could not be the original." In fact, the duke was referring to the other Gainsborough portrait of 1783, but nonetheless some concluded "that it was owing to this letter that the Earl of Dudley declined the offer made to him by Agnew." Perhaps, on the other hand, the earl was simply teaching the art dealer a lesson.

A fortnight after the auction, *The Times* reported, "the interest in the sale of the Wynn Ellis collection, of which we gave the details last week, continues to be kept up with considerable vigour in the various differences of opinion which have arisen as to the portrait of the Duchess of Devonshire." Whether or not it was the genuine article, Sir William Agnew was already recouping some of his investment by selling tickets to see the portrait at a shilling apiece and had received subscriptions for engravings to the value of £3,000 in just two weeks. Sir William's extravagant bidding for the painting would become the stuff of legend, and ever afterwards he retained a reputation as a man who was prepared to pay inflated prices for works of art. In Oscar Wilde's *The Picture of Dorian Gray*, published in 1891, Basil Hallward remarks to Lord Henry Wotton, "You remember that landscape of mine for which Agnew offered me such a huge price, but which I would not part with?"

Worth watched the excited, milling crowd for a few moments and then turned to Junka and told him to buy a pair of tickets. He later recalled that Junka, whose appreciation of fine art was exactly nil, was initially unwilling to waste time on such an unprofitable activity, but Worth insisted and Junka sullenly pushed his way to the front of the throng, which parted with some alacrity as the huge figure approached.

Once inside the building, the pair followed the line of people to the upper gallery, until finally they stood before the great picture, separated from the jostling spectators by a thick velvet rope. William Pinkerton later described his reaction, based on Worth's own account: "Then and there the idea occurred to him that if he had possession of the picture that he could, by holding the picture off, effect the release of his brother by making the owner of the picture go on the bond for his brother and then let his brother skip out of the country." It was a brilliant ruse. With the portrait "hostage," William Agnew, a figure of adamantine respectability who was later knighted for services to art, could be forced to post bail for John Worth, probably through a third party. John could jump bail and no one would dream of suspecting Henry Raymond. Back at the apartment, Worth summoned Joe Elliott and outlined the operation. As he later told Pinkerton, he "would go to an acquaintance, a solicitor of shady reputation who was an ex-convict, and instruct him to call on the prisoner [John Worth] in the jail, and hand him a small canvas clipping cut from the side of the picture. The attorney was then to go to Agnew & Co. and say to them that he had a client in Newgate prison who could give them valuable information concerning the Gainsborough picture. The prisoner in jail was to say to them, that if his liberty was effected, he would guarantee to return the picture, and as an evidence of good faith and that he was telling the truth, he was to produce the piece of canvas cut from the side of the picture which they could fit on the frame as a test."

William Agnew might be a pillar of London society, but Worth knew enough about human nature to be confident that he would do anything to get back such a valuable commodity, even to the extent of compounding a felony. Morality was an elastic quality when money was involved. Little Joe quickly agreed to the plan. Junka, who preferred blowing up safes and bashing policemen to the delicate business of art theft, was dubious, noting that a picture was "a clumsy thing to do anything with," but he was quickly brought into line.

Although Worth had seen the *Duchess* only once, the painting had had a profound effect. "All England was talking about it. All London was flocking to see it. The picture was the sensation of the hour. This was enough for Worth. He made up his mind to possess it."

But Worth was not the *Duchess*'s only suitor. The Earl of Dudley, worsted by Agnew at the Christie's sale and unwilling to accept the dealer's subsequent offer, had not given up hope of possessing her. That very evening, the aristocrat came to Agnew's gallery and gazed at the painting in reverence—Lord Dudley was, as it turned out, the last person to see the *Duchess* before she vanished—but by now the portrait had already been promised to another. Ferdinand de Rothschild had privately put in a bid, but it had been topped by Junius Spencer Morgan, the wealthy American banker resident in London, whose son, John Pierpont Morgan, was well on his way to becoming one of the richest men in the world.

Junius Morgan was an art connoisseur and owned an impressive array of works by Reynolds, Romney, and Gainsborough. His taste for fine art had been inherited by his son, whose collection would eventually become the largest private assemblage of art ever created. Having read of the extraordinary auction in *The Times,* the elder Morgan decided to buy the famous painting as a "princely gift" for his son, with precisely the right dynastic connotations. In the early 1870s the elder Morgan had hired a genealogist to trace his ancestry and discovered that his mother, Sally Spencer, was distantly related to the noble Spencers of Althorp through a common ancestor—an ambitious sheep farmer from Northampton called Henry Spencer. Delighted with this discovery, Morgan had books and charts printed up to display his illustrious newfound pedigree, for the banker was a social climber with a head for heights. The relationship was distant, indeed almost imperceptible, but "the connection was enough to fuel that peculiar brand of Anglomania mixed with ancestor worship that was much in vogue." Junius Spencer Morgan was himself representative of the breed of wealthy (often American) individuals of the period, who sought to demonstrate their taste and refinement by buying up valuable (often English) artworks, the better to show that they, too, had attained the all-important rank of gentleman. A Gainsborough automatically conferred status, but how much more magnificent that possession was if one could claim kinship, however remote, with its aristocratic subject.

The elder Morgan's interest may have been further stimulated by the knowledge that the Rothschilds, rivals to the burgeoning financial power of the Morgans, were also in the market for the *Duchess.* Sensing a potential public-relations coup, Junius Morgan was one of the first people to visit Agnew's gallery after the sale. Herbert Satterlee, his son-in-law and chief sycophant to the Morgan family, described how "Mr. Junius Morgan dropped in to see the picture and asked Mr. Agnew the price and thereupon bought it, telling the dealer that it was for his son Pierpont, who had begun to collect pictures in New York." Morgan agreed to pay $50,000 (the equivalent of some $620,000 today) for the painting, providing William Agnew with a reasonable profit and doubtless putting the nose of Ferdinand de Rothschild out of joint for a second time. Agnew was enjoying all the attention and made one stipulation: "he had to consent, however, to leave the picture on exhibition some weeks longer." In return, the elder Morgan insisted that both the sale of the picture and its price be kept "absolutely secret."

So, in a technical sense, the *Duchess* was already the property of Junius Morgan when, at around midnight on May 27, 1876, Adam Worth set out in his most fashionable attire, as he later put it, to elope with the duchess. Junka Phillips was brought along as best man, and Little Joe as chief usher. On one level, the escapade had all the hallmarks of the crook's handiwork: a characteristic amalgam of daring, rebellion, and greed, carried out with speed and efficiency. But what began as a clever act of thievery would eventually take on a far more elaborate meaning.

As Worth stood before the painting in the dark gallery that night, he might have pondered the words of a previous occupant, for it was in this very chamber, on March 18, 1768, that the writer Laurence Sterne, another of Thomas Gainsborough's subjects and one of the great satirists in the English language, had breathed his last. In his most celebrated book, *Tristram Shandy*, Sterne had written with characteristic wit of the way an idea can grip the mind when once it has taken root: "It is in the nature of a hypothesis, when once a man has conceived it, that it assimilates everything to itself, as proper nourishment; and from the first moment of your begetting it, it generally grows stronger by everything you see, hear, read or understand . . ." Stealing the Gainsborough was for Worth the first act in a strange hypothetical relationship, the idea of which would grow stronger in his mind, evolving from conception to conviction to obsession.

Henceforth, the stories of Adam Worth and Gainsborough's *Duchess* would be one.

TWELVE

A Wanted Woman

THE TIMES
SATURDAY, MAY 27, 1876

The picture which had already become famous for having been sold for 10,100 guineas (£10,605), the highest price ever paid at auction for a portrait, has now been rendered still more so by having been stolen from the gallery in which it had only recently been placed for exhibition, No 39b Old Bond Street. The greatest excitement arose in the neighbourhood when it became known yesterday morning, soon after 7 o'clock, that this extraordinary and daring robbery had been committed. The large printed placards in the windows inviting attention to the picture were soon surrounded by little crowds, who read with no small astonishment the written notice that during the night some malicious person had cut the picture from the frame and stolen it. From inquiries made on the spot it was found that the picture had been very neatly cut from the stretching frame after it had been removed from the gilt frame in which it hung against the wall, near the window above the doorway on the first floor. The stretching frame was seen leaning against a sofa opposite the now empty gilt frame, and it showed that no unpractised hand had operated on the canvas, as the picture itself had been completely removed. The gilt frame had the nails simply bent back and not extracted so that the thief or thieves lost no time in needless trouble. The apartment in which the picture was exhibited showed scarcely any marks of what had been done, beyond some crumpling of the drapery hung in front of the picture. The room is not more than 10 ft square, having only one window opening on to Bond Street. The one window was found to be open about two feet, and on examining the lead outside there was distinctly visible the mark of a nailed shoe. The window had no blind to it, consequently if any light had been used during the work of the thieves it would in all probability have been noticed by the policemen in the street, who were aware that no one resided in the house after the doors were closed and the premises left locked up for the night. All the doors were found fastened as they had been left. The window, however, would enable the thief to drop his booty in the shape of a roll of very moderate size into the hands of a confederate.

These matters are now in the hands of Superintendent Williamson, of the police, and the detectives, and as we learn that with his advice Messrs. Agnew have offered the large reward of £1,000 for information leading to the recovery of the stolen picture, some speedy intelligence may be looked for. It must be tolerably evident that such a robbery was not contrived with the view of selling the picture, as that would be a thing next to impossible, and the mere offer of it would be certain to bring the thieves to detection in almost any part of the world. The description given of the picture at the time of the sale, and the engraving in the *Illustrated News* must have made it known far and wide.

It is very rarely that robbery of valuable paintings in this way has been attempted, and rarely, if ever, we believe, without discovery in the end. In the present case it is to be hoped that a picture of such remarkable notoriety and interest will be recovered uninjured, and the audacious thief or thieves brought to justice.

The airy confidence of the *Times* writer was not in evidence in other quarters of the metropolis. William Agnew was flabbergasted at the loss of his valuable investment, not least because he had agreed to pay the great engraver Samuel Cousins the enormous sum of 1,500 guineas, "double his usual amount," to make another engraving. Junius Spencer Morgan was equally displeased to be deprived of the painting he believed was his already.

The authorities were understandably embarrassed that such a daring theft could have taken place in the heart of London. Agnew's neighboring art dealers lost no time in voicing their concern at the lack of security the theft indicated. Two of these, Messrs. H. and J. Jacobs, wrote to *The Times* to express the general consternation. "Being inhabitants of Bond Street, and having property of our own, we are at a loss to know how such a daring robbery could have been effected without the knowledge of the police, and of the watchman who is paid by the various tradesmen to protect their property." Suspicion immediately fell on the dozy night watchman, who, *The Times* unfairly reported, "is said to have given himself a holiday on the night of the theft and, of course, he could throw no light on the subject."

Inspector Williamson of the Yard was left the unenviable task of scouring London for a small thief, knowledgeable in the art of stealing paintings without damaging them, who may or may not have hidden in the gallery after closing time and who probably wore hobnailed boots. Circulars and photographs of the missing painting were sent to police forces "all over the known world," and advertisements were placed in many European newspapers. According to one report, "the hue and cry raised in Bond Street spread to every civilized quarter of the globe, and all nations, peoples and languages were talking of the loss of the dead master's work." The Pinkertons pronounced Scotland Yard "mystified."

No one thought to suspect Henry J. Raymond, the wealthy American gentleman living just a few hundred yards away and now thoroughly enjoying his new acquisition and the frenzy he had caused. But the police and *The Times* had been correct in one aspect: Worth had no intention of trying to sell the *Duchess,* now even more widely recognizable thanks to the Scotland Yard posters which festooned London offering £1,000 for its return and his arrest. Similar posters were also printed up by Scotland Yard in German and (appallingly bad) French for distribution in Europe.

While Worth was admiring the *Duchess* in his Piccadilly lair and congratulating himself on his own brilliance, news arrived that removed the reason for stealing it in the first place. John Worth, thanks to one of the few strokes of good fortune ever

The army document on the left contains handwritten and printed text:

> *W.* | **34** Battery. | **N. Y.**
>
> *Adam Worth*
>
> *Sergt.*, Batt'y L, 2 Reg't N. Y. Light Art'y.*
>
> Appears on
>
> **Battery Muster Roll**
>
> for *Sep. & Oct* , 1862
>
> Present or absent ....
>
> Stoppage, $..........100 for ....
>
> Due Gov't, $..........100 for ....
>
> Valuation of horse, $...........100
>
> Valuation of horse equipments, $.......100
>
> Remarks: *Died at Seminary Hospital Georgetown D. C. on Sep. 25th from the effect of wounds received at Battle of Manassas Augt 30th 1862,*
>
> *This organization subsequently became 34 Indpt. Battery, N. Y. Light Art'y.
>
> Book mark :..........................
>
> (858) ....*L. S. Fitch* Copyist.

Fredericka "Marm" Mandelbaum (*above*), professional "fence," who played mother and "saloniste" to the New York underworld. This sketch, with plainly anti-Semitic overtones, illustrates Marm's "heavy features, powerful physique and penetrating eye"

American Civil War army document (*left*) recording the "demise" of Adam Worth on September 25, 1862, from "wounds received at Battle of Manassas" (also known as the Second Battle of Bull Run)

"Marm" Mandelbaum's dinner party, with the hostess at far right. "She entertained lavishly with dances and dinners that were attended by some of the most celebrated criminals in America, and frequently by police officials and politicians who had come under the Mandelbaum influence"

Sophie Lyons, self-styled "Queen of the Underworld" and "notorious confidence woman," whose best-selling memoirs chronicle the career of Worth, her lifelong friend

Jack "Junka" Phillips, the gargantuan English criminal employed by Worth as butler, bodyguard, and safebreaker. This picture, showing Junka tied to a post, was labeled "an unwilling photograph" by Pinkerton's detectives

"Piano" Charley Bullard, Worth's partner and soul-mate, "one of the boldest operators that has ever handled a jimmy" and a virtuoso musician with "fingers so sensitive he could open a combination safe with his hands alone"

Adam Worth, 1892, in one of the few extant photographs. Note the arranged breast-pocket handkerchief, combed hair, and buttoned collar of the incarcerated dandy, after weeks of intensive police interrogation during which he claimed to have been tortured

Charles "the Scratch" Becker, the master forger of Worth's gang, seen here in a rogues' gallery identification card from Pinkerton's National Detective Agency

William Pinkerton [seated], flanked by Pinkerton's detectives in the "bandit-chasing days" of the 1870s. "When Bill Pinkerton went after a man he didn't let up until he had got them"

Joe Chapman, the lugubrious former bank clerk who had "but one vice—forgery; and one longing passion—Lydia Chapman"

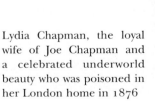

Lydia Chapman, the loyal wife of Joe Chapman and a celebrated underworld beauty who was poisoned in her London home in 1876

Georgiana, Duchess of Devonshire, painted by Gainsborough "in the bloom of youth" around 1787. "I could light my pipe at her eyes," remarked one of the many admirers of the popular, scandal-plagued duchess

Kitty Flynn, aged twenty-three, after a photograph by French photographer Félix Nadar. This "unusually beautiful girl" became Worth's lover and presided as hostess in his illegal Paris gambling den [Courtesy: Katharine Sanford]

The West or Western Lodge, Worth's London headquarters, "a commodious mansion standing well back on its own grounds out of the view of the too curious at the west corner of Clapham Common"

The Shamrock, Worth's 110-foot yacht, named in honor of Kitty Flynn, his Irish lover

enjoyed by this feckless man, had suddenly been released from Newgate prison, to his own and his brother's immense surprise. At considerable expense, Worth had retained a solicitor named Beasley to help defend his brother, and while the master criminal had been laying plans to abscond with the *Duchess,* Beasley had been hard at work. The solicitor later became a highly respected judge in London and deservedly so. In his enthusiasm to make an arrest, Inspector Shore had had John Worth extradited as the principal in the alleged forgery. Beasley pointed out that the description provided of the man who had actually cashed the forged check (Little Joe) "in no way answered the description" of John Worth, and since the police had not accused him of passing the forgery, he could only have been legally extradited as "an accessory after the fact." Just hours before the Gainsborough was stolen, Beasley had obtained a writ of habeas corpus, and the following day, to the fury of Inspector Shore, John Worth was released and told to leave the country within thirty days or face arrest again.

His older brother, mindful of John's chronic bad luck and Inspector Shore's wrath, moved fast. Within twenty-four hours of quitting Newgate prison, John Worth had been bundled onto a boat sailing for the Continent, with instructions to make his way back to the United States as soon as possible, and stay there. Delighted as he was to see his brother set free, Worth now found himself in a fresh quandary. As he put it, he "had the picture and his brother's liberty as well." Getting John out of harm's way was the work of a moment, but disposing of the portrait, with profit but without getting caught, was clearly a much more complex matter. Even the most disreputable art dealer would be insane to handle so hot a property, and returning the painting to claim Agnew's reward was an equally dangerous course. Worth toyed with the idea of simply giving the painting back, but to give John Shore that pleasure, after the trouble the Scotland Yard detective had put him to, was simply not in Worth's nature. He was, moreover, enjoying the illustrious presence of the famous Duchess of Devonshire, his illicit guest. The painting was securely hidden beneath the mattress of his four-poster bed, sandwiched between hardwood boards; from time to time, he would take her out and admire his conquest. He would not, he decided, send "the noble lady" back to her rightful owners—quite yet.

In the meantime, William Agnew was becoming more agitated with every passing day, particularly since ugly rumors were beginning to circulate that the dealer might himself have had a hand in the disappearance. Some were claiming that Agnew had discovered, too late, that the painting was a fake and consequently it had been "burned to save the dealer's reputation as an expert." The anonymous writer of this particular slur goes on to insist slyly, "No one who knows the high standing of Mr Agnew as a businessman can but be aware that this preposterous story not only is without foundation, but is wholly improbable." Preposterous or not, like all rumors, this one was taking on a life of its own. Other "wise ones had it that the article stolen was an imitation, and that the genuine canvas was in safe keeping."

So far from eliciting any concrete information about the theft, Agnew's offer of a £1,000 reward had prompted a massive, emotional, and quite useless response from the English public. From every corner of the land, letters and telegrams flooded in to the Bond Street address; they came from the helpful, the criminal, and the merely barmy.

A Mr. Mortimer from Blomfield Road, North London, wrote on May 28, politely informing William Agnew: "I have a very good clairvoyant . . . and with your kind permission will bring her to the gallery and see if she can trace the valuable painting which is such a loss to the public. I know I cannot obtain her services until after Thursday . . . I make this early appointment because the fewer persons touch the frame the more likely she will be to trace the culprit." He added a postscript, heavy with conspiracy: "You had better keep this a secret, or it may prevent her tracing it."

Others were quite specific in their assertions and accusations. "No doubt you will think it strange my writing to you in thus manner," advised another correspondent, "but having had a Dream last night that your valuable picture has been taken away by a Gentleman living at The Time House, Newton, Yorks, a Mr Villiers, I think it would be advisable for you to send there. You will please keep this letter as I shall keep a copy of it so that if it is as I have said you will be able to know the writer. I hope you will take note of this and send as I am so impressed with it that it is right." Daniel Berman, from Leeds, simply sent a black bordered card with the suggestion: "Could they not have hid it in a metal tube and sunk it?"—which, since it left Agnew to search every expanse of water in the world, did not really help very much.

The Agnews' archives contain scores of such suggestions, proving that Victorian society included quite as many cranks as our own. Some clearly saw an opportunity for criminal profit. "Australia" insisted: "I shall not take a fraction less than 1,000 pounds" in exchange for the painting and suggested a rendez-vous with William in Eaton Square. "Now Mr Agnew you must come alone and have no one watching. You will only have one person to deal with and no personal injury will be offered to you—it will be entirely your own fault if you are not in possession of your picture $1^1/_2$ hours after you meet me . . . remember I have my freedom to look after . . . and if arrested I should have to suffer the punishment of the English law, which would be about five years I suppose." "Australia" further warned that he had left instructions with his wife to destroy the painting in the event of his arrest and signed off with some wholly misplaced homespun philosophy: "A woman will do anything for the man she loves." Another writer suggested that if William Agnew would bring £1,000 in gold to a street corner in the East End of London at midnight on a given day, he would get his painting back. Very sensibly, Agnew declined an offer that would surely have seen him blackjacked down a dark alley, robbed, and possibly killed. It is easy to imagine this simple East End mugger waiting patiently at the corner for his victim to arrive. The art dealer wearily passed the letters on to Williamson at Scotland Yard. Some were briefly investigated; most were ignored.

Sprinkled among the nutters and criminals were a few letters expressing genuine anguish at the theft and reflecting the extraordinary impact of the painting, and its sale, on the general public. Of these, perhaps the most heartfelt came from one Marguerite Antehuester. "Sir, Although unknown to you, the news of your great loss tonight has so touched me that I feel unable to resist assuring you of my profound sympathy and I cannot but think the crime has been committed by a madman—for days past I have dreamed of the delight of seeing the Gainsborough, and when news reached us tonight of its abstraction I can hardly say whether sorrow or indignation had the largest share of my heart . . . pray forgive a stranger for thus addressing you but I do feel intensely interested, as does everyone else, in that wonderful picture."

The distraught Ms. Antehuester was hardly exaggerating, for the mysterious fate of the *Duchess* had suddenly become a parlorgame whodunit and few were without an opinion. For years afterwards, a steady trickle of false sightings, unsolicited advice, and commiserations continued to arrive at Agnew's London office. Until the theft, Gainsborough's *Duchess* had been the preoccupation of educated Londoners, a passing fancy of the chattering classes; suddenly Georgiana's raunchy past was revivified by modern scandal. "The interest, not to say anxiety, felt by the public as to its probable fate was so keen as to cast into the background all other things. It eclipsed all contemporaneous events, and so great was the desire to know what the picture was like that reproductions, more or less accurate, appeared in the public prints, and were much appreciated on presentation almanacs by the customers of grocers and bookmakers," one observer noted. "Nothing but the poisoning of a favourite race horse or the disappearance of a famous dog could have aroused equal concern in the average British mind," puffed the *Midland Daily Telegraph*.

The image of the duchess was everywhere, her possible whereabouts avidly discussed by everyone, from dukes to costermongers. Georgiana's lewd reputation was now celebrated in musichall ballads and scurrilous doggerel, while "impresarios paid the leading beauties of the variety stage to put on replicas of the famous Gainsborough hat." Thanks to Adam Worth, the fame of the duchess was now universal. As one newspaper observed wryly, whoever had stolen the painting had also "accomplished a task before which Ruskin might have paled—he made known the names of Gainsborough and of Georgiana, Duchess of Devonshire, to millions who would never otherwise have heard of them. So, in some sense, he was an apostle of culture."

If, before the theft, the *Duchess* had achieved iconic status, now women positively wanted to *be* her. She became the haute-couture statement of the hour. The theft proved a blessing to London's hatmakers, since "at most of the public ceremonials a large proportion of the ladies dressed upon the model which the painting provided." Vast ostrich-feather hats became the rage on both sides of the Atlantic, and in New York "the Gainsborough hat . . . was so fashionable among women [that] one fashionable modiste went so far as to call it the 'Lady Devonshire style.' " A Duchess of Devonshire hat gave its wearer a stylish, even somewhat risqué image and was used by literary types to denote a particularly flamboyant sort of woman. In Sir Arthur Conan Doyle's *A Case of Identity,* Watson describes Mary Sutherland as wearing "a large curling red feather in a broad-brimmed hat which was tilted in a coquettish Duchess-of-Devonshire fashion over her ear." This was not the last time Sir Arthur would find himself indebted, directly or indirectly, to Adam Worth.

Vain as he was, and delighted to be the anonymous object of so much attention, Worth was also disturbed by the hullabaloo. He knew that the loyalty of Little Joe Elliott and even more of Junka Phillips (moronic but also avaricious) was dependent upon hard cash. Already they were demanding that the *Duchess* be made to pay, but entering into negotiations with William Agnew for the profitable return of the painting in the midst of such pandemonium would be to court disaster. So Henry Raymond, charming and prosperous man of the world, decided the time had come to take one of his excursions, this time accompanied by his new, portable paramour. A large Saratoga trunk was equipped by a skillful and discreet carpenter with a concealed panel in the bottom in which the painting could be accommodated with comfort and, while London still buzzed with rumor, the *Duchess* and her proud new consort inconspicuously slipped out of London and took ship for New York.

THIRTEEN

My Fair Lady

Worth's former partners in crime, and love, Piano Charley Bullard and Kitty Flynn, had preceded him to the United States. The former was now in prison, serving time for the Boylston Bank robbery; the latter was in business, biding her time before the next social conquest. Calling herself Mrs. Kate Flynn, Kitty sought to sever contact with her former criminal associates and, as proprietor and main attraction of a men's boarding house, had transformed herself once again, this time into a comely, impoverished, and wholly respectable New York matron. Or possibly not.

The young "widow" Flynn, according to one account, rented "furnished rooms on the upper floors to single 'gentlemen' and let out her parlor rooms for card parties, small dances, lovers' trysts and private dinners for businessmen." Worldly and charming, Kitty soon attracted a reputation as "an influence peddler and go-between in financial deals." Every time a broker made a deal under her roof, Kitty got a cut. William Pinkerton considered Kitty "dissipated" and remembered her establishment as "a sort of semiassignation house somewheres up town." She was, he later told his brother, "at one time considered the mistress of a Police Magistrate in New York, I think it was Justice Ottovard." This may be no more than idle, if intriguing, tittletattle, but it would have

been entirely in character for Kitty to select a man such as Ottovard, one of the city's powerful lawmakers, as her next lover.

After disembarking in New York, Worth immediately went to
visit Kitty and the two girls, as he would repeatedly over the coming years. "Adam told me he always went to see them when he was
here, and admitted they were his daughters," William Pinkerton
later wrote. Worth was plainly still infatuated with Kitty, but he
made no attempt to win her back from Justice Ottovard. The
bond of conspiracy between the two former lovers, who had once
shared every secret and ambition, was broken. As he sat politely
sipping tea in Kitty's parlor, Worth made no mention of the noble
lady who lay faithfully at the bottom of his large trunk.

Certainly he was in a strangely euphoric mood when, on June
10, he checked into New York's Astor House and penned a chatty
letter to Messrs. Agnew & Co., brimming with impudent self-satis-
faction. This was the first of ten letters sent by Worth over the next
two years, all of which remain in Agnew's archive. It must have
irritated the pompous art dealer no end to be thus addressed by a
man who had only recently relieved him of the world's most expensive painting, but Worth was clearly determined to cause Agnew's the maximum possible annoyance.

"Gents," he began, expansively, "A knowledge of safety has
an exhilarating effect on one's nerves after the mental strain I
have just passed through, and cannot fail of being appreciated. I
arrived in the SS *Saythia* on Tuesday last, bringing with me the
Duchess of Devonshire." This hail-fellow-well-met introduction
was followed by some jaunty observations about the weather, his
general state of well-being, and his satisfaction with the facilities at
Astor House.

"Now to business," he went on, as if bringing a friendly chin-
wag to order: "This picture is worth, say, $50,000, and by this
advertisement [i.e., the well-publicized theft] its value is greatly
enhanced, so much so that one half that sum would be a modest
sum for its return.

"Now, first, I am safe and secure from arrest. Second, this
work of art is concealed. No one but MYSELF knows of it. At the

same time it is perfectly safe from harm. I can get quite a sum for it here. I heard a dealer from Frisco said he'd give $10,000 if by chance it was offered for sale here, and others expressed near the same sentiment.

"Knowing this I feel under no meanness and for $25,000 I will return it undamaged. Being personally safe I am open to negotiate with any person you may send or employ—in this country, of course.

"It was a big risk, but it has the magic words: 'There's money in it.'

"I want no underhand work as you cannot scare me, and it is a game in which I hold the winning card. The picture is in excellent condition. Of course, I rolled it with the painted side out, so I can assure you it is in good order."

The effect of this astonishing missive on its recipients can only be surmised, but in terms of sheer devilry, effrontery, and sly humor, it is one of Worth's masterpieces.

As well as disguising his handwriting and adding a few persuasive illiteracies, Worth now attached a new alias, signing the letter "Edward A. Chattrel" and giving a postal address for correspondence.

Was Worth serious about returning the painting, or was he simply playing with his victims? William Agnew had already contacted the New York picture dealer William Schaus and Robert Pinkerton, William Pinkerton's brother and head of the detective agency's New York office. As soon as the letter was received, detectives were sent to scour the registration books of Astor House, but naturally found that Chattrel's name "does not appear on the register, nor does [sic] any of the clerks or employees in the office of the hotel know him." No postal box was registered in the name of Edward Chattrel, but a twenty-four-hour watch was placed on the post office just in case. "Our impression, on first reading Mr. Chattrel's note," wrote Schaus, "was that it was a hoax, and that impression is now considerably strengthened." Needless to say, Worth had already moved to another hotel, and never went near the post office. It seems likely that his first letter was an act of characteristic hubris, designed to baffle his pursuers and exasperate William Agnew, while notifying them who held the "winning card."

For the moment, Worth had no intention of parting with his *Duchess,* and over the next few months he visited his old haunts, shopping for expensive clothes, dining at the best restaurants, and generally playing the part of a visiting English gentleman. By this point, it should be noted, Worth, habitual dissembler that he was, had adopted a distinctively upper-class English accent. The German-Jewish immigrant and naturalized American would remain resolutely British, in elocution and manner, for the rest of his life.

Happy to be on American soil for the first time since the Boylston job in '69, Worth and the *Duchess* now set off on what might best be described as a triumphal tour of the country. First stop was Boston, scene of his childhood, where he visited his brother John while staying at the Adams House, which he declared to be "the best managed hotel in the United States." This was followed by a discreet visit to Piano Charley Bullard in Concord prison, and then on to Illinois, where Worth spent a few weeks relaxing and indulging his taste for blood sport in a resort known as Klineman's Cabin on Lake Calumet, "which was greatly frequented by hunters." A few weeks later, thoroughly rested, he headed back east to Buffalo, New York, where his sister Harriet now lived with her husband.

Underworld informants had long ago told the Pinkertons of Worth's central part in the Boylston Bank robbery, and Worth was still a wanted man in America. One night Worth was entertaining his sister and brother-in-law, a shady lawyer named Lefens, in his rooms at one of the Buffalo hotels. Midway through the party, Worth felt the need for some fresh air, but as he walked through the lobby he realized he was being watched by a man from the other side of the room. "He felt sure it was one of our people," William Pinkerton later recorded, after Worth had recounted the incident in detail. "His sister was upstairs and not wishing to alarm her he dodged the man, went upstairs, told his sister he was suddenly called away and [told her] to get out of the room." Back down in the lobby, Worth tried to saunter off but the watcher spotted him and gave chase. Once outside, Worth broke into a sprint but then stopped abruptly when he caught sight of "two big policemen standing on the corner. The man made a signal to them and one reached out to grab him, knocking off his hat. They were both big stout men, as big as I am, and he started to run and as they ran after him one of them slipped and fell and the other fell over him and he got away." The episode had unsettled him, and Worth and his *Duchess,* who had sensibly been stashed at the railway luggage office, were on the next train out of town. America was still a dangerous place, with the Pinkertons on his trail and one of the world's most recognizable paintings in his trunk. Worth was also running low on spending money again.

For the first time Worth appears to have given serious consideration to the possibility of returning the portrait, and his next letter to Agnew's from the United States, "found in the letter box at Five, Waterloo Place Dec. 30. 1876," has the unmistakable ring of urgency. The facetious, mocking tone is gone, as are the deliberate mistakes and hastily selected alias, to be replaced by a curt, almost legalistic set of demands.

December 15, 1876
Gentlemen:
We beg to inform you of the safe arrival of your picture in America, and enclose a small portion to satisfy you that we are the bona-fide holders and consequently the only parties you have to treat with. The portion we send you is cut from the upper right-hand corner looking at it from the front, which you will find matches with the remnant of the frame.

From time to time, as we negotiate with you, we will enclose pieces which will match the piece we now send you so that you can have the whole length of the frame. The picture is uninjured. There being no extradition between this country and England, we can treat with you with immunity.

This communication must be strictly confidential. If you

decide to treat for the return of the picture, you must keep faith
with us; as, on the first intimation we have of any police interfer-
ence, we will immediately destroy the picture. You must be convinced by now of the uselessness of the police in this matter.

The picture being on this side of the water, almost any
lawyer can negotiate with you without being liable to prosecution for compounding a felony. We would like to impress you
with our determination which is, NO MONEY, NO PICTURE.
Sooner than return, or take any great risk in returning it, we
would destroy it.

Now as to terms. We must look at this as a commercial
transaction. It represents to you a money value of 10,000 pounds
sterling. The extraordinary advertisement has certainly added to
its value. If it was again exhibited in London, thousands would
go to see it that never would have thought of going before the
elopement of the Duchess. If we come to terms you can exhibit
it here (New York) and you will certainly clear two thirds of the
money you pay for the recovery of it.

We want 3,000 pounds or $15,000 in gold. No other money
will be taken but English sovereigns. Insert an advertisement in
the London *Times* if you will treat on these terms, viz., "NEW
YORK, letter received etc. etc." or whatever you have to say, as
we have *The Times* by every mail. The rest is simply a matter of
detail, and can be arranged by letter hereafter. It lays entirely
with you whether you have it back or not.

If this letter is shown to the police, we will know that you
are not inclined to keep faith with us, and will act accordingly.
For obvious reasons you will be careful in wording the advertisement.

Worth signed the letter NEW YORK, and added that all further correspondence would be sent under that name.

The letter was vintage Worth: methodical, organized, imperious, and remarkably impertinent. The legal tone suggests that it
may even have been drafted by his brother-in-law, the lawyer
Lefens. Agnew hardly needed to be told that the thief had been

good enough to increase the value of his painting by stealing it, nor how to word a careful reply, and it is fascinating that Worth, ever the snob, wanted it understood that even on the other side of the world he still read *The* London *Times,* the newspaper of the British elite.

The letter was also partly a bluff. Worth had no intention of destroying the painting; indeed, the piece of canvas sent as proof of theft had been carefully cut from the portion of the picture beneath the frame, so as not to damage the work: Worth was no Mrs. Maginnis. This letter contains Worth's first reference to the "elopement of the Duchess"—a humorous remark, but also an indication that the portrait had come to mean more to him than a mere "commercial" property. While Agnew might find his tone distinctly galling, the fragment matched with the remnant on the stretcher and proved the writer was no hoaxer. In contrast to his earlier nonchalance, Worth now gave no clues to his whereabouts.

Agnew's, after conferring with their solicitors, Lewis & Lewis, and with Scotland Yard, placed an advertisement in the personal columns of *The Times*: "New York, Letter received. On further proof are prepared to treat."

William Agnew knew he was compounding a felony, whatever Worth's reassurances, but he wanted his picture back. Worth promptly sent "a longer piece of the upper part of the picture, to match the piece now in your possession," adding that "from time to time in our negotiations we desire to send a small piece to prevent any mistake or your wasting your time on bogus possessors." It was a considerate, if ironic remark, for Agnew's was still being deluged by hoaxers, amateur detectives, crooks, and crackpots. This letter concluded by recommending that Agnew's place another notice in *The Times* immediately if he was satisfied and wished to proceed, since "it is certainly in the interest of both parties to bring the affair to a close as soon as possible."

Agnew complied, and on March 6, 1877, Worth sent yet another letter, on the elegant stationery of the Grand Hotel, announcing that "in order to facilitate matters" he had dispatched a man to London who "has our confidence" to negotiate the return of the painting and avoid the delays caused by the transatlantic postal system. "The Picture is over here in our possession. You will hear further from the bearer of this letter in a day or two," Worth wrote, enclosing another fragment of canvas "which will be found to fit the last piece you received." But Agnew's did not hear from the mysterious messenger and after three weeks the art dealer placed another advertisement: "New York. Am waiting to hear from you further. Have received your letter and wait appointment."

Suddenly the thief was getting cold feet, perhaps fearing some sort of an ambush by Scotland Yard. After several more tense weeks, Worth reestablished contact, but the terms had now changed. He was no longer willing to send someone to London to haggle on his behalf, given "the penalties for the crime of compounding a felony in England." If Agnew's wanted the picture back, then someone would have to come to New York and get it. "It is out of the question to get anybody to come to you about negotiating for it, as it might get the party so doing into trouble." Worth was not prepared to put his subordinates in the way of unnecessary danger, but he was also unwilling, as ever, to relinquish control of events. "The only way that I know of is by you sending a trustworthy man over to N.Y. with a draft for the amount, and paying it, on the picture being shown to him . . . Please answer as usual."

The affair was now coming to a head. William Agnew refused to come to New York and Worth was not about to put himself at the mercy of Scotland Yard by coming back to London, although he made it appear that he had already done so. In his next letter he stated unequivocally:

> I have vainly endeavored to think of some safe way of negotiating the return of the Lady on this side of the water [i.e., England] according to your desire (although it would be considerable expense to bring it over again). But I cannot see my way clear to doing so without putting myself in your power, and that I will not do.

Consequently we must fall back in our original position—namely that it must be arranged in America. If your desire be to recover the Lady only, on the terms mentioned before, and not the punishment of the abstracters, it can make very little difference to you where the negotiation takes place. If you persist in your determination to deal only on this side I shall be compelled to drop the matter.

Agnew was equally adamant: "NEW YORK, No danger to you whatever. There can be no necessity for voyage, which, indeed, I cannot make."

From May to August there was silence. Then on August 8 a letter postmarked London arrived at Agnew's office. "Finding that it was impossible, as you said, for you to go to America, the parties have gone to the expense of sending the 'Duchess' back to this country . . . too much time has already been wasted on the affair, and the parties wish it settled at once." Worth had returned to London with the painting, but his attitude had clearly changed. His next letter, dated August 21, was abrupt to the point of rudeness:

I really cannot suggest any way of returning the Noble Lady, and if you cannot, I am afraid we shall have to drop the affair entirely . . . We have been trying to think of some plan in which we can safely do it on this side of the water, but can think of no way with safety to ourselves. As I said before, if you cannot find some means of doing it, why then we will not trouble ourselves any more about it. If you really mean to act squarely with us and want the missing lady back, you have only to suggest some safe method and we will adopt it.

Agnew, realizing he had been presented with an ultimatum, put another coded advertisement in *The Times*, on August 23, agreeing to do whatever the elusive NEW YORK wanted. But it was too late. Worth had changed his mind. He never again contacted the art dealer, and all William Agnew had to show for his months of delay tactics were a few carefully clipped fragments of canvas and a handful of peremptory letters.

Agnew had certainly been in contact with Inspector Shore of Scotland Yard, and Worth may have got wind of the danger thanks to his spies in the force. One newspaper, noting his wavering tone many years later, concluded he had been toying with Agnew all along. "It seemed evident that he was not really anxious to surrender the masterpiece or make any revelations. He wished merely to excite curiosity."

Kitty Flynn was undoubtedly part of the key to Worth's change of heart and his sudden decision to keep the portrait. The former Irish barmaid and the late Duchess of Devonshire, whose piquant history was now enjoying a second lease on life after the theft, had many of the same character traits: an extraordinary zest for life, a healthy disrespect for the opinions of others, and thus a freedom of spirit that would always be denied the bitter and complex Worth. The physical resemblance between the two women was equally striking. The best portrait of Kitty shows her with a teasing, pouting expression which might have been borrowed directly from Georgiana. The *Duchess*'s golden tresses, flashing eyes, her curvaceous figure and vivid determination to enjoy herself, and others, were all echoed by Kitty in her prime, and the former hostess of the American Bar had long and rightly considered herself one of nature's aristocrats.

Like some criminal Pygmalion, Worth had sought to mold Kitty into a flawless replica of his ideal woman—elegant, pliant, and socially acceptable—and he had succeeded. Yet there was a part of Kitty he could not touch—her very vitality—and thus his creation had betrayed and abandoned him. Worth's "Fair Lady," as in every version of that enduring myth, had shown she did not need him. Galatea had taken flight. He had sought to control and hold Kitty, and for the first time in his life he had failed. Gainsborough's *Duchess*, by contrast, was docile and maneuverable, a perfect painted captive in a way Kitty had declined to be. In the Greek myth, Pygmalion found love when his beautiful statue came to life; Worth perhaps found some remnant of love by transferring his affections from flesh, blood, and spirit to canvas, oil paint, and artifice.

One writer who speculated on the motives of the man who stole the Gainsborough wondered if he might be "a *fin de siècle* scoundrel . . . a mad enthusiast [who] had stolen the portrait to worship its grace and tender beauty in the still watches of the night, when pale moonbeams lit up the rounded form and revealed fresh depths in those lustrous eyes. Folly and crime there might have been—let there also be love." The writing was pure Victorian schmaltz, the effect somewhat emetic, but the suggestion was entirely apt.

Half a lifetime later, Worth remarked that the portrait had been "a white elephant on his hands for years that he could not get rid of." This claim was manifestly false. Over the next twenty years, he could have reopened negotiations with Agnew's for the return of the portrait at any stage, but he did not.

In time, the rumor that Worth was the thief gained currency in the underworld and many a dubious character offered to help arrange its return, for a consideration. He turned them all down, preferring to face disgrace, penury, and imprisonment rather than part with the *Duchess*. The painting became his permanent companion, as constant and demure as Kitty had proved fickle and independent. When he traveled, she came, too, in his false-bottomed trunk; in London he slept with her, literally, the *Duchess* pinned beneath his mattress.

Still, there was more to this strange relationship between a master thief and his stolen Old Master. As Worth's obsession grew, the painting came to exert a hold over him, a symbol and reflection of his own artificial existence. In Georgiana's powerful image, he found a voyeur's keyhole through which he could spy on the privileged society to which he aspired but of which he could never truly be a part, any more than Georgiana could return to life. She was a fetish, representing the pinnacle of his dreams and the evidence of his exclusion. The most desirable object a man of wealth could own, here was a prize he could never display—unlike his racehorses, yachts, and luxurious homes—an icon of his power and powerlessness. When Worth remarked that he could not "get rid of" the painting, he was betraying his own impotence. Like a murderer preserving body parts, he clung to this ultimate testament to his crimes, for the arrogant gaze of the *Duchess* crystallized all his strength and frailty. She was his captured enemy standard, tangible evidence of his hatred for and power to undermine respectable society, an object of overwhelming beauty to crown Worth's ugly trade, a focus of longing and loathing. But when he looked on that lovely, scornful face, did he not see a pitiful reflection of his own con trick, a tawdry, superficial creation that was not even skin-deep? As the years rolled on and the painting slowly merged with his own conception of himself, Worth perhaps came to realize that his fabricated world was founded on the *Duchess* and her symbolism. "Feasting his eyes on the coveted object in secret," in the words of a contemporary, he clung to the great painting as if his life depended on it, because it did.

Worth's relationship with his stolen *Duchess* altered and deepened over time—from affectionate pride and admiration to dependence and fixation—but we can trace its genesis with some precision. He had hit on the plan to steal the painting while brooding on Kitty's departure from London, but it was in the summer of 1877, more than a year later, that he abruptly and permanently broke off all negotiations for its return—the exact moment when Kitty's life took a new and, for Worth, a freshly devastating turn.

Just as he seemed to be closing on a deal with Agnew's, word reached Worth that his onetime lover, the "canker" in his breast and probably the mother of his children, had found a new suitor in New York and planned to marry him. This final rejection also pushed Worth into matrimony, but of a very different sort: his elopement with the *Duchess* was now transformed into a fullfledged marriage that would last a quarter of a century.

FOURTEEN

Kitty Flynn,
Society Queen

That delightfully salacious newspaper, the *New York World,* now sadly defunct, would later conclude with a sly wink that, while playing the role of hostess to a gang of villains at the American Bar in Paris, Kitty "perfected herself in the arts and graces that enabled her to make her second and most brilliant matrimonial coup." She was only twenty-eight and exceptionally beautiful when, as the newspapers reported, she "captured a matrimonial prize which many of New York's proudest society women would not have disdained." With two children to support, and her ambition for fame and fortune burning as bright as ever, Kitty was plainly on the lookout for a new husband, so when Juan Pedro Terry sauntered elegantly into her life, she summoned up every art and grace in her portfolio. Juan Terry could hardly have been more ideal: he had handsome blue eyes, Irish blood, the beard of a sprightly conquistador, a taste for luxury, and a courtly demeanor. He was, moreover, staggeringly rich.

Juan was the son of Thomas Terry, an Irish adventurer whose ancestors, like Kitty, had quit the damp sod of Ireland to make their fortune in the New World. Thomas, or Thomaso, Terry was born in the city of Caracas, Venezuela, on the 24th of February 1808, and "baptized in the local church of San Pablo." An ener-

getic and resourceful youth, he began building up a fortune by
exchanging tracts of land for cheap jewelry, and in 1830 he settled
in Cienfuegos, Cuba. There he met and fell in love with Teresa
Dorticós y Gómez de Leys, the French-born daughter of a Havana
sugar planter, and asked for her hand in marriage. Teresa's enor-
mously wealthy father, don Andrés Dorticós y Casson, the gover-
nor of Cienfuegos, took one look at the beguiling but hardly de-
pendable figure of Tom Terry, and exploded. Not only did he
refuse his consent, but he ordered his field hands to give his
daughter's impertinent suitor a sound thrashing and throw him
off the premises. Terry promptly eloped with Teresa, and they
were married on October 31, 1837. Thomaso simply ignored the
ensuing uproar, and "when he heard that his father-in-law had
referred contemptuously to him he remarked quietly and ear-
nestly, 'I shall be richer than he is some day.' "

And so he became. "Every transaction in which the young
Venezuelan was concerned proved immensely profitable. His
sugar plantations gave an abundant yield. The lands for which he
had exchanged trinkets became valuable plantations." Remaining
loyal to Spain during the Cuban insurrection, Terry was rewarded
with vast parcels of confiscated land at low prices, which "proved
veritable gold mines," and within five years he was the largest
sugar planter in Cienfuegos, richer by far than his now amiable
father-in-law. Some of his fortune may have been made in an even
more unromantic way, for according to one report he supple-
mented his income from sugar with a side business in the slave
trade. Nonetheless, Thomas Terry exchanged his Venezuelan
passport for American citizenship, and as "one of the wealthiest
men in the Americas," he and Teresa traveled the world, collecting properties and having children, amassing, by and by, roughly
a dozen of each. "The Terrys owned houses in New York and a
mansion in Paris on the Rue de la Boétie, in prime expatriate
territory off the Faubourg Saint-Honoré, and dwelt also in several
castles of the Loire Valley, including, for a while, the magnificent
Château de Chenonceau."

Tom Terry was a prodigiously generous father to his multitude of children and handed out regular dollops of cash. Juan Pedro, the youngest, came to New York in 1875 with a gift from his father of $900,000 in cash, "with which he went into Wall street and when he was through with a certain transaction in gold he was half a million richer." An adept speculator, Juan was "distinguished for his business ability, but fond of a life of luxury and pleasure." Both aspects of his character immediately endeared him to Kitty Flynn.

Kitty may well have kept from her suitor the less respectable details of her history, which only leaked out many years later, but if Juan knew that the object of his adoration was a onetime barmaid who had been married to a bigamous burglar and had, for many years, shared her affections with her husband's friend and partner in crime, he does not seem to have cared one jot. His own family history was quite as romantic and roué as Kitty's, and with millions in the bank, he knew society could titter all it wanted. Indeed, the widow Flynn's racy past may have added to her fascination in the eyes of the wealthy, fun-loving *flâneur* and speculator. Juan was also a bland and vacillating man whose will, weak at the best of times, was no match for the Irishwoman's gumption. Kitty had more than enough chutzpah for them both.

According to Sophie Lyons, the two met at an art dealer's on Twenty-third Street in Manhattan, where Kitty, perennially short of money, had gone to sell the last of the paintings from the American Bar. "Young Terry was infatuated with Kate's queenly beauty, and he laid siege to her heart so ardently" that she agreed immediately to marry him. Sophie's romantic memory being what it was, it seems rather more likely that, as newspapers later reported, they met at the widow Flynn's boarding house one evening when Juan, on the spur of the moment, invited his hostess to attend a charity ball with him. "She was pretty and fascinating, and caught the imagination of the Cuban," the papers reported.

The only hitch in their fast-blooming love affair was that Kitty was still legally married to Charley Bullard, who was also illegally married to someone else. The intervening years had not been happy ones for the musical felon. On September 13, 1878, he had managed to escape from the prison in Concord to which he had been consigned for his part in the Boylston Bank robbery. "His conduct as a prisoner was uniformly docile and good for many months, until one day he surprised his keepers by a seemingly inexplicable outbreak of insolence and riotous disturbance. For this offense against discipline he was confined overnight with five other rioters in the cells for refractory prisoners. The next morning it was discovered the birds had flown. Bullard had somehow fitted keys to the locks of the cells, released his confederates and found a way of escape."

At liberty in New York, and in a drunken euphoria, he had sent an "insulting postal card" to General Chamberlain, the prison warden at Concord jail, "stating that the Manhattan Bank robbery was planned by him." After bumming around New York for a while, Bullard had made his way to Toronto, where he slipped back into some low-level crime, but "his ill-gotten gains soon melted in his hands." Long imprisonment followed by heavy drinking had sapped his once-legendary abilities as a sneak thief and pianist. The man who once had "fingers so sensitive he could open a combination safe with his hands alone" now had the shakes so badly he could hardly open a bottle, let alone play the piano with any skill.

The thief of the Merchant Express and the Boylston Bank was reduced to petty pilfering and finally came to grief "while penny weighting a watch chain in a jewelry shop," for which he was arrested and sent to the Canadian Penitentiary at Kingston for five years. This time he found himself well and truly incarcerated, and it was here, in the winter of 1880, that Bullard finally received the news that Kitty had divorced him.

The following spring, Kitty and Juan Terry were married by Judge Morgan in a civil service at Jefferson Market Court in New York, "greatly to the consternation of his family," who had been making their own investigations into Kitty's past. Of all the levels of hypocrisy in this tale, the fury of the Terrys when presented with an Irish barmaid as a relative is among the most impressive.

To his credit, and like his father before him, Juan Terry simply ignored the bleating of his nouveau-riche relatives and moved his new wife into luxurious apartments in Stuyvesant House, New York. The widow Flynn may initially have been attracted by Terry's wealth, but they were well suited to one another and the result was, as Sophie Lyons reports, an "exceedingly happy marriage." Kitty's two daughters, "who had grown up to be beautiful girls," were informally adopted by their wealthy new stepfather. Juan Terry "permitted Kate's daughters to use his name and saw that they were properly educated with private lessons in the arts and sojourns in schools in New York and on the Continent in keeping with their rich-gypsy existence." New York society might snigger as word of Kitty's lowly origins leaked out, but the extent of Terry's fortune was sufficient to ensure that such carping was short-lived. Within a few years Mrs. Terry had become a noted figure in New York society and a sought-after guest at the city's social functions.

Her good looks, her wealth, and her exciting past earned Kitty the envy and attention of the masses, but another aspect of her character ensured that she quickly became a regular feature in the pages of the more scurrilous New York newspapers: her newfound and obsessive taste for litigation. The gangster's moll who had happily turned a blind eye to the illegal doings of Worth and Bullard now recruited the law to her side. She sued hard and she sued often, and was sued in turn.

Where Worth had, for obvious reasons, made every effort to avoid setting foot in court, Kitty was strangely drawn to the legal fray, perhaps out of a desire to show herself on the right side of the law, having spent so much of her early life, if not actively, then at least by association, on the wrong side. Kitty was no criminal; she was not even a natural dissembler. She was an actress, and the courts were her stage. While her legal imbroglios did not always show her in the best light, the attendant publicity and revelations added to her social cachet—a manner of social self-advancement not unknown in modern times.

Her first experience in the New York courts involved one Miss Alcevinia, or "Vinnie," Atwood, a young lady of dubious reputation, who appeared to be on uncommonly, not to say infuriatingly, intimate terms with Kitty's new husband. The facts are disputed, as with all such domestic spats, but *The New York Times* reported the incident thus: "Returning from a shopping tour on the afternoon of Nov. 10, 1881, Mrs. Kate Louise Terry found in her room in the Stuyvesant House, a letter addressed to her husband, Mr. Juan P. Terry. As the address was in feminine handwriting she opened the letter, and found it contained a request for money to enable Miss Vinnie Atwood to make a trip to some place called Burlington where she desired to interview the father and mother of some man who had done her a wrong." The *New York World* reported that Kitty had actually extracted the letter from her husband's pocket, "the tone of which indicated a degree of intimacy not pleasing to his wife."

The redoubtable Kitty, who thought nothing of opening her husband's letters and was no stranger herself to the intricacies of divided love, took to the warpath. "She wrote a reply, signing her husband's name, took a cab and drove to the vicinity of Miss Atwood's flat. She sent the missive into the house and receiving no reply, followed it in person." Kitty testified that she had found Miss Atwood and some other women "sitting smoking and drinking," and that when she demanded an explanation for the letter, she was assaulted. Miss Atwood's account was probably more accurate, given what we know of Kitty's incendiary personality: "Mrs. Terry, as soon as she entered her rooms, began to curse her and throw miniature images &c at her." A brief but ferocious bout of fisticuffs ensued, "in the course of which crockery was broken and Mrs. Terry's face was bruised."

Kitty stormed off to the police station at the 29th precinct, and Miss Atwood was arrested on a charge of assault and battery, to which a further charge of grand larceny was added after Kitty claimed her rival had also stolen from her the sum of $1,000. Justice Smith was plainly baffled by the fracas, and to Kitty's fury, the theft charge was dismissed. Miss Atwood was briefly held on the charge of assault, and when she was finally acquitted, she promptly filed a countersuit against Kitty, "complaining that Mrs.

Terry had acted maliciously, and had injured her in her social reputation and standing, for which she asked $25,000 damages."

When the cat-fight came to court more than a year later, New York was agog. Kitty insisted that Miss Atwood was a slut, "a person of bad character, and therefore could not have been hurt in reputation," since she had no social standing to damage. Miss Atwood's lawyers, in turn, subjected Kitty to "a similar cross-examination, the design of which was to show that she must be an untruthful woman because she was formerly the wife of Charlie Bullard, alias 'Piano Charlie,' one of the Boylston Bank robbers, and therefore the associate of his friends. She was asked if she knew certain notorious criminals and she said she did not."

Kitty launched into an impassioned defense of her misspent youth. "Her marriage to Bullard, alias Wells, she said, occurred when she was only 17 years old. He represented himself as a millionaire, and she married him after having known him only three weeks." The jury found in Miss Atwood's favor, but, perhaps moved by Kitty's account of life with a wicked bank robber, ordered her to pay just $800 in damages, a mere trifle, given the size of the Terry bank account, and a great deal less than the $25,000 demanded. What Juan Pedro made of the legal tangle between his new wife and a woman we can only assume was his mistress is not recorded, because the Cuban millionaire, showing eminent good sense, had gone on holiday. Kitty, however, seems to have regarded the verdict as a moral victory. "The court experience seemed to whet the appetite of the ex-barmaid for legal disputes," the *New York World* later reported, "and ever since then she frequently figured in the New York courts."

In 1888 she was back in the dock, accused of assaulting her servant, Mary Anne Coogan, and fought the charges in a lengthy court battle. Then in 1891 she was entangled in yet another case when she refused to pay rent owed to a Fifth Avenue boarding-house keeper, one Mme. Lavalette. Kitty, it appears, had rented this woman's rooms a few years earlier but "afterwards went South . . . leaving her rooms at Mme. Lavalette's locked. Mrs. Terry was informed anonymously that Mme. Lavalette was not only using her apartments but also her clothing.'' Kitty, furious, refused to pay the landlady and also took her to court, and won.

Such incidents reflected a vital aspect of Kitty's character. She now had the fine clothes, the grand apartments, the gilded carriages, but she was still the salty, high-spirited woman who wouldn't set herself on a moral pedestal, or pretend to be better than she was. There was no double life for Kitty Flynn, and if that meant showing the world she was still prepared to duke it out with chambermaids or her husband's mistress, so be it.

Meanwhile, Juan Pedro and Kitty lived the flamboyant life of a wealthy young couple, holding dinner parties and dances, attending the opera, and generally showing off to their peers. Despite his brief and lucrative flutter on the stock exchange, Juan Pedro was never tempted to repeat the experiment and did not a hand's turn of work for the rest of his life. When not in court, Kitty traveled the world in lavish style with her husband and children, much as she had done with Worth and Bullard, but this time there was no subterfuge. Kitty Flynn, the poor girl from the Dublin slums, had finally achieved the status she had always dreamed of: she was now a society duchess in her own right.

FIFTEEN

Dishonor
Among Thieves

W orth prided himself on his loyalty to his minions, a lofty principle they repaid with egregious betrayal. Little Joe Elliott and Junka Phillips would never have agreed to help steal the Gainsborough had they foreseen they would not be richly compensated for their work, and Worth's unexplained and unilateral decision to keep the painting for himself both confused and angered his partners in crime. To shut them up, Worth handed them both a wad of cash, knowing only too well that this was only a short-term solution. With the *Duchess* in his possession, he was an obvious target for blackmail, and Worth was enough of a realist to know that his fickle friends would sell him out if it suited their purposes. Just weeks after the theft, Little Joe was back demanding more money, explaining that he needed to go to America immediately. Once again, love was uppermost in Joe's mind: he wanted to go back to his wife, and he wanted Worth to pay his passage. Knowing that he needed to keep Elliott sweet and concluding that he would be safer with his accomplice on the other side of the Atlantic, Worth consented.

Amazingly, Kate Castleton still had room in her heart for her husband, and the two were reunited. But if Kate remembered Elliott fondly, so did the New York Police Department, and in

April 1877 he was arrested. On his way to the Tombs, the notorious New York lockup, Elliott briefly escaped, but was recaptured in Poughkeepsie. On the evidence of the Pinkertons, he was charged with "being the perpetrator of a forgery amounting to $64,000 on the Union Trust Company in New York, having forged a New York Life Insurance Company check." The Pinkertons also fingered him for robbing a Boston jeweler of $4,000 in uncut gems several years earlier. Little Joe was speedily tried, convicted, and sentenced to seven years in Sing Sing. With touching loyalty, Kate Castleton continued to visit her husband in prison; with equally profound disloyalty, Elliott decided that this was the moment to cash in on the Gainsborough theft by betraying Adam Worth.

According to the Pinkerton files: "While in prison he sent for Mr. Robt. A. Pinkerton, and tried to make terms with him for his release, offering to restore the Gainsborough portrait, and told Mr. Pinkerton the history of the robbery and the names of the parties connected with it. These facts were communicated to Mr. John Shore, Superintendent of Criminal Investigation Department, New Scotland Yard, London, England, and only confirmed what Mr. Shore and the London Police Department had then suspected concerning who the perpetrators of the deed were."

Elliott's treachery was little help to him, since he had no idea of the whereabouts of the painting and "could not control it or deliver it, as he claimed he could, [so] the matter was abandoned." Scotland Yard had more respect for Worth than to imagine he would be rash enough to keep the painting on his premises, so while Elliott's testimony was a useful confirmation of their suspicions, it was insufficient to nail the thief. It is not clear precisely at what point the Pinkertons and Superintendent Shore of the Yard became convinced that Adam Worth, alias Henry Raymond, was responsible for the deed, for it appears that Elliott was not the only person passing on information to the authorities. "Gradually certain facts leaked out in regard to the robbery," the Pinkertons recorded, "which put the London police in possession of information as to who the perpetrators of the robbery were, but they had only hearsay evidence and no proof whatever. Every possible ingenuity was used by Scotland Yard detectives to find the hiding place of the picture and fasten the crime on the thieves, but all efforts failed."

With Worth "back at the old stand" in Piccadilly, as Shore wrote to Pinkerton, the Scotland Yard detective was growing more and more frustrated at his inability to bring the thief to book. "He became such a 'bugaboo' to the English police that they eventually tried to drive him out by stationing a policeman in front of his door, and watching and reporting everyone who entered his house." But to no avail. Inspector Shore's extreme measures came close to police harassment; at least that was how Worth chose to interpret such efforts to interfere in the smooth running of his criminal network. Worth believed he still owed Shore for arresting his brother, and this sort of victimization was quite intolerable. The time had come "to get even with him"; Inspector Shore would have to be removed. A more brutal and less sophisticated man than Worth might simply have arranged for the Scotland Yard detective to be knocked on the head one dark night and thrown into the Thames, but that was not Worth's style. He planned a far more witty and humiliating fate for the irritating detective.

Superintendent Shore may have been a prominent and powerful man in Scotland Yard, and a dedicated if rather plodding policeman. But he was also, like most characters in this tale, a man of double standards. He might represent the strict moral face of the English constabulary, but he was also a notorious womanizer and frequenter of London's brothels. Shore maintained that he went to such places only to gather information, but Worth, and even William Pinkerton, knew better. As the American detective delicately put it, "Shore was in the habit of what we would call in this country 'chasing chippies'; that is, running after girls of a low order."

Shore's favorite brothel was run by one-legged Nellie Coffey, the widow of a burglar and pickpocket named Big Jack Casey who had been murdered some years before. Nellie had lost her leg in the New York riots, and now made her living, in Pinkerton's words, by "keeping a brothel or assignation house in the Borough, a low district of London." On the side, for a consideration, she passed on useful information to John Shore, one of her most regular clients. They met often at a pub "called the Rising Sun, at the head of Fleet Street in London, where they had private dining rooms . . . This woman had a fund of information and was very useful to him," Pinkerton reported. "She told us everything that was going on around the drinking house of Bill Richardson, a resort for thieves, and all the gossip about London thieves." Worth regarded underworld informers and Scotland Yard detectives as like species of vermin, so he now planned to put an end to Shore's career and silence the overtalkative Nellie with a single blow.

Worth later told Pinkerton, in detail, of the plan by which he intended to rid himself of the persecuting Shore. "He said they had gotten a broken down swell and located him at a neighboring place, paying his hotel bills, and had him there for weeks waiting an opportunity to catch Shore. This man was readied up to go and make a charge that a woman had robbed him of a piece of jewelry, which was supplied to him for this purpose, and some money. The woman was to have been traced to the house of Coffey, and an officer was to go into the house to arrest the woman and find her there with Shore. An exposure was to follow." Shore would be disgraced, Coffey's establishment would be closed, and Worth could carry on his nefarious business unimpeded.

The "old swell" was an elderly con man of good birth known to Worth for many years, who had recently fallen on hard times and taken to the bottle. For weeks Worth drilled the old thief in his role as a raffish gentleman who had fallen victim to a light-fingered whore. He deprived the old gent of alcohol and took him for long walks in London's parks to clear his fuddled brain. And while Shore's detectives were keeping watch on Worth's movements, Worth's spies were tailing the superintendent, with instructions to report back the moment Shore was seen going to Coffey's brothel with a prostitute.

When word finally came that the detective was on his way to pegleg Nellie's, Worth rushed to the hotel where his accomplice was being kept, only to find that the old man had left his post and repaired to a nearby pub, where he was now gloriously, incoherently plastered. So far from being able to give the police a convincing story, the ancient swell could not even stand up. As Worth later explained, with admirable detachment, "he had got tired of waiting at his post and went off and got drunk."

Instead of being angry, Worth seems to have found the entire episode hilarious. He paid off the old man, who, once sober, was most apologetic, and even told him he could keep the expensive suit he had bought him. Shore never knew how close he had come to disgrace, and although Worth made no further attempt to frame his adversary, the animosity continued to blaze between them.

Worth's battle with Shore redoubled his determination to keep the Gainsborough, and he later claimed, not quite convincingly but as further proof of the link between his greatest theft and his hatred of the law, that "had Supt. Shore treated him in a half-way decent manner that the picture would have gone back long ago." William Pinkerton later asked Worth why he had expended so much energy trying to entrap a detective who was, after all, only doing his job. "I told him I thought he was drawing a long bow on Shore," Pinkerton recalled, but Worth's response was adamant: Shore was an asinine, boozy sex maniac who "would never have amounted to anything" without the Pinkertons to help him.

In spite of his prodigious generosity, when Worth felt he had been wronged or betrayed, he was implacable in exacting revenge; he regarded retribution as his right. One who learned this to his cost was the French banker Monsieur Meyer, who had caused the arrest of John Worth in 1876. Meyer had only been defending his interests, but Worth was deeply resentful, the more so when yet another of his associates was arrested as a result of Meyer's vigilance. On a trip to Paris many years later, Worth was walking along the rue St.-Honoré when he passed the offices of Meyer & Co.

Remembering the trouble Meyer had once caused him, Worth made some investigations and learned that the banker's safe was a cinch to open and was, moreover, currently full. That night, 250,000 francs were stolen from Meyer's vault. "This robbery was perpetrated at night, the safe having been forced open with jimmies," the Pinkertons reported. "Of this robbery Adam Worth was the originator, and it satisfied his vengeance as it ruined M. Meyer almost completely."

As if the avid attentions of Scotland Yard and his continuing feud with John Shore were not enough, Worth faced another problem rather closer to hand: Junka Phillips was demanding to know what had happened to the Gainsborough, and insisting that if Worth would not sell it, he would. "From time to time [he] had borrowed money from Worth for his interest in it," but the bulky burglar had started to dun Worth for cash on a regular basis, and his formerly submissive attitude was becoming positively intimidating. Finally Worth told him he had sold off the Gainsborough painting "for a bagatelle," handed him £50 as his share, and told him there would be no more. But Junka, who made up in persistence what he lacked in intelligence, was not to be put off.

On the basis of the Gainsborough theft, Junka regarded himself as a master criminal in his own right, and tried to persuade Worth to finance a job of his own devising. Worth, he said, should provide money to a pair of crooked clerks in a bond office in London, who would repay the investment by lifting redeemable bonds "not out of the vaults but by stealing from other clerks." The threat of what would happen if Worth failed to underwrite the scheme was implicit. For a master criminal like Worth, such "sneak thieving" was small-fry and, given that he knew neither of Junka's clerks and must rely on Junka's word alone for their competence, extremely risky. He therefore "refused to have anything to do with it." Junka was livid and told Worth he did not believe the Gainsborough had been sold. "Phillips demanded that the picture be produced and he would pay his indebtedness, and buy out Worth's interest." Again Worth declined, but to calm the enraged thug he agreed to meet him a few days later at the Criterion

Bar in Piccadilly, where they could talk over the situation. When the day of the rendezvous arrived, Worth, "suspecting treachery, secretly took a position, watched Phillips's movements, and found that he was accompanied by two well known detectives from Scotland Yard. Under the circumstances, neither Worth nor the picture put in an appearance." Through Joe Elliott's treachery, John Shore was already aware of Junka's role in the theft, and with promises of leniency, and a monetary reward, the Scotland Yard detective had persuaded Junka to help him trap Worth.

Incensed by Junka's duplicity, Worth planned his revenge with studied care. He sent a message to the English thief's home, saying he had been unavoidably delayed, and arranged to meet him the next day. When Junka arrived at the Criterion Bar, he was accompanied by "a fighting man" and in a most belligerent mood. A little way down the bar, Worth caught sight of Inspector Greenham of Scotland Yard, one of Shore's trusted deputies, in heavy disguise and wearing the unmistakable expression of a man who is drinking alone but is straining every muscle to overhear what is being said. Clearly Junka thought he could trick his former patron into making an admission in front of a witness. While the fighting man stood a little way off, Junka began to accuse Worth of involving him in the theft of the Gainsborough painting. Worth listened politely as Junka tried to prod him into talking about the robbery, but uttered not a word. Subtlety not being part of Junka's makeup, the hoodlum finally did what came most naturally; as Worth later recalled, he "commenced to abuse him and struck him."

For the first and only time on record, Worth broke his own cardinal rule. "He jumped up and struck Junka fair in the eye, and Junka slipped and fell, and while he was down he kicked him in the head four or five times." Under any other circumstances, Worth would have made a discreet exit and settled with Junka later, but this was a far remove from any normal commercial exchange. An uncouth Philistine was attempting to deprive him of his beloved *Duchess,* and in an upsurge of chivalry, Worth leaped to her defense. Even the most pacific of men feel justified in resorting to violence when a woman's honor is at stake. And no one could accuse Worth of cowardice. Weighing in at just five feet four and 150 pounds, Worth had probably never hit anyone before in his life on the understandable basis that he was likely to be thrashed in return. Six-foot-four Junka, on the other hand, was a former wrestler and prone to violence, who could break a safe open with his bare hands. The sight of the dapper little man beating seven bells out of this colossus clearly stunned the fighting man into passivity, for he offered no assistance to his companion, and it was not until Inspector Greenham intervened and Worth was pulled off his unconscious former bodyguard and butler that the bout ended. Realizing that he had been rumbled, Inspector Greenham gave up any pretense at disguise and "denounced him for striking an old man like Junka." Worth hotly responded that it "looked to him like Junka had Greenham there for the purpose of involving him in trouble." With that, Worth dusted off his jacket and stalked haughtily out of the bar.

The principled villain was plainly embarrassed to have broken his own code of nonviolence, for he only once discussed the incident, and then reluctantly. But Junka, who specialized in clubbing his victims senseless with heavy objects, was no mean adversary and had in fact proffered the first blow after trying to entrap him. Junka certainly seems to have got the message after he regained consciousness and was escorted, blearily, out of the Criterion Bar by his apologetic fighting man. He troubled Worth no more, and "they never met again up until the day of Worth's death."

SIXTEEN

Rough Diamonds

Adam Worth, or more precisely Henry Judson Raymond, Esquire, worthy gentleman of Piccadilly, was not the sort who liked to be seen getting involved in barroom brawling. What with Scotland Yard breathing down his neck and his former associates betraying him left and right, London was becoming distinctly uncomfortable, and good criminal help hard to find. Joe Chapman was still in a Constantinople jail; Carlo Sesicovitch and Little Joe Elliott had vanished. Charles the Scratch Becker was still in London, but fast becoming an encumbrance. Becker might be a superb forger, but he was also, Worth concluded, a spineless coward who was liable to run to the police at the first sign of trouble. The Bank of England had recently employed a new technology, "a combination of the artist, printer and chemist," which made forging checks all but impossible. Becker's forgeries had been highly successful in the past, but his talents were out of date, while his neurotic tendencies made him increasingly dangerous. Johnny Carr, an experienced thief, warned Worth to "be on his guard when dealing with a blackguard like that and give him none of the best of it."

"On account of [Becker's] tendency to squeal," Worth decided that he "would have nothing more to do with him."

With his *Duchess* pinned down beneath his mattress at night,

Worth seems to have retreated from friendship and human company. His social acquaintance grew ever wider, but the circle of his close and trusted colleagues shrank steadily, thinned out by fate, betrayal, and his own withdrawal. He was not a genuine part of the high society he emulated or the low society he truly represented, but a being suspended between the two, trapped by his own moral ambivalence, of which the Gainsborough was an ever present, tangible reminder.

Worth's sense of isolation was increased by news of Piano Charley Bullard. His old partner had finally been released from prison in Canada, but instead of reuniting with Worth, he had elected go into partnership with Max Shinburn, who had also been through some ups and downs since the days of the American Bar. The Baron had made another fortune safecracking in Europe, and with the proceeds he had formalized his aristocratic posturing by purchasing a castle in Holland to go with his assumed title of Baron Shindell. But Shinburn was an inveterate gambler, and the combined effects of Monte Carlo and ill-advised investments on the Paris Bourse had reduced his finances to a low ebb. "He might have lived in his fine feathers to the end of his life, but could not restrain his passion for gambling," as one police account noted, and Worth recalled with glee how, on one occasion, he "came to London . . . with a twenty pound note, and said 'Here is where I have got to.'" On the underworld grapevine Worth learned that Shinburn had emerged from retirement, entered into partnership with the recently released Piano Charley, and was now planning to revitalize his criminal career. Prison had dulled what few wits Bullard had not already pickled in alcohol. Worth rightly concluded that Shinburn had duped his former partner and would simply abandon him if circumstances required it. After Shinburn linked up with Bullard, Worth's dislike for the Baron turned to loathing, a feeling that was strongly reciprocated.

With the old gang in shreds, Worth concluded, it was time to seek out new colleagues and browse alternative criminal pastures. In the spring of 1878 Worth had taken on as accomplices one

Captain George (his Christian name remains unknown) and a young thief named William Megotti. Together they broke into the money car on the Calais-to-Paris express train, removing Spanish and Egyptian bonds valued at 700,000 francs. From Worth's point of view, the job was a success, but Captain George, showing traits similar to the idiotic John Worth's, managed to get himself arrested in Paris. The imprisoned man appealed to Worth for funds to pay a defense lawyer, but then promptly made a full confession to the French police, naming Worth as the principal organizer. Worth was sentenced to twenty years' imprisonment, in absentia. The profits from the train robbery were undoubtedly useful, but now France, too, was out of bounds.

At the same time, the Pinkertons reported, Worth was suspected of being involved in a "number of dynamite explosions which took place at that time in Europe," usually involving boats scuttled for their insurance value. In fact, the authorities later admitted, "he was entirely innocent of these crimes." They were carried out, it later transpired, by none other than Max Shinburn. But Worth's reputation had evolved to such an extent, and Scotland Yard's determination to catch him was now so intense, that virtually every major crime was assumed to be his work.

In the circumstances, it was time for Worth and his *Duchess* to take a holiday. With a gallantry indicative of how far he had anthropomorphized the painting, he bought a fine hunting coat ("the very best of the lot") in which to wrap his trophy, which was then stashed securely in the secret compartment at the bottom of his trunk. For a combination of superstitious, romantic, and cautionary reasons, Worth refused to let the painting out of his immediate possession. According to Sophie Lyons, "he feared to leave it in storage lest someone recognize it. So he carried the roll of canvas with him about the world."

There is an uncanny resemblance, in Worth's behavior, to that of Captain Nemo in Jules Verne's *20,000 Leagues Under the Sea,* but whether the culture-hungry crook read the book, published ten years earlier, will never be known. Captain Nemo is the archetypal criminal aesthete whose gallery contained "thirty or so paintings by famous masters . . . a veritable museum, in which an intelligent, prodigal hand had brought together all the treasures of nature and art." Nemo, Captain No-name, also cuts himself off from society, while vowing revenge on it, setting up his parallel world in the *Nautilus* submarine, a subaquatic Mr. Hyde. "I'm not what you would call a civilised man. I've broken with all of society for reasons which I alone can appreciate. I therefore don't obey its rules," says Captain Nemo, words that might as easily have been uttered by Worth. Verne's antihero is a civilized man rejecting civilization, and there is no doubt Worth saw himself in the same light. Where Verne's villain has his *Nautilus* and his sumptuous gallery to prove his superiority and rebellion, Worth had his false-bottomed trunk; where Nemo has thirty Old Masters, Worth had one.

In 1880, soon after Kitty's marriage, Worth and his *Duchess* set sail for Cape Town, South Africa, where the air was clear, the countryside beautiful, and Shore and his cohorts—indeed, the law in any shape—were enticingly absent. Worth later said he had come to South Africa "partly on business, partly on pleasure." Having surveyed the criminal landscape, he had concluded that uncut diamonds represented an excellent, portable, and easily exchangeable form of cash. As an accomplice he brought along one Charley King, described in the Pinkerton files as "a noted English crook." Apart from his criminal talents, King had the added advantage that he knew nothing about the theft of the Gainsborough, and remained completely ignorant of the unlikely traveling companion stashed in Worth's Saratoga trunk. Worth was not about to be blackmailed again.

The diamond fields, offering quick profits and "crystallized romance" or ghastly toil and heartbreak, depending on your luck, had already proved a magnet for a diverse mixture of visionaries and vagabonds. "Rabbis, rebels, rogues and roués from Russia and the Riviera, transports from Tasmania, convicts from Caledonia, ex-prisoners from Portland, brigands from Bulgaria, the choicest pickings of the dirtiest street corners in all of Europe . . . unfrocked clergymen with the air of saints and the souls of sinners . . . It was a hoard that increased and multiplied, and would have made a fine haul for the devil." Two more crooks in the multitude would not stand out, and with diamonds being hauled out of the earth at a prodigious rate, the thieving opportunities were tremendous. The fastidious Worth was not about to get his hands dirty grubbing around for gems amid the flies and baked dust. As Cecil Rhodes and his ilk were already proving, the best way to extract a large fortune from the mines was to let others do the digging.

This was the height of the ostrich-feather boom, thanks in part to the continuing craze for vast ostrich-feather hats of the type made glamorous by the Duchess of Devonshire, which were still firmly in fashion following the notorious theft of the Gainsborough portrait. Pairs of ostriches could fetch as much as £200. Even the locals had taken on a little of the Georgiana look, for, as one observer noted, "large ostrich feathers are frequently to be seen curling gracefully round the slouched felt hat of some stalwart young farmer." According to the *Standard Encyclopedia of South Africa*: "As there were no restrictions on immigration, [Worth] entered the country without difficulty and set up business as an ostrich feather buyer." Worth and King checked into the best hotel in Port Elizabeth and, as so many years earlier in Boston, began to build up a cover. "He opened an office, hired a clerk, bought a shipment of feathers and had them crated to a London warehouse." In the guise of a respectable man of business, Worth could now travel the country without suspicion, apparently seeking "inland agents" for his feather business, while in reality planning one of his most ambitious robberies to date.

"While looking about," according to the Pinkertons, "Worth studied the manner in which diamonds in the rough were brought from the De Beers and other mines in South Africa" to the coast, before being shipped to England. The mine owners were no fools, and elaborate precautions were in place to prevent just such a robbery as Worth intended. From Kimberley the diamonds were transported in a convoy of horse-drawn coaches, accompanied by heavily armed Boers. The timetable was worked out to the minute, ensuring that the shipment arrived just as the steamer for England was ready to sail, thus avoiding the necessity of keeping the diamonds in one place for any length of time where they might prove a temptation to criminals. Worth "looked the situation over carefully, and concluded that the most feasible way to get possession of the consignment from the mines was through what would be called in America a holdup robbery." They recruited a third accomplice in Cape Town, "an American sea captain, who was then in hiding, he being wanted in America for sinking his ship at sea for the insurance."

The three duly set out one evening, full of misplaced confidence and, in the case of two of them, cheap whisky. They would intercept the coach at night on a deserted stretch of road, by stringing a rope across the way to trip the horses. They would then capture the driver, overpower the guard, and help themselves to the diamonds. The plan was straightforward but failed to take into account the armed men guarding the diamond convoy. As the Pinkertons reported, "the horses were thrown and the coach tipped over, but before they could carry out their plans, the big Boer guard in charge, who was armed with a repeating Winchester rifle, commenced firing in every direction, driving the thieves to cover."

Banditry was evidently not Worth's forte, yet he seems to have had a penchant for this particularly unsophisticated form of robbery. This was not the last time he would attempt to pull off a highway robbery and regret it.

The operation was an unmitigated failure. The attempted holdup "created quite a sensation" when the battered coach arrived safely at the coast, and convinced the diamond mine owners of the need to post extra guards on convoys. The American captain, who had come within inches of receiving a bullet in the head, proved to be rather less than the "game fellow" Worth had thought. He announced he was no Dick Turpin and returned to Cape Town. Charley King, too, as Worth later put it, "had weakened and got scared off." Worth, however, "decided to remain to have another trial at it and see what he could do."

King was given instructions to return home but keep a close watch on the London papers. Should a South African diamond robbery be reported, he should send Worth "£200 immediately to Brindisi." If Worth did manage to pull off the heist, this would certainly be reported in London, and Worth was planning an escape via the port on Italy's Adriatic coast. Mindful of the time when Little Joe Elliott had had to pawn his gold teeth to get home, Worth did not want to be left short of traveling cash. "His intention," as he later explained to Pinkerton, "was to take the long route home from there, which was a round-about way and would take him nearly 60 days to get home." For the next few months, still posing as a feather buyer, Worth hung around Port Elizabeth, studying the situation. From various sources he learned that, in spite of the precautions taken by the mine owners, the convoy was periodically delayed by bad weather, floods, and other unanticipated obstacles. Since the convoy was timed to arrive at Port Elizabeth just before the steamer left for England, a delay of even a few hours meant that the diamonds had to be stored in the safe of the Port Elizabeth post office until the next boat was ready to leave. If Worth could delay the shipment long enough, and simultaneously find a way to break into the safe, he could make up for his earlier, irritating failure.

The assistant postmaster was "an old gentleman, very social in his habits, and Worth cultivated his acquaintance" by buying him drinks and allowing him to win at chess, night after night. After a few months, the postmaster and the ostrich-feather merchant were firm friends. On one of his trips out of town, nominally in search of ostrich plumes, Worth "took three parcels out on the road and sent them registered mail, addressed to himself, and came in on the same train with the parcels." He then waited until his new friend was about to close up shop and the post office was empty of customers, and "pleaded that it was of great importance that he receive the packages which had been locked up for the night. The assistant postmaster agreed to get them for him, and went back to get the books, and while his back was turned, Worth managed to get wax impressions of the keys to the safe for registered packages, received the packages which he had shipped to himself, and went about his business."

With one part of the plan now in place, all that remained was to ensure that the diamond shipment was delayed. Not far from Port Elizabeth "there was a deep stream, where the coach had to cross by the ferry, which was operated on wire rope cable: nearby was a small tavern, and Worth waited until time for the coach was come, which was in the evening, and then cut the rope, which allowed the ferry to drift down the stream with the current." The convoy was delayed by eight hours as the ferry was laboriously poled back up stream and another cable attached. Sure enough, when the convoy arrived in Port Elizabeth, the steamer for England had sailed, and the packages of uncut gems were, as usual, placed in the post-office safe as a precaution. "The next night he entered the post office and abstracted from the safe diamonds and other valuables to the amount of $500,000."

"The swag," as he later told Pinkerton, "consisted largely of packages of diamonds, money and government bills, all of which were valuable."

The assistant postmaster was immediately suspected of the theft and placed under arrest. There was no proof he had played even an indirect part in the robbery, but the police found evidence that "he had been embezzling money letters which passed through his office." He was tried and sentenced to five years, but even though "experts from England were sent out to investigate the case," of the real thief there was not a trace—which was less than surprising, since he had left Port Elizabeth several hours before the theft was discovered. "Knowing that anyone who attempted to leave the country would be under suspicion, Worth quietly went up the country from Cape Town pretending to be in search of investments and purchasing ostrich feathers."

After a month, Worth, this time with a large parcel of diamonds as well as the *Duchess,* set sail for Suez and then Brindisi. He was extremely short of ready cash and praying fervently that, as agreed, Charley King had sent money to Italy for his return passage. The old thief, however, scenting money, had gone one better and, "seeing the thing in the papers, instead of wiring the money to his account in Brindisi, for the purpose of declaring himself in with the money, started for Brindisi himself." The two crooks could not find each other in the bustling port, and after he had waited more than a week, Worth pawned "some article which he had and took the other route home." When the apologetic Charley King finally arrived back in London, Worth was forgiving. Despite the fact that he had played no part in the final theft, and had disobeyed Worth's orders by failing to send the money, Worth nonetheless gave him £1,600, "more for the purpose of buying his silence than anything else."

Worth's next act, on returning to his Piccadilly pad, was equally a mixture of generosity and self-interest. His brother John Worth, the criminal incompetent who had already caused so many problems, was down on his luck, threatening to return to England and keen to participate in another criminal enterprise—a prospect which, given John's dazzling ineptitude, was distinctly troubling to his older brother. Almost half the proceeds from the South African heist were handed over to John Worth, on condition that he abandon a life of crime and settle down in America. John agreed, moved to Brooklyn, and to Worth's deep relief and surprise, he never again attempted to break the law.

Some years later Pinkerton reported what Worth had said and done about his younger brother: "He said that John was a damn fool for a crook and he stopped him at it a long time ago; that he had been used by Becker and others, and that he had given John a considerable sum of money at the time of the mail robbery in Cape Town [sic], and with that had kept John clean and above board, and he hoped he would never again be engaged in any crooked transaction." Worth plainly felt a deep responsibility for his sibling, but it was less for the sake of John's immortal soul that he persuaded him to go straight, and rather more because, given John's gullibility and general incompetence, he was too much a liability as an accomplice.

Worth's generosity also reflected his extraordinary good humor on his return to London. For one thing, he had hit on an excellent and highly profitable way to dispose of the diamonds. The traditional method was to work back such stolen goods through a series of fences until they reached the open market. Not only was the process risky, since any one of the links in the chain could turn informer, but it meant that the diamonds fetched a fraction of their full worth. In a stunningly audacious move, Worth decided to cut out the expensive middle men by selling the diamonds himself.

From America Worth recruited one Ned Wynert, alias Johnny Smith, described by the Pinkertons as a "clever, educated fellow and entirely unknown to the London police." Wynert was an astute, reliable rogue, but an inveterate womanizer. According to Shinburn, who never missed an opportunity to slander his rivals, Wynert was "married to a lady of a very respectable family. He treats her shamefully, spending all of his stealings on other women." For Worth's purposes he was the ideal henchman, as discreet in criminal matters as he was intemperate in emotional ones. Worth set up his new partner as a diamond merchant under the name Wynert & Co., in Hatton Garden, the heart of London's jewelry trade. "By putting their goods at a shilling or two on the pound less than the standard prices in London, they found no trouble in disposing of all their goods to merchants who came to London from Amsterdam to buy." To Worth's great pleasure, some of the gems were even sold to the very merchants who had already bought them once, on consignment, before he stole them. The final take was estimated at £90,000. As Sir Robert Anderson of Scotland Yard noted, a different sort of man might have been content to go into early retirement after such a coup. "If I had ever possessed ninety thousand pounds of anything, the Government would have had to find someone else to look after burglars," the detective once remarked. "But Raymond loved his work for its own sake" and was already plotting new schemes.

The Gainsborough was his talisman, seldom far from his grasp and hungry eye, and it was thus with rich ironic pleasure that he read of the continuing saga of the *Duchess of Devonshire,* who miraculously reappeared time and again, in London, Vienna, and

New York, raising the hopes of Messrs. Agnew & Co. and sending Scotland Yard off on a series of fruitless trails. "It has been 'discovered' nearly a dozen times," *The Times* wryly reported.

"I believe I have found the missing picture of the Duchess of Devonshire in Ambrose's travelling art show which was here on May 3," wrote one informant. On another occasion it was confidently reported that "while a gang of men were engaged in dismantling some premises in New Bond Street . . . [an object] was discovered in the corner of a disused cellar, and this, upon examination, turned out to be the portrait of the Duchess of Devonshire, which was cut out of its frame in May 1876, and disappeared under mysterious circumstances." Upon further examination, of course, it turned out to be nothing of the sort, but instead one of the many replicas available for a few shillings. Another correspondent believed he had "seen the thief cheating at roulette" in a London club, a perfectly possible contention backed up with no evidence whatever. One J. Meiklejohn, a former Scotland Yard detective, claimed to have struck a deal with the "custodians of this article" and insisted that "under no circumstances would they part with it for less than fifteen hundred . . . they would sooner burn it than give it for less." Needless to say, the negotiations came to nothing and the corrupt Meiklejohn was eventually jailed for a variety of "racing frauds."

In a bid to rekindle negotiations for the return of the painting, and presuming the portrait was still in America, Agnew's had dispatched an art expert, David P. Sellar, to New York, where he placed several advertisements in the newspapers, hoping to reestablish contact with the thief. "Negotiations can be opened for the restoration of the 'Noble Lady' who mysteriously disappeared from Old Bond Street in 1876, Address L.S.D.," read an advertisement in the *New York Herald*. (L.S.D. referred, as he later explained, to "pounds, shillings and pence.") A helpful art dealer suggested the message was too cryptic, so Sellar tried a more blunt approach: "New York.—If the present owner of Gainsborough's celebrated picture 'The Duchess of Devonshire' which was taken from Old Bond Street in 1876 will address LSD *Herald* up-town office, negotiations for its restoration can be resumed." If Worth was unaware of the two advertisements, which is unlikely, he could hardly have missed the articles about Mr. Sellar's "secret" visit that soon began appearing in the press. "What his precise instructions are, what price he is willing to pay, and what progress he is making towards the recovery of the picture, Mr. Sellar naturally keeps to himself . . . he has confident hope that the all-powerful influence of money will secure the success of his visit."

It did not, for Worth was not to be enticed, and had no intention of relinquishing his Noble Lady. With each fresh false alarm, faithfully reported back by his spies at Scotland Yard, and with each new attempt to repossess her by the authorities, his affection for the portrait grew and his determination to keep her for his own private pleasure redoubled.

SEVENTEEN

A Silk Glove Man

With his diamond profits, Worth could now look beyond mere bourgeois respectability, toward the life of a fully paid-up member of the English aristocracy. If Victorian mores stressed hard work, dependability, and Christian family values, at least one segment of the elite was nonetheless distinguished by doing no work at all and pursuing a regime of boundless self-indulgence. Victorians talked of duty and morality, a cast of mind perhaps best exemplified by Queen Victoria herself. But what truly distinguished the most conspicuous members of the ruling class was a perfect and undiluted dedication to pleasure. Queen Victoria's son, later Edward VII, was the most visible exponent of this heady style of existence, in which Worth now participated, as if to the manner born.

The Prince of Wales and his Marlborough House set (not so very far removed, in its habits and personalities, from Georgiana's Devonshire House set in the previous century) elevated conspicuous consumption to an almost full-time occupation: shooting parties, house parties, boating parties, trips to Paris and the German spas, gambling, evenings at the opera or more often the music hall, and late-night champagne-doused card parties. While birth and breeding were useful passports to this exclusive world, the only essentials were vast wealth and a determination to spend it on enjoyment. One historian has noted that, "as the first gentleman of the land, Edward's tastes and habits, including his liking for the 'nouveaux riches,' set the tone in high aristocratic circles." Worth's riches could hardly have been newer, whereas his taste for luxury was evident to the most casual observer, and he slipped through the barriers of class with consummate ease, utterly disguised by his stolen money. The circle of those who could afford such pleasures was necessarily small, and although it is entirely possible that the future king and the monarch of the underworld rubbed shoulders, there is no evidence they ever met. But there is also no doubt that the highest in the land would have found, in the very lowest, a kindred spirit.

The 1880s were years of consolidation and prosperity for Worth. He grew portly, and his mustache evolved in shapes ever more luxurious and rococo, for he had become what Pinkerton called a "silk glove man," a gentleman crook and sporting gentleman of leisure luxuriating in his loot and a cut above the vagabonds and rascals with whom he had once associated. From Hatton Garden, Ned Wynert, now his right-hand man, ran the day-to-day criminal business, while Worth enjoyed his yacht and his horses, traveling whenever the fancy took him, gambling and entertaining his friends, some criminal but many of unimpeachable respectability. To his growing string of thoroughbreds he now added "a pair of the finest horses in the country, having purchased them," recalled Harold Lloyd, one of the many lawyers on the Worth payroll, "at a public auction, outbidding the late Lord Rothschild and Baron Hirsch." In addition, "tucked away in the New Forest, he had a shoot of some 400 acres with a nice shooting box, where he entertained on a large scale." The money flowed in, and just as quickly out again, but "even his heavy losses at Monte Carlo could not seriously affect a fortune which was being steadily increased by all sorts of illegal undertakings." As yet further proof of his social standing, he purchased "a very fine house on the front at Brighton, where he entertained lavishly."

In November 1881, soon after disposing of the diamonds from the South African heist, Worth struck the Hatton Garden post office in central London and bagged yet another clutch of gems. "About five o'clock on the evening of November 16th two registered mail bags containing diamonds consigned to various merchants in Amsterdam and elsewhere on the Continent were sealed up and hung on iron hooks behind the counter of the post-office in question ready for dispatch."

As Worth, in disguise, sauntered up to the counter, an accomplice, probably Wynert, slipped "down the steps leading to the basement and turned off the gas at the meter," with the result that "the office was plunged into total darkness. For apart from the fact that at this season of the year night had already fallen, the fog outside was so thick it could be 'cut with a knife.' " By the time the postal workers got the lights on again, it was too late; "Worth, the moment the gas failed, had vaulted lightly over the counter, seized the bags, slung one over each shoulder, and made his way outside and into a four-wheeled cab in waiting."

The uncut diamonds, quickly divided and mounted to prevent them being traced, were then sold just a few feet away from the scene of the crime by Wynert & Co., for an estimated £30,000. The general public was soon made aware, indirectly, of Worth's heist, for the robbery "had the effect of causing the authorities of the postal department to place in almost every post office the wire-net protection of the counters with which we are all familiar, and from the inconvenience of which we have all suffered."

On such special occasions Worth was prepared to participate in the action himself, but more usually he was content to be the financier, coordinator, and chief beneficiary of his schemes, leaving others to carry out the various forgeries, burglaries, and robberies that filled his bank account and inflated his ego. "I made an average of £63,000 a year for three years," he later bragged to an acquaintance. The English-born jailbird Eddie Guerin, fresh from the French penal colonies, visited Worth in London in 1887, the year of the Queen's Jubilee, and was stunned to find his old friend and fellow felon transformed into a wealthy representative of the British upper class. "If ever a man in this world could be pointed out as an exception to the rule that no crook ever makes money it was Adam Worth," Guerin later mused. "He owned an expensive flat in Piccadilly, he entertained some of the best people in London, who never knew him for anything but an apparently rich man of a Bohemian nature."

Sir Robert Anderson, the head of criminal investigation at Scotland Yard, rightly concluded that Worth's criminal professionalism reflected a hatred of the Establishment just beneath his respectable veneer: "he loved . . . to pit his skill and cunning against the resources of organised society; and this regardless, in some instances, at all events, of the actual pecuniary benefit accruing to himself." Even Shinburn, in a rare moment of admiration, conceded that "Raymond loved his work for its own sake: and although he lived in luxury and style, applied his energies to the last in organising crimes."

Bank robbery remained a staple form of income and Worth made no secret of his belief that the bank he could not get into and the safe he could not crack had yet to be invented. "From year to year the safemakers produced stronger and better safes, which they called burglar-proof safes," Max Shinburn observed sardonically. "The crooks followed suit by inventing tools wherewith they were able to beat them . . . The Bankers of that period vied with each other to install burglarproof work in their banks, which they were ever ready to show with pride to their customers or to any passing crook." On the pretext of wanting to place valuables under the protection of the latest technology, Worth would case the latest inventions and then pass the information on to his underlings, with the result that "the burglar kept pace with the safemaker and was able to beat anything the latter could produce."

It is easy to imagine Worth at the heart of this criminal web, "one of the cleverest framers-up in the whole world," in the words of a contemporary. Rich, cautious, and contented, he sits in a leather armchair, calculating his profits, his famous stolen painting always within reach, his icon of imposture. He flitted back and forth across the Atlantic at will, and while the London police sought to keep track of his movements he would often vanish completely for long periods.

"It is an odd thing, but everyone who disappears is said to be seen in San Francisco," Oscar Wilde once observed, and, sure enough, early in 1886 the San Francisco chief of police reported that Worth had led "a mob of all round crooks" to the West Coast for a fresh criminal spree. Knowing Worth's refusal to brook betrayal of any sort, it seems clear he was as yet unaware of the perfidy of Little Joe Elliott, who had been released from prison the year before. Elliott now rejoined him, along with Dave Lynch and Dick Bradley, a brace of experienced thieves who had proved themselves in the past, and one Charlie Gleason, an elderly Australian convict. The gang made a rendezvous at Mulholland's pub in New York City before heading West.

On January 9, this crew of "Eastern Experts" blew the safe of a Sacramento bank and extracted about $4,000. "It was a clean job with no evidence to convict," complained Captain I. W. Lees of the San Francisco Police Department to William Pinkerton. "Raymond seemed to be the moneyed man, and bought the Eastward bound tickets for the whole five. Joe [Elliott] also displayed at times, considerable money."

After dividing the spoils, the gang broke up. Little Joe headed to Oakland to visit the parents of Kate Castleton, by whom he was still smitten, in the hope of a reconciliation with his former wife. "He is still dead in love with Castleton and will show up wherever she is," noted Guerin. "Castleton won't have him, but Joe says she will weaken in the end." She did. They remarried, but fought again—for Joe's jealousy "grew worse than ever." This led to several embarrassing incidents, including one in which Joe "slugged one of his wife's admirers three times bigger than himself." Finally they broke up for good and Joe became "absolutely reckless." In 1889 Elliott was arrested in another forgery case and sentenced to fifteen years. As one criminal philosopher observed of the bizarre romance between the crook and the actress: "It was surely the irony of fate that the first day he arrived in Auburn Prison to begin his term his beautiful wife should be starring at the local theater. The knowledge of it absolutely broke Joe's heart; he never came out of jail alive."

After a tense and dangerous "dispute with the baggage man" in San Francisco, who tried and failed to get Worth to open his trunk (containing the *Duchess*), Worth had headed back East and recrossed the Atlantic. He did not travel directly to London, however, but disembarked at Ostend, where, by prearrangement, he met up with a group of his men, including Gleason and old John Carr.

Two weeks later, the gang struck again, this time lying in wait for a tram car transporting jewels and cash from Brussels to Ostend. When the tram stopped briefly in a siding, Worth's gang "twisted the lock off the car and got into the mail car and took the funds, which amounted to something like two million francs." The Belgian police moved with surprising swiftness, and Worth was astonished and enraged to find himself among the dozens of potential suspects rounded up for questioning. Once again, bluster pulled him through: why, he asked his interviewers, would he bother to be involved in such a crime when, as a wealthy London sporting gentleman, he was winning a fortune at the card table? He showed evidence of his latest winnings as proof, and the police, with some reluctance but convinced of Worth's affluence, allowed him to leave on the next boat for England—where the stolen money was waiting.

That same year the pregnant Kitty briefly suspended her trail of litigation in New York and also returned to Europe to settle with Juan Pedro in Paris. Their six years of marriage had been happy, and wildly self-indulgent, punctuated by expensive foreign trips, the sole purpose of which was the conspicuous display and disbursement of their wealth. There was nothing Worth, or for that matter the Prince of Wales, could teach Kitty about the pleasures of extravagance. Soon after taking a large apartment in the center of Paris, the Terrys received the news of the death of old Thomaso Terry. The Irish-Venezuelan adventurer turned Cuban-American magnate had finally succumbed to gout, leaving an estate worth some $50 million. With his share of the inheritance added to his already considerable fortune, Juan Pedro was now worth some $6 million. Sadly, he did not live to spend more of it or to enjoy his child. On October 17, 1886, the debonair Juan Pedro Terry, who had loved Kitty for her feisty personality and sharp tongue, inexplicably died while on a trip to Menton. Now a widow and seven months pregnant, Kitty was distraught, though suddenly immensely wealthy in her own right. In his will Juan Pedro left Kitty one-fifth of his estate, the rest to be invested in securities, preferably U.S. government bonds, from which Kitty would derive the income until their unborn child came of age and inherited the lot. A baby daughter, Juanita Teresa, was born in Paris two months after Juan Pedro's death. As soon as the child was old enough to travel, Kitty collected her money and headed back to New York with the avowed intention of spending it. Worth had no doubt heard of Kitty's bereavement and windfall, for he continued to keep tabs on her every movement, but with a fortune of her own, a young daughter, and courtiers lining up by the score, she was now further from his reach than ever.

It is a truth universally acknowledged that a successful criminal in possession of a good fortune must be in need of a wife. Worth had begun to tire of the bachelor life and yearned for the respectability of a solid Victorian marriage. One of the recipients of Worth's fabled generosity was a poor but genteel widow who lived with her two daughters in Bayswater, where Worth had briefly taken lodgings. "He became, in time, much attached to this woman and her children, and lavished every luxury on them, including the education of the girls in the best French schools. For years the family never suspected their benefactor was a criminal, but supposed him to be a prosperous diamond importer"—which, in a manner of speaking, he was.

When the older daughter's education was completed, Worth asked for her hand in marriage, and was accepted with alacrity. Sophie Lyons, who was periodically employed by Worth to carry out petty thefts and other criminal work, did not think much of his choice. "She was a beautiful woman, but a weak, clinging sort of creature—very different from strong self-willed Kitty. Although passionately fond of her, Raymond's attitude towards her was always that of the devoted father rather than the loving husband."

Lyons, who clearly carried a torch for Worth herself, clung to the belief that Worth never truly loved anyone but Kitty Flynn, and she was surely right. He was fond and protective of his young, rather feeble wife, and resolved that she should never learn of his true character, but after the loss of Kitty and, perhaps just as powerfully, his acquisition of Georgiana, Worth seemed to have lost his capacity for powerful emotional bonds, let alone genuine love. He seldom discussed his wife, even in his most confessional moments. To Pinkerton he referred to her in terms of wardship rather than marriage, as "one of the little girls that lived in the lodgings where I used to live when I first came to London." Indeed, most details concerning Mrs. Henry Raymond, including her name, remain mysterious, but in time she bore Worth two children, a son and a daughter, in 1888 and 1891, in blissful ignorance of her husband's dishonesty. Theirs was not a grand passion such as Worth had known with Kitty, but by all accounts he was "devotedly attached to her and squandered money on her in every way." Worth still believed money could assuage all desires, and the marriage was another stark expression of his strange, fraudulent priorities: even to his wife he maintained an impenetrable mask of respectability, believing that, by so doing, he was behaving in a moral manner and protecting her from harm. When she finally discovered the truth, the effects were, inevitably, tragic.

Worth moved out of his bachelor apartment in Piccadilly and began to live full-time in the West Lodge by Clapham Common, a more appropriate home for a wealthy family man, "standing in fine grounds of its own, and boasting a numerous but mysterious company of guests and a retinue of servants. Every one of them was his tried confederate; and none but such ever gained entry into the premises."

Marriage seems to have subtly altered Worth's attitude toward his stolen painting. Hitherto the portrait had never been far from his grasp: in London, he would sometimes stash it "under the roof of a summer house at his place at Clapham Park"; while traveling, it came with him in the false-bottomed trunk, and when aboard *The Shamrock* "he hid it in the chartroom amongst the logs." The thought of surrendering the painting never crossed his mind, but he plainly felt uncomfortable keeping it in the marital home and so, at the end of 1886, he set out with the *Duchess* in his trunk to find her new and safe accommodation in America. It seems unlikely that the new Mrs. Raymond ever set eyes on her husband's peculiar keepsake.

Taking with him "the proceeds from the big Tramway robbery at Ostend," and posing as a London bond broker traveling in the grandest possible style, Worth took the Allen Line ship for Canada with the *Duchess,* a cache of diamonds, and additional cash stashed in the bottom of his trunk. The trip was nearly a disaster, for unbeknown to Worth another criminal, a Swedish thief called Adolph Sprungley, was also on the boat.

In mid-Atlantic, Sprungley began breaking into passengers' cabins and liberating them of various valuables while they dined, causing consternation on board. Worth did not want Sprungley, or for that matter the Canadian authorities, to find what was in the bottom of his trunk, so he decided to disembark at Rimouski and travel the rest of the way to Montreal by train.

The police, however, had carefully examined the ship's manifest for any passengers making a sudden change of plan, and were waiting in Montreal when Worth's train arrived. Spotting the Mounties as his carriage pulled in, Worth moved quickly and prised away one of the boards of the train carriage. He had deposited most but not all of the diamonds and cash in the partition when the train came to a halt. Mr. Raymond, protesting vehemently, was escorted from the platform to a waiting room. Bizarrely, the Canadian police failed to uncover the Gainsborough, but they did find the few gems remaining in his pockets and immediately arrested him as the steamship thief and impounded the diamonds.

Worth later recounted that "he made a great bluff and de-

manded a solicitor and telegraphed to London for a firm of solicitors for reference." Finally, with great reluctance, the French-
Canadian police let him go, less, as he claimed, because he had
"scared them out of the thing" than because Worth's diamonds
did not match any of the items stolen from the ship. The gems
were confiscated and Worth happily paid a fine for failing to de-
clare them.

The police grudgingly apologized for detaining the now gracious Mr. Raymond, and firmly told him to leave the country
immediately. But Worth was not heading south without the rest of
his valuables. According to the Pinkertons, "after his liberation,
Worth succeeded in tracing the car on which he had left the jewelry, having taken the number of it, and when the car was put in
the yard for the night, he entered it and regained possession of
the missing diamonds, which he afterwards safely smuggled
into the United States." Delighted to have won his liberty, and
generous as ever, Worth even gave a small diamond ring to the
Pinkerton detective, George Skeffington, who had interrogated
him but obligingly failed to recognize him in the Canadian jail.
Worth "would have given him more but was afraid of tipping his
hand off as being a crook if he gave too much." The scrape had
cost him "several thousand dollars' worth" of diamonds, a small
price to pay for his freedom. "At a small cost of a few thousand I
was able to save my principal," or the bulk of his hoard, he later
boasted.

Safely in New York, Worth wrapped the Gainsborough in
clothes and stashed it and the Saratoga trunk in a Brooklyn warehouse, not far from where his brother John had married and
settled down to raise a family. The stolen portrait was by now, it
seems, deeply ingrained in his mind and personality; he no longer
needed to see it on a daily basis, but simply to know that it was his.
Worth returned to the United States several times in the next six
years and on each occasion he would retrieve the *Duchess* and view
it anew, before replacing his Noble Lady in the false-bottom trunk
and shifting her to another warehouse. In this way the Gainsborough duchess moved from Brooklyn to Manhattan, then back to

Brooklyn, and finally to a warehouse in Boston, where she would lie, unseen, for a decade.

Back in London again at the start of 1887, Worth was riding on the leaf of his silk hat—wealthy, respectably married, and increasingly powerful. Never in any doubt that he was a more adept crook than any man alive, he would periodically carry out a robbery to keep his hand in and demonstrate his prowess, if only to himself—he being the only critic whose opinion he truly valued. On "one occasion he walked out of a London bank with £35,000 worth of gems belonging to a well-known actress, getting possession of them by the simple expedient of presenting a forged order for their delivery."

It is a sign of Worth's status among his fellow criminals that he even set himself up as a peace broker when disputes arose between his minions, as happened in the celebrated feud between Eddie Guerin and Sophie Lyons. Guerin had developed a violent hatred for Lyons, believing she had given him up to the French police, an event which led directly to his incarceration on Devil's Island. "Sophie Lyons was a pimp," Guerin later declared. "She battened on crooks, sucked their life's blood, and then bartered away their liberty to the police." Worth made a point of trying to reconcile his two old friends. As Guerin recounted, "I was walking down Oxford Street, London, one day . . . in company with Harry Raymond [when] whom should we run into but the fellow whom Sophie Lyons had married quite recently, none other than my old friend Billy Burke"—a fellow known to William Pinkerton as a "noted American bank sneak."

"We went to have a drink together and over it Harry, always a good sort, said to us: 'Now, you boys, you don't want to start quarreling. Shake hands and be good friends. We'll have dinner tonight and see if we can't do a bit of business together.' " Worth planned to invite Sophie along, too, "thinking, no doubt, it would be a good thing to patch up our quarrel." Guerin, still raging at what he perceived to be Lyons's treachery, failed to materialize on the grounds that the "dinner might have been like an Irish wake by the time I had finished with it if I had found Sophie there."

When Billy Burke encountered Guerin some years later and asked why he had not appeared at Worth's reconciliatory party, Guerin's response was straightforward and to the point. "I didn't say anything in reply—I just slugged him." Despite his civilized manners and opposition to violence, Worth moved in a world of hard men of which he was, for all his scruples, perhaps the hardest, if least pugnacious.

Peacemaker (in this case, unsuccessfully), job provider, receiver, by the end of the 1880s Worth had become a sort of criminal paterfamilias, offering counsel and crime on contract. "Thieves came to him for help," according to one such individual. "Was there a bank official to be bribed or a skeleton key to be made? Adam Worth solved both problems. Did a particular job require the services of an expert burglar or forger? Adam Worth had a large supply of either on hand. He knew where to find the right man for every job." But his fame was also rapidly extending beyond the criminal fraternity to a wider public.

In 1888 the celebrated and corrupt chief of the New York Police Detective Bureau Thomas Byrnes, a man for whom Worth had as little respect as he had for John Shore, published an article in the *New York World* naming Adam Worth as "The Most Famous Criminal of All" and illustrated it with a picture of a sinister-looking fellow in a top hat. "Adam Worth," Byrnes wrote, "the most noted of the American criminals abroad, resides in London. He is a fugitive from justice from the United States, having been concerned in the Boylston Bank robbery of Boston. This robbery occurred about eighteen years ago, but there is an indictment against Worth for the burglary of the Boylston Bank still standing, and it is this indictment which keeps him out of the United States. He had an interest with Marsh and Bullard, went to London and on the money taken from the Boylston Bank bought a residence there and is now living in grand style. Worth is the owner of a fine steam yacht, and each season entertains his friends aboard of it cruising up and down the Mediterranean . . . He looks up jobs for nearly every American thief of any note who goes to the other side, and those who go from here who are not acquainted with him are sure to get a letter of introduction to him. The work which Worth lays out is generally located on the Continent, as he is afraid of the English police, and dare not work in London, as he desires to make the city his home. He receives a percentage from all the successful burglaries he plans, and also has option on the goods, as he is an extensive 'fence' as well as 'putter-up of jobs.' "

Byrnes knew as well as Scotland Yard that the fugitive Adam Worth and the prosperous Henry Raymond of Clapham Common were one and the same. The article was intended as a warning shot across Worth's bows, an implicit threat that the police on both sides of the Atlantic were on his trail. What it truly demonstrated, however, was their inability to bring him to book. The files on Worth were bulging, but still the police could not pin him down. Instead of being sent into a panic, as intended, Worth was delighted with the largely accurate portrayal of his life-style, and instead of being cowed, he became cockier still. Indeed, to show how little he was afraid of the English police, he tipped off Charlie Gleason, the Australian, when his Scotland Yard spies told him the old fellow was in imminent danger of arrest. Gleason very sensibly vanished to the Continent, and Worth made certain that Shore knew who was behind the tip-off. As Pinkerton noted, the enmity between Shore and his arch-enemy was approaching a climax.

A story told by Sir Robert Anderson of Scotland Yard illustrates just one of the many methods by which Worth contrived to establish an alibi for every occasion. As Sir Robert recounted: "A friend of mine who has a large medical practice in one of the London suburbs, told me once of an extraordinary patient of his. The man lived sumptuously, but was extremely hypochondriacal. Every now and then an urgent summons would bring the doctor to the house, to find the patient in bed, though there was nothing whatever the matter with him. But the man always insisted on having a prescription, which was promptly sent to the chemist . . . I might have relieved his curiosity by explaining that this eccentric patient was a prince among criminals. Raymond knew that his movements were a matter of interest to the police, and if he had reason to believe he had been seen in dangerous company he bolted home and 'shammed sick.' And the doctor's evidence, confirmed by the chemist's books, would prove that he was ill in bed till after the hour at which the police supposed they had seen him miles away."

Goaded to distraction, Shore increased the surveillance on the Worth mansion in Clapham Common. In a letter to William Pinkerton, the English detective noted that Worth had recruited a man named Sunter, "who has been known to me for some years as an expert thief-tool maker." The master thief and his underling "have fitted up the place with an anvil, forge &c. sufficient for them to make any implement they may require. This house is permanently under the observation of police, in fact a constable is posted outside at all times," Shore reported, through gritted teeth.

On May 22, 1888, the detective finally lost patience and the police staged a raid. In the basement of the house they found the machine shop, and a complete set of burglar's tools neatly stacked along the walls. Shore had hoped to find more incriminating evidence—the Gainsborough or other stolen goods, forgery paper, or at least Worth himself in cahoots with some known criminals—but the house was deserted. Worth, his investment in bribery paying dividends again, had been warned off by his police spies and, after sending his pregnant wife to stay with her mother, had hurriedly taken a short vacation. He returned to find that Shore, out of spite, had confiscated all his burglar's tools, even though they could prove nothing in a court of law. In a magnificent act of brass-necked effrontery, Worth sued Shore for breaking into his "office" and demanded the return of his valuable household tools. The case, naturally, was thrown out, but Worth was satisfied merely to have forced Shore to appear in court.

Inspector Shore may not have been the brightest policeman (even Pinkerton considered him a fool), but he was nothing if not dogged. His latest run-in with Worth had ended in a draw, but Shore now waited, and watched, firm in the belief that Worth, whose temerity was increasing by the day, would eventually make a mistake. For once, he was right.

EIGHTEEN

Bootless Footpads

Worth had successfully escaped the clutches of the law, but the same could not be said of most of his colleagues, thanks, in large measure, to the work of William and Robert Pinkerton, who had all but cornered the market in bank-robbery prevention. The number of U.S. banks was increasing rapidly, from 754 in 1883 to 3,579 in 1893. Nitroglycerine had made it easier to blow open their safes, but the authorities, ably backed by the Pinkertons and improved safe designs, were becoming more efficient at defending their property. As Max Shinburn remarked: "It was nip and tuck between the safe makers and the crooks, as to which should gain the upper hand." In time, the Pinkertons would found the Protective Association of American Bankers, through which banks would pay for their special protection. It was a worthwhile investment, for Billy Pinkerton, the Big Man, or the Eye, as he was known—a reference to the Pinkertons' motto—had become a towering figure among detectives, as skillful in championing the law as Worth was adept at breaking it.

As the burglar Josiah Flynt recalled: "The guns leave the Big Man's territory alone, if they can. If there was two banks standin' close together, an' one o' them was a member of the Bankers' Association an' the other one wasn't, the guns 'ud tackle the other one first. The Big Man protects the Bankers' Association banks."

Eddie Guerin thought that "the Pinkertons did more than all the detective forces of the world combined together to smash up the big bank robbers."

Pinkerton's National Detective Agency had left the early days of mere bounty-hunting far behind, to become the most effective and, after the bitter labor disputes of the 1880s and early 1890s, the most detested detective force in the United States. Many considered them to be hired strike-breakers, private police in the pay of the large industrialists. The Pinkertons insisted, in the words of an official report into their activities, that "the practice of employing Pinkerton guards or watchmen by corporations in cases of strikes or labor trouble has grown very largely out of the sloth and inability of the civil authorities to render efficient and proper protection." They had a point, but the participation of Pinkerton's men in the Burlington strikes of 1888 and then the Homestead riots of 1892 was among the ugliest chapters in the agency's history.

William Pinkerton, a man of unabashed conservative views, played a key role in those events, but he was always happier in the saddle, hunting down the bandits and thugs who terrorized the West. Whenever a train robbery was reported, William was usually the first to hasten to Denver and organize pursuit of the fresh breed of desperadoes: the Farringtons, the Burrows brothers, "Texas Jack" Searcy, Charles Morgan, the McCoys, Harvey Logan, alias "Kid Curry," and, of course, Butch Cassidy and Harry Longabaugh, the Sundance Kid.

No area of criminal endeavor was beyond the scope of the Pinkerton brothers: outlaws, blackmailers, fences, forgers, fraudsters, killers, and cattle rustlers learned to respect and fear them. The bankers were not alone in seeking the Pinkertons' protection. When the Jewelers Security Alliance took on the agency as their detective corps, they were offered another punchy motto: "Prevention, Pursuit, Prosecution and Punishment." Other detective agencies might be "principally constituted of thieves, pickpockets, blackmailers and porch climbers," but Pinkerton's prided itself on absolute incorruptibility.

Robert and William jointly ran the agency after their father's death in 1884, in sharply contrasting ways. Where Robert, a dry and meticulous man, ruled the New York office, buried in paper work, William still operated out of Chicago and points west. The older brother was the more outgoing and expansive of the two, and the more formidable. He shared his father's immunity to fear, but unlike the unbending Allan, William Pinkerton had a strangely subtle view of the criminal mind. He harried his quarry with the perseverance of a monomaniacal bloodhound, but he brought to his work an unlikely admiration, even affection, for the criminal classes. When the talented, and plainly insane, train robber Oliver Curtis Perry stole $8,000 by sawing through the side of a moving train, William made no secret of his awe. "There are few if any men who possess the daredevil courage to accomplish what this train robber did," he said, shortly before Perry was nabbed by the detectives.

As one historian has remarked, William had an "instinctive altruism" sharply at odds with his public image as a pitiless lawman compounded of rawhide and scar tissue. He might speak of crooks as vermin, but in a way that was extraordinary for the time, he tended to treat them as human beings. He had no objection to hurting criminals but tried to avoid hurting their feelings. This was not always to their advantage.

In 1871, the Pinkertons had collared the notorious train-robbery gang led by Hillary and Levi Farrington, after a series of gun battles in which William was shot in the side before clubbing the gang into submission with a pistol butt. Hillary Farrington, an enormous backwoods outlaw whose mother appeared to have mated with a grizzly bear, was restrained in a pair of custom-forged manacles and loaded onto the paddle steamer *Illinois,* headed for Columbus, Kentucky. On the way Pinkerton offered to buy his prisoner a drink in the bar. Farrington readily accepted, but asked to be taken through the back door to the boat's saloon, via the deck, because he was embarrassed by the handcuffs and "didn't like to be seen under the circumstances." The sensitive Pinkerton agreed, but no sooner had they reached the deck than

Farrington attacked him. They wrestled for Pinkerton's gun, which went off, sending a bullet across the detective's scalp and tipping the massive Farrington over the rail and under the churning paddle wheels, where he was diced into a number of very small pieces, none of which was ever found.

It was one of the few occasions when Pinkerton's kindness had gone awry, but he continued to treat his prey with a mixture of sympathy and severity. Some years later, when a group of criminals was pardoned and released, it was suggested that William Pinkerton, the felon's friend, should give a party in their honor at the "Crooks Club." It was a mocking dig, but Pinkerton would probably have enjoyed nothing more, for such men were by now his closest acquaintances.

The criminal world had become markedly smaller and more unpredictable since the days of Worth's apprenticeship in New York. One commentator noted in 1888 that "the Canadian government looks to the Agency entirely, and there is constant correspondence between Robt. A. Pinkerton at the New York office and the police authorities of London, Paris, Berlin and other great European cities." Rogues' galleries depicting criminals were common in police stations throughout the United States and Europe, information flowed internationally with increasing ease, and Inspector Byrnes's best-selling and self-flattering *Criminals of America* had made life distinctly uncomfortable for many of those named and pictured therein.

The invention of the Bertillion method of criminal identification was another breakthrough. In 1883, Alphonse Bertillion concluded that certain parts of the human body do not change over an adult's lifetime and cannot be hidden by even the most elaborate disguise. The Bertillion method, which was introduced widely in Europe, involved the careful measurement of a criminal's vital statistics, which could then be filed and distributed to aid identification. Before the invention of fingerprinting, the Bertillion method was hailed as a crucial contribution to crime-fighting, until about 1903, when the "science" was seriously undermined by the discovery that two prisoners at Leavenworth not only had the same name, William West, but had identical Bertillion measurements. By this time Scotland Yard had introduced fingerprinting, and the Pinkertons and European police authorities soon followed suit. Worth himself had decided that America, while a splendid place to visit and to hide a grand English painting, was no longer a good venue for business. As he subsequently explained to Pinkerton himself, "he had looked about this country, and had looked at the bank work as put up in this country, and it looked to him impossible."

With such technological advances as the telephone, which, as Guerin noted, "plays sad havoc with your chance of escape," and the increasing sophistication of crime-fighting techniques, it is hardly surprising that the ranks of Worth's criminal fraternity were thinning out fast. As Shore noted, Worth was becoming increasingly "fidgety over the ill-luck which is attending so many of his American clients." By 1890 such notable burglars as Langdon Moore, Banjo Pete Emerson, George Bliss (who had once extracted more than two million dollars from the Ocean National Bank), Joe Killoran, and Western George Leslie, New York's King of the Bank Robbers, were either dead or in prison. Of Worth's inner circle, Ned Wynert, a Lothario to the last, had suffered the traditional adulterer's fate, gunned down in flagrante delicto by an enraged husband; Joe Chapman, finally allowed to leave the Turkish jail, was now a semilunatic; Becker was lying low in the American Midwest; Captain George languished in a Parisian jail; and fickle Joe Elliott and Carlo Sesicovitch had died in American ones. Even old Junka Phillips was out of the picture, having been arrested in 1886 in Quebec "for uttering spurious Bank of Scotland notes" and sentenced to ten years in prison. It was not an encouraging roster.

Worth's twitchiness at the misfortune of his American clients was most particularly a reference to the sad fate of poor, battered Charley Bullard. The partnership between Piano Charley and Max Shinburn, resented by Worth from the outset, had proved largely unsuccessful despite a number of criminal forays in Belgium and Holland. Bullard was still drinking heavily, and Shinburn, deter-

mined to regain his grand life-style, tended to fritter away whatever they managed to steal. "The urge to speculate made him
something of a plunger on the Bourse," and what little was left
over from the Baron's speculations was lost through "gambling
and extortion by a blackmailer threatening to reveal his identity."
Pinkerton ran into Shinburn in Belgium in the 1880s and found
him "with resources sadly depleted." According to one associate,
"Max and Charlie [sic] after having made and spent fortunes in
some of the most gigantic robberies known on two continents,
were broke."

The Baron was hoping for one more big theft to establish
himself as Worth's equal and reclaim the life of luxury he craved.
Shinburn's *crime de résistance* would prove a humiliating, hilarious,
and costly catastrophe, not just for himself, but for hopeless,
drink-befuddled Charley Bullard as well. Many years later it was
suggested that Worth himself may have had a hand in the Baron's
downfall. According to one, uncorroborated, account, he had
grown "tired of supporting his old pals and determined to rid
himself of his unwelcome parasites" by setting them up to commit
a major crime and then betraying them. Although Worth may well
have known of their plans, since he maintained friendly contact
with Bullard, there is no evidence of treachery on his part. Indeed, he seems to have been quite stunned at the ensuing events.

The target selected by the Baron was the Provincial Bank in
Verviers, Belgium, a rural establishment containing an ancient
safe which Shinburn was confident could be broken into without
difficulty. Piano Charley was easily persuaded to go in as an accomplice and was promised $6,000 if the heist was successful.
Shinburn later admitted that he "hoped to realize at least
$100,000 for himself."

The bank was situated within a courtyard at the heart of the
town, protected by a large wrought-iron gate. The door to the
bank was constructed of oak at least a foot thick and secured by a
lock later described by the Belgian press as "immense." Armed
with revolvers, the pair set out one midnight to case the premises.
"They planned to rob the bank the following night," according to

the Belgian prosecutor, "after having made a thorough inspection of the interior." Shinburn picked the lock of the outer gate and then set to work on the inner door, unscrewing the keyhole plate and placing the four screws in the pocket of his waistcoat. Once that door had been opened, the thieves removed their boots and left them on the doorstep, so they could tiptoe through the bank without leaving any traces.

But while Shinburn and Bullard were inside sizing up the safe, a night watchman happened to pass by the outer gate and, noticing it was ajar, shone his torch inside. The robbers' boots were clearly visible on the doorstep. The watchman, realizing what was happening, gathered up the shoes and set off to alert the police. Moments later the thieves reappeared, having seen all they needed to, and Shinburn had almost finished screwing back the keyhole plate when Bullard pointed out that their footwear had vanished. Shinburn could not find the fourth screw despite frantically emptying his pockets. "To save time rather than attempt a search in the darkness, Shinburn took some wax from a ball of that material in his pocket, and filled the hole, drawing his finger nail through the substance to give it the appearance of the top of the screw." The pair then fled in their socks, just as the Belgian police arrived in force. The Baron "fired a pistol at one of the gendarmes but missed him, and was immediately overpowered." Bullard somehow managed to break free, gamely cantering off into the darkness and firing his gun skywards in a vain effort to scare off his pursuers. He was tackled and handcuffed before he made it to the end of the street.

Although the American criminals appeared to have been caught red-handed, the Belgian police were baffled. Having searched the suspects, they found no stolen goods and only a tiny ball of wax in Shinburn's waistcoat. While they strongly (and rightly) suspected this had been used to obtain an impression of the interior of the keyhole, they could not prove it.

With typical insouciance, Shinburn insisted the courtyard gate had been left open and that he and his friend were footsore after a long day sightseeing in the town, and had merely removed their boots in order to sit down for a rest on the bank steps. Mr. Bullard, he explained, had started shooting at the police officers because he believed he was being mugged, spoke no French and was, moreover, prone to alcoholic hallucinations. One look at raddled Piano Charley confirmed that at least the latter part of this tale was thoroughly credible.

Shinburn was an adept liar, and the police, lacking proof, were on the point of setting the two men free when one of the officers suggested they call in what would now be considered forensic experts for one final examination of the bank interior. As the Belgian papers reported, "one of the experts requested an opportunity to examine Shinburn's ball of wax. To his surprise a small screw was deeply embedded in the wax. A locksmith tested the door in the yard, whereupon he noted that one of the screw holes was filled with wax, and the screw missing."

The missing screw was the same type as that found in Shinburn's pocket, and on minute examination the keyhole plate showed scratch marks from tampering. Inspector Byrnes of New York, meanwhile, had received photographs of the pair and immediately "identified them as notorious burglars and jail breakers for whom the police in this country had been looking." After a swift trial before the Court of assises in Liège, they were sentenced on February 21, 1884. Charley got twelve years' hard labor, and Shinburn, as the ringleader, got sixteen and a half.

Worth was busy arranging his own criminal affairs at the time of these events, but he observed them with horror from London. He already had ample reason to dislike Shinburn, and the Baron's part in bringing down his former partner seems to have caused the crook particular anguish. He railed against Shinburn's stupidity and bemoaned Charley's fate, but he was powerless to intervene.

As the years of Charley's incarceration dragged by, the aging pianist, deprived of his dual supports of alcohol and music, declined visibly. Like Worth, he had never forgotten Kitty Flynn and seems to have entertained the hopeless illusion that she might now come to his aid with her new wealth. The Pinkertons recorded that he even made a "vow to reunite with the rich widow Terry" and noted "she is immensely rich, but whether she will consent to reunite with her convict husband, those who know her best are unable to tell." The last photograph of Piano Charley shows a pitiful figure with straggling beard and staring eyes, a grim cipher of the once-glamorous rake. Worth provided his former partner with what little succor he could, bribing the wardens to slip him small packages of food and messages of support. But by 1891, as Bullard began the seventh year of his sentence, the old thief was plainly dying.

Worth wanted to see his friend again, and perhaps even to plead, if not in person, then with cash, for his release. Bullard was adept at getting into prison, but no slouch at getting out of them again, as he had shown in 1868 and again in 1878. Worth may have thought he could spring Charley from Liège prison: almost equally pleasurable would be to leave Shinburn behind.

The Prison de Louvain at Liège was, like most penitentiaries of the time, a place of lavish nastiness, designed to crush all rebellion out of its inmates rather than reform them. Only the most resilient or resourceful survived its rigors unbowed. Piano Charley, aesthete and lush, was neither.

One day in 1892 Worth suddenly announced to his wife that he was going on a short foreign business trip, bade farewell to his young children, and headed for the Continent. As always, Worth's motives were a mixture of the altruistic and the criminal: he intended to see and perhaps try to free Charley Bullard, but he was also nursing a new scheme to liberate the Belgian banks of some cash.

The first part of the plan came to nothing, for by the time Worth reached Liège, Charley Bullard was already dead and presumably playing the piano in Hades; the second part was to prove Worth's undoing.

NINETEEN

Worth's Waterloo

Perhaps it was the emotional trauma of Bullard's death that caused Worth to undertake a crime he would not have contemplated in his more rational moments. His taste for highway robbery had been demonstrated in South Africa, and maybe he thought a little light larceny would take his mind off things for a while, or perhaps he had simply become so vain that he considered himself immune to ill fortune. Even the Pinkertons considered it bizarre that a man of Worth's intelligence, who had stolen enough to live comfortably for the rest of his life, should stoop to petty crime once again. "Worth was living 'on top of the wave' in England, he had become wealthy," William Pinkerton reflected. "One would have thought that with this amount Worth could have retired, but the gambling propensity was so strong within him, and the desire for other fields led him into a still further life of crime."

After leaving London early in September 1892, Worth first headed for Switzerland, where he had arranged a rendezvous with a crook and former habitué of the American Bar named Oscar Klein, before heading on to Liège via Cologne and Aix to pick up some customized burglar's tools from a local blacksmith. A week after leaving London he arrived in Liège and checked into one of the city's more expensive hotels. The scheme hatched by Worth as he wandered around the city mulling over Charley's demise was straightforward but exceedingly rash. Most of the currency delivered to the Belgian city was brought by rail, Worth learned, before it was transported to the various banks by an express van guarded by an armed driver accompanied by a young boy. The driver was responsible for the safe delivery of the strongboxes, while the urchin ran lesser errands. After a few days of observation, Worth worked out that the driver and the boy sometimes went off simultaneously, leaving the van briefly unguarded. As he later explained to Pinkerton, if he sent a package to be delivered at a point near one of the larger banks, he could ensure that "the boy would be sent with this while the man went in the bank, leaving the wagon alone."

For the first time in several years, and for reasons best known to himself, Worth decided to carry out this theft personally rather than delegating the job to others, but obviously he needed accomplices. He recruited two known crooks, Johnny Curtin, a fugitive American bank robber whom he summoned from England, and Dutch Alonzo Henne, a local sneak thief with a solid underworld reputation. Curtin was a plausible but wholly unreliable rogue of saturnine good looks and long brown whiskers, whose charm was matched only by his avarice. The forty-two-year-old Curtin had served time for various crimes in Chicago, Sing Sing, and the Eastern Penitentiary in Pennsylvania, and had a reputation as "one of the most notorious burglars and shoplifters in America," before crossing the Atlantic in 1886 with two other criminals, as the police reported, to "make a tour of the continent, as they had considerable work laid out for them by Adam Worth, a noted receiver of stolen goods to whom all the American thieves go, on their arrival in London, for points." Curtin had won Worth's admiration and approval some months before when he was arrested while attempting to pass off a forged check and then swallowed the evidence en route to the police station.

Big Dutch Alonzo, one of the most villainous-looking men in Europe, was brought along as backup. He might appear terrifying, but, as Worth later reflected bitterly, "Alonzo, in spite of the fact that he had a great reputation for being a staunch fellow, and everything of that kind, was the biggest coward that ever lived when it came to doing anything daring."

For several days Worth coached his partners in their appointed roles: Curtin was to be the legman, ready to whisk off the bag which Worth would fill from the express-van strongbox, while Alonzo would act as lookout. The day before the robbery, Worth purchased a padlock identical to the one on the wagon strongbox, and a new overcoat, should a quick disguise become necessary. On the morning of October 5, 1892, the trio set out, and in its early stages the plan ran smoothly. At 9:30 a.m. the driver climbed down from the coach to deliver a strongbox to a Monsieur Comblen at 31, Boulevard Frère Orban, while his boy disappeared up a side street to make the bogus delivery. Worth, as he later recounted, "jumped on the seat and tore the lock off" the van's strongbox and "in less time than this takes to write," as one paper later reported, emptied the contents into a small sack.

"Alonzo was to be on the lookout to give the signal one way and Curtin the other, but when he looked about he saw both of them walking away." Either Worth's reflexes were going, or greed had got the better of him, for instead of taking to his heels at once, he "got off the van with as many packages as he could carry in his arms and started up the street." The reason for the disappearance of both Curtin and Alonzo was immediately apparent. Just as the robbery was taking place, one "Monsieur Decorty, a railway employee, happened to be passing who noticed the event." Worth's two accomplices saw Decorty staring with his mouth open, and scrammed. The railwayman recovered from his surprise "and, seeing the malefactor running away, set off in pursuit crying 'Stop! Thief!' "

At precisely that moment, the van driver returned to his vehicle and "he too set off after the robber." For a middle-aged man, Worth could put on a good turn of speed when the occasion demanded, as this one clearly did. "The fugitive already had a considerable distance on his pursuers," one newspaper later reported, "which he gradually increased." Meanwhile, police officer Charbonnier had heard the shouting and he, too, joined the chase. Worth's age, countless expensive dinners, and the weight of his haul soon made it an unequal race. Realizing the pursuers were gaining ground, Worth "hastened to rid himself of the objects he had just stolen, hurling them onto the pavement and making a bee-line for the rue Saint-Veronique," where he hoped to hide in the crowd. As Worth ruefully explained to Pinkerton years later, he was "two blocks away" from the scene of the crime before he was tackled from behind by the far younger and fitter policeman, who, aided by two more citizens and panting from the chase, clapped him in handcuffs.

Arrogant to the last, Worth tried to brazen it out. His name was Edward Grey (which the police transcribed as Edouard Grau), he said, from London, England, and he demanded to be released immediately. His spontaneous choice of alias may conceivably have been a reference to Charles Grey, the Duchess of Devonshire's onetime lover. But the Belgian police were cannier than their French Canadian counterparts had been a few years earlier, and were not going to be put off so easily when, as the magistrate put it, they had him "en flagrant délit de vol," red-handed.

In its edition of the following day, *La Gazette de Liège* described the attempted robbery as "an audacious coup, brilliantly planned" and allowed some sly racism to intrude on its reporting. "Grau is a strong fellow, with a vigorous and intelligent air. His face, of the characteristic Semitic type, is furnished with a dark mustache which, like his hair, is beginning to turn gray. It appears almost certain that he is lying in his declarations and that he has given a false name. He has given contradictory responses to other questions." *Le Soir* noted that "he was dressed in gentlemanly fashion and carried on him a considerable amount of Belgian cash," and *La Meuse* pointed to his "conventional attire" and noted that "all his effects carry the marks of British makers."

When his hotel room was searched and business cards found embossed with the name Henry Raymond and his London address, he admitted he had been living under that name for twenty-five years. Next, the police produced the burglar's tool from the scene of the crime, "the extremely solid 'Pince Monseigneur' [crow bar], wrapped in a leather sheath, which had been used for the theft." Worth now spun the baffled police a remarkable tale: he was, he said, a fifty-two-year-old mechanic, originally from Munich, who had come to Belgium via "Cologne, Mulhouse, Strasbourg and other German and Swiss towns." The burglar's tool he had purchased from a blacksmith in Aix the previous week. Hoping to put his interrogators off the scent, he offered them a sop, saying he had not worked for two years in London but had lived on the proceeds from a few petty thefts. Prior to that, he claimed, he had worked legitimately as a diamond salesman for the firm of Wynert & Co. in London. One moment he admitted carrying out the robbery of the wagon, the next he denied it. Deprived of sleep, he began to contradict himself.

"There is evidence to suggest that we are in the presence of a bold bandit who has strong motives for staying completely mute," *La Gazette* reported as the interrogation continued, adding: "Grau is a Jew, but whether German, English or American, remains unknown."

For two days the police hammered Worth with repeated questions. "Who are you? Where do you come from? Where did you last work?" Exhausted, Worth finally lost his temper and he told the Belgian police superintendent he would rather die than say anything else. "If you knew the truth I would be put away in prison for eternity," he growled, with a flash of the ego he could never suppress. Realizing that he had already said too much, at this point Worth clammed up and, despite the alternate threats and inducements of the police, he declined to utter another word. "He refuses to disclose his identity for family reasons," the police reported. In this, if nothing else, Worth was being perfectly honest, for his principal concern seems to have been to prevent his wife from finding out about his predicament. Despite the evident treachery of his accomplices, Worth insisted he had acted alone. "With the loyalty for which he was famous Raymond [Worth] steadfastly refused to reveal the identity of the confederate to whose folly he owed his own arrest, and Curtin escaped to England," the starry-eyed Sophie Lyons later wrote. In fact, it appears that Worth's refusal to finger his accessory was directly intended to protect his family, since he had asked Curtin to look after his wife and children in the event of his arrest.

All of which left the authorities in a quandary. Inquiries made at the Guillermins railway station revealed that "this individual had been seen several times over the previous weeks, wandering around the shopping areas. A sub-conductor had even seen him the week before, closely following a delivery wagon in the quai de Fragnée." The man in their custody was plainly a criminal of some sort, but precisely what sort it was impossible to tell; Worth had hoped to come away from the van robbery with up to "a million francs or $200,000," but in fact the packages he had stolen also contained "valuable state papers," which raised the possibility that he might be a spy. "The official value of the papers is 60,000 francs, but the real value is a great deal more," one newspaper stated; others estimated the contents of the box were worth at least half a million francs, given their importance.

Five days after Worth's arrest, he "continued to maintain an almost complete silence [and] as for the question of whether he carried out this brazen robbery with the aid of accomplices or whether he planned it alone, that too remains unknown . . . the robber continues to pretend his name is Edouard Grau." Finally, the investigating magistrate at the Liège High Court, Théodore de Corswarem, took the step of circulating to European and American police forces a description of the suspect, complete with Bertillion measurements and a photograph, along with a request for information.

"This fellow speaks and writes very good English," Corswarem advised, "as well as German and French with an English accent. He is stout, strong and of a sanguine temperament, hair cut short, side whiskers and mustache in the Russian style, whiskers completely gray, moustache less so, brown eyes, high forehead, prominent nose." While Worth had lavished money on racing horses and champagne parties, he had clearly neglected his dentistry. "Teeth irregular and discolored," wrote the Belgian judge.

"On the right side of the upper jaw one tooth is missing and one is decayed, on the same side of the lower jaw another tooth is missing and another decayed, on left side of upper jaw the two little molars are missing and the first big molar is very much decayed," and so on. Since Worth was still resolutely refusing to open his mouth for any other reason, his teeth were almost the only solid evidence the Belgian police had to go on. The circular concluded with a plea from Judge Corswarem to his "legal colleagues and all police officials to do their utmost to establish the man's identity, find out his antecedents and anything else concerning this person, and to communicate them as soon as possible."

The authorities were beginning to panic, for, as a contemporary noted, "neither the police nor the detectives knew him. The evidence against him was not very strong. He stood a good chance of being acquitted." A week after his arrest, as it became ever clearer that the authorities were still in the dark, Worth's spirits began to lift and he regained his voice, dropping boastful hints and taunting his captors, in the apparent belief that he would not be prosecuted and might as well have some fun. "Interrogated on the subject of his nationality, he said that if they really wanted to know they had only to look back over the history of an important and celebrated robbery committed, some time ago, on the railway at Ostende de Malines." The Belgian journalists picked up the scent. "Investigations have been made in this quarter," reported *La Meuse*. "If he is one of the perpetrators of this robbery, which we remember, there is every reason to believe that this bold bandit is an Englishman. He has retained his 'sangfroid' throughout, and is enjoying himself thoroughly at the trouble his anonymity has caused the investigating magistrates."

While the Belgian police waited to hear from their colleagues in Europe and the United States, word reached them that an elderly criminal by the name of Max Shinburn, currently imprisoned in the local jail, was only too anxious to identify the miscreant. The Baron, it seems, "had got hold of the newspaper containing an account of the arrest [and] from the description he

suspected that the prisoner was his intimate enemy, Adam Worth
. . . He lost no time in communicating with the authorities [and]
made a bargain with them which was doubly advantageous to him
inasmuch as it secured his own release and convicted the man he
hated."

Shinburn laid out Worth's striking criminal history in lavish
detail, noting virtually every theft he had carried out or commissioned since the Civil War. The resulting document, which remains in the Pinkerton archives, was a masterpiece of treachery,
hypocrisy, and revenge. Over the years Shinburn had learned
from Charley Bullard the complete details of his rival's career,
and he now provided the astonished Belgian police with chapter
and verse on the Boylston Bank robbery, the American Bar, the
South African robbery, and even the theft of the Gainsborough
portrait, which "had never passed out of Worth's hands and is to
this day under his control." Shinburn noted, with only slight geo-
graphical inaccuracy, that Worth "lives in extravagant style in a
house in Piccadilly above the store of Fordham [sic] and Mason,"
and conceded that "Adam Worth is without doubt the most successful burglar of the present time . . . no one has ever got the
best of him; on the other hand, he has the reputation of having
got the best of everybody in his line of work with whom he has
ever had any transaction."

Warming to his betrayal, Shinburn then launched into what
can only be described as wholesale character assassination. "His
policy is to deal with weak men in his line of business, [with]
whom he may do as he likes without question; this is evident in
looking over the men with whom he has been connected. He does
not recognize the principle of honesty among thieves, and he has
never been in a job where he has not taken some mean advantage
of his pals. This he may have been entitled to do in consequence
of always having been the head and soul of every job he has been
into, but, if so, it ought to have been understood before the job
was undertaken." Worth's alleged treachery included substituting
poor-quality diamonds for good ones when dividing spoils, "weed-

ing the swag," and generally diddling his accomplices out of their fair share.

Pointing out that he had "known Worth, alias Raymond, since his boyhood days," the Baron even saw fit to spice his perfidy with some more personal remarks: Worth's appearance is "rather Jewish," Shinburn sniffed, and he is "very fond of wearing much flash looking but valuable jewelry, especially a number of diamond, ruby and emerald rings on his fingers . . . his legs are what is termed bow-legged." Not knowing that Ned Wynert was dead and William Megotti in jail, Shinburn included Worth's erstwhile associates in his diatribe, which concludes with a sparkling piece of hypocrisy: "It may be said with truth that this trio of thieves are the most unprincipled towards their own kind that exist at the present day, and it is to be hoped that they will soon have meted out to them their just deserts by an often outraged law."

The representatives of the Belgian law were not so much outraged as stunned by the unexpected windfall, but as they pondered whether to believe Shinburn's claims, corroboration arrived from other quarters. Thomas Byrnes of the New York Police Department politely suggested that the description fitted that of Adam Worth, the Boylston Bank robber and, in his own words, "the most famous criminal of all." This was followed by another missive from an elated Superintendent John Shore of Scotland Yard, which sealed Worth's fate. Shore would dearly have liked to catch Worth himself, but this was the next best thing, and he offered the Belgian authorities everything he knew about Worth's life and crimes, including the Gainsborough robbery. The result was closer to a personal denunciation than an objective package of evidence and, as Worth himself put it, somewhat ruefully, "Shore blistered me from one end of the line to the other and made me as bad as possible" in the eyes of the Belgian authorities.

The people who knew most about Adam Worth, the Pinkertons, maintained a complete silence, making no attempt to provide de Corswarem with the volumes of information they possessed on his activities, an omission for which Worth would be eternally, demonstrably grateful. As he later told Pinkerton, and Pinkerton told his brother, "he expected every day to see a report from this country from our agency in regard to him, and he knew that it must have been my influence that stopped the report. I did not say yes or know [sic] in regard to this, but let him go on thinking so." In fact, William insisted, "we were not called on for the report." This was patently untrue, for the Belgian authorities had lost no time in contacting the largest detective agency in the United States and, indeed, a copy of de Corswarem's circular is in the Pinkertons' archives to this day. On November 3, 1892, William Pinkerton wrote to John Shore, thanking him for forwarding a copy of Worth's photograph. "To tell the truth he has changed so that I would hardly have known him . . . He is growing very old and does not look like the dapper chap he was when I saw him in London eighteen or nineteen years ago. Should the Judge of Instruction call for any particulars I have no doubt that Robert in my absence will supply him with anything he wants." Shore also made a point of writing to Robert Pinkerton, who promptly replied, stating, "I will write to the Judge of Instruction at Liège, Belgium, advising him as to what I know about Adam Worth." But he did not, and neither did William.

It seems likely, then, that Worth was correct in his supposition that the Pinkertons had decided not to provide the Belgians with the agency file on Worth. Pinkerton and Worth had met at least twice, in the American Bar in Paris and later in the Criterion Bar in London; the Eye turned a blind eye. Today, this would be considered scandalous, but then law enforcement ran on a less rigid basis. William Pinkerton upheld the law, but in a highly personalized way, and he was not above bending the rules if circumstances, or individuals, required it. On such shifting sands was the rock of Victorian morality built. Pinkerton did not give up Worth for the simple reason that he liked him, respected his talents, and knew he was in scalding-hot water.

"I know what your institution has done," Worth told Pinkerton many years later, "and I know they had an opportunity of knocking me at the time I was in Belgium during my trouble in

Liège." It was, he said, "a debt of gratitude that he could never get over." Eventually, Worth would repay Pinkerton in full, by providing him with the most celebrated detective coup of his career.

TWENTY

The Trial

Even without the Pinkertons' help, the Belgian authorities now had enough information on Worth to be confident of a successful prosecution, and a trial date was set for the following spring. The Belgian press excitedly advertised the forthcoming attraction: "Session of 20 and 21st March—the affair of the theft from the mail wagon by the Englishman Adam Wirth, alias 'The Prince of the Safecrackers.' Defending attorney: Jules Janson."

Word that Henry Raymond, the prominent London gentleman, had been unmasked as Adam Worth, international criminal, quickly spread to both the English and the American press. "Henry Raymond, a well known sporting man, was arrested on a railway train at Liège, Belgium . . . while stealing bonds valued at £4,000," the *New York World* reported. "He lived in high style in London, enjoying the proceeds of many larcenies . . . and belongs to a clique of American thieves well-known to Paris and New York detectives. He figures in Inspector Byrnes's book on criminals as Adam Worth." *The Daily Telegraph* noted that "the man Wirth . . . was a member of a notorious band of American thieves, two of the members of which were tried at Liège in 1884 for breaking into the Modera Bank at Verviers. Wirth, who was concerned in some of the most daring bank robberies of recent years, passed under various aliases, and was known to the American police during his stay in the United States as the 'Prince of Cracksmen.' He spent considerable time in London, where he lived in extravagant style, and acted as the receiver of an international agency of thieves." The press had yet to establish a connection between Adam Worth and the stolen Gainsborough, but Inspector Shore lost no time in telling William Agnew that the search for the *Duchess* might soon be over. The Scotland Yard detective arranged a meeting with the art dealer and laid the known facts before him.

Thus it was that, as Worth sat gloomily awaiting trial in a fetid jail cell, he received word that none other than the American consul had arrived to visit him. The official "claimed to represent a prominent police official in America, and offer[ed] to pay him $3,000 and effect his liberation from imprisonment for information that would lead to the recovery of the Gainsborough portrait." The official Agnew's history, perhaps not surprisingly, makes no mention whatever of this offer, but there is little doubt the art dealer was behind it. Worth, however, "declined to have anything to do with the matter, claiming that he knew nothing about the picture, and that all stories to the contrary were false."

Soon another, more credible offer arrived. Worth's own solicitor told him he had been contacted by the "English authorities" and claimed to bring "word from the Home Secretary in Belgium that his release would follow the return of the picture." Again Worth flatly refused not only to make such a deal but to "admit to his own lawyer that he knew anything whatever about the picture." The lawyer pleaded with him, but Worth was adamant.

Perhaps, as Pinkerton surmised, he feared the offers were merely a ruse, for it is hard to see how a London art dealer (however well connected) could have prevented the Belgian authorities from bringing to trial a man with an extensive criminal record who had been caught committing a major robbery. Worth was clearly in the most desperate straits of his career, but his refusal to cooperate in any way with either the "English authorities" or this nameless "prominent police official" suggests a willful obstinacy as much as caution. The painting was in a Boston warehouse, but during the seventeen years that Worth had traveled the world with his *Duchess* in his trunk, his yacht, and his bed, an extraordinary bond had grown between them which meant far more to him than money, more, even, than his freedom.

During her lifetime, Georgiana had bewitched a generation. Long after her death, through images like the Gainsborough, the strange power of her personality continued to seize the public imagination. Through his theft of the painting, Worth had become the custodian of that myth, attached, even shackled to Gainsborough's duchess by a psychological covenant he would not and perhaps could not break. Worth's double life had crashed around him, but he still had the painting, the last symbol of the grand con trick he had played so well. With the duchess on his arm, as it were, he had swaggered through gilded halls undetected; she had been his passport to high society, and the hurdle that held him from it. The law and the world might now know him as Adam Worth—rogue, impostor, villain, and liar—but for as long as he had the *Duchess* he was still, in his own perception, Henry J. Raymond, worthy gentleman and mighty thief. A photograph taken by the prison authorities early in 1893 says much about Worth's state of mind. Tieless but in a suit, a handkerchief protruding from his breast pocket, he stares directly at the camera, a picture of arch defiance, controlled and deeply menacing.

To the intense frustration of William Agnew, no doubt, Worth vigorously denied any knowledge of the painting's whereabouts. The *Duchess* was his badge of superiority and invincibility, proof that he remained as ever one step ahead, and he now penned numerous letters, in elaborate code, to his allies, lawyers, and friends, requesting help in his predicament. Many replied, also using code and false names, sending money, moral support, and the latest underworld gossip. Each letter was intercepted and scrutinized by the baffled Belgian prison authorities. From his wife and her appointed protector, Johnny Curtin, there was an ominous and total silence, but succor did arrive from another, poignant quarter.

Kitty Flynn—the widow Terry—now wrote regularly to her for-

mer lover, sending large amounts of money with cheering messages. She signed herself "Turquoise." Already a dab hand in
legal matters, she also helped to organize Worth's defense. Somehow the authorities rumbled the true identity of Turquoise and,
perhaps through Shinburn, learned of Kitty's strange amatory history connecting Worth and Bullard. The police quizzed Worth
closely on his relationship with Kitty, but the thief, gallant as ever,
staunchly denied they had ever been lovers. When it was suggested otherwise, he angrily refused to discuss the matter further.
An English gentleman, even one exposed as a fraud, does not
discuss his love affairs.

As the trial date approached, Worth's defending lawyer, Jules
Janson, paid a visit to his notorious client and set the exceedingly
bleak prospects before him. The police, Janson pointed out, had a
mountain of evidence indicating that Edouard Grau, alias Adam
Worth, alias Henry Raymond, was a career criminal of rare distinction. As for the robbery in question, the prosecutors had assembled several reliable witnesses, not to mention a record of Worth's
incautious remarks while in custody. The lawyer's advice to Worth
was stark: admit to robbing the mail wagon, but deny everything
else emphatically, and throw yourself on the mercy of the court.
Worth should claim the admissions he had already made were
extracted under duress. Above all, Janson recommended, play
down the "Prince of Cracksmen" stuff. Somewhat chastened,
Worth agreed.

On the morning of March 20, 1893, the Liège court of assizes was
packed with lawyers and members of the public "eager to see the
defendant who has been the subject of such extraordinary publicity." Sleepy, comfortable, bourgeois Liège had never seen a case
like it. Eastern Belgium was not noted for crime: the occasional
domestic assault and a little corruption was about the most its
courts expected to deal with from one end of the year to the next.
A mysterious, dangerous, many-named international thief attempting a daylight robbery in one of the city's busiest streets was
a rare treat indeed. Reporters for the Liège newspapers jostled for

the best view as Monsieur Beltjens, the portly public prosecutor, swaggered into court, looking supremely confident. Worth followed, in manacles, but doing his best to keep up appearances. Six months of imprisonment had taken a toll, and as he stood in the dock it was noted that he had "lost much of his gentlemanly bearing." On Janson's advice, Worth had reluctantly shaved off his handlebar mustaches and, "deprived of the magnificent whiskers which had furnished his face, the accused had singularly lost his dapper appearance." As the newspaper *La Meuse* observed: "This is no longer the gentleman of last October: but if the face has lost some of its earlier distinction, the man has nonetheless retained his polite and correct manner." Monsieur Beltjens may have done his homework, but Worth was also prepared for the coming tussle and determined not to be outdone in the matter of courtroom politesse.

The proceedings were short, confusing, and often hilarious, as Worth tergiversated, trying to throw Beltjens off with a combination of charm, equivocation, calculated self-incrimination, and straightforward perjury.

PROSECUTOR BELTJENS: "When did you go to America?"

WORTH: "When I was five or six years old."

PROSECUTOR: "But you were only three when your father emigrated?"

WORTH: "Quite possibly, yes."

PROSECUTOR: "How long did you stay there?"

WORTH: "Until 1870. Then I traveled to England, but I did not stay there long. I then went to the Cape, to the diamond mines."

PROSECUTOR BELTJENS: "You say you left London on 27 September 1892?"

WORTH: "Yes."

PROSECUTOR: "Were you not invited to Switzerland by a man called Oscar Klein?"

WORTH: "I met him in Bâle, where a contact in Geneva had said I would find him. I stayed in Bâle until the day I left for Liège, stopping for a few hours in Cologne and Aix on the way. I arrived here on 4 October on the express train at 8:30 in the morning."

PROSECUTOR: "What did you notice on your arrival?"

WORTH: "I saw the post office parcel delivery coach. Since the parcels were all stamped, I said to myself that they must contain something of value."

PROSECUTOR: "Is that when the idea of the robbery occurred to you?"

WORTH: "Yes."

PROSECUTOR: "How did you spend the day on October 4?"

WORTH: "I walked around the town, I purchased a padlock to see if the key might not fit the padlock on the van strongbox, and an overcoat because it had rained and I didn't have one with me."

PROSECUTOR: "Did you not buy the overcoat so that you could put it on as a disguise after the robbery to cover your tracks?"

WORTH: "No."

PROSECUTOR: "That's what you told the examining magistrate."

WORTH: "Quite possibly, but it wasn't true."

PROSECUTOR: "Where did you spend the night?"

WORTH: "With a woman."

This was not, as it happened, true, but it had the desired effect. Once the audience had stopped tittering and being scandalized, Monsieur Beltjens resumed his cross-examination.

PROSECUTOR: "How did you carry out the robbery?"

WORTH: "I saw the driver leave the van and go into a house. I climbed up onto his seat and forced the lock with a tool. I had followed the van all the way from the station."

PROSECUTOR: "When you were arrested, you refused to say who you were or where you came from. You even told the police superintendent that you would rather die than admit where you had last worked, adding 'If you knew that, I would be put in prison for the rest of eternity.' "

WORTH: "I didn't say any of that."

PROSECUTOR: "You claim you have no previous convictions?"

WORTH: "I've never been convicted, or arrested for that matter."

PROSECUTOR: "You tell us this is the first robbery you have ever committed?"

WORTH: "Most certainly."

PROSECUTOR: "Did you not tell the police superintendent that you are a mechanic by training, but that you have lived for the last two years on the proceeds from thievery?"

WORTH: "I never said anything of the kind, but I was chained up for twenty-two hours, and therefore I said a whole lot of things, but I didn't say that. I did say, in order to stop them from torturing me, that I would say anything they liked."

PROSECUTOR: "We are not in the habit of torturing people here."

And there, for a while, Monsieur Beltjens paused for effect, having thus reinforced the might and civilization of the Belgian kingdom. Worth had admitted the robbery, but made it sound like a spur-of-the-moment act, the uncharacteristic behavior of a foreigner in a strange land. Beltjens now moved to his second phase of attack: trying to prove that Worth was a rich and dangerous criminal with a long record of malfeasance and numerous, highly undesirable associates. He set off on a new tack.

PROSECUTOR: "When you were implicated in the robbery at Ostend in 1886 you said, at that time, did you not, that you had no need to steal anything because you were winning 1,500 francs a week playing baccarat in the winter and betting on horses during the summer?"

WORTH: "That's right. I found it a bit more lucrative than working as a mechanic."

The laughter at Worth's insolence did not deter the stolid Beltjens, who now charged into the thicket of Worth's innumerable aliases, a most complicated area of inquiry which Worth did his best to render still more confusing.

PROSECUTOR: "You gave various false names when you were
   arrested. Why?"
WORTH: "First of all I said I was Edouard Grau. It was the first
   name that came into my head, because I didn't want you to
   know my real name."
PROSECUTOR: "You admit that you behaved in an extremely
   irregular manner?"
WORTH: "Yes, I was playing about, but I didn't do anything
   illegal."
PROSECUTOR: "Why was it that you happened to choose the name
   of Grau and of Henry Raymond, names of infamous criminals
   in America?"
WORTH: "During the war between France and Germany in 1870, I
   wanted to go to Paris but, because of my German origins, I was
   denied a passport, so I took the name of Raymond and came to
   France, where I continued to be known as Raymond, as I was in
   the Cape."
PROSECUTOR: "Do you know this fellow Raymond?
WORTH: "Yes, he was a friend of mine."
PROSECUTOR: "Did you know that he was a robber?"
WORTH: "I had heard it said, but I never saw him steal anything."
PROSECUTOR: "Did you not also know that this fellow Raymond had
   another name: Adam Worth?"
WORTH: "At that time it was myself who used the name Adam
   Worth."
PROSECUTOR: "Did you never hear it said that in America this
   Adam Worth also had the reputation of being a ruthless thief?"
WORTH: "No."

The judge, jury, spectators, and even Monsieur Beltjens were
now surely baffled as to who, precisely, stood in the dock. Beltjens,
thoroughly discomfited, pressed doggedly on.

PROSECUTOR: "In America did you not know Bullard and
   Shinburn, who were tried here in 1884?"
WORTH: "Yes."

PROSECUTOR: "These were both professional thieves, were they not?"

WORTH: "I knew that Bullard was, but not Shinburn."

Worth had not yet learned of Shinburn's treachery and still sought to protect him, despite the antipathy he felt toward the man. He may also have hoped that Shinburn would provide a similar character reference. There was little point in attempting to defend Bullard's good name, even supposing such a thing had ever existed.

PROSECUTOR: "Oscar Klein, who you said was a friend of yours, was also a professional criminal?"

WORTH: "Yes, I knew that he lived off theft and swindling."

PROSECUTOR: "What intimate relations you have with professional thieves! Bullard was a particularly close friend, was he not?"

WORTH: "Yes, I went to visit him in Paris, where he ran a bar on the rue Scribe."

PROSECUTOR: "Was he not convicted in Paris for running a secret gambling parlor in this very same bar?"

WORTH: "Yes."

PROSECUTOR: "While he was in prison, did you not run the bar?"

WORTH: "I bought it from him. Bullard was extremely wealthy. He had £10,000 in the bank. I had £12,000 myself. I had just returned from the Cape."

PROSECUTOR: "Did you know how Bullard earned his money?"

WORTH: "No."

PROSECUTOR: "So, this is yet another association with a crook! How much did you pay for the bar?"

WORTH: "100,000 francs."

PROSECUTOR: "You not only have a peculiar set of friends and acquaintances, but bizarre ways of corresponding with them. You received letters in prison signed Turquoise, Comedian, and Edouard Grau, the very name which you yourself had adopted."

WORTH: "These are the names of comic actors in London. I

wanted to make sure that you didn't find out about either my acquaintances or my business."

Monsieur Beltjens was running out of steam. He suggested that Worth had purchased the new padlock to replace the forced lock on the strongbox and give himself time to escape. No, said Worth, he had not. Beltjens pointed out, with heavy sarcasm, the "remarkable similarity" between the Ostend robbery and the crime in question, and insisted that Worth had been in Liège for at least a month before October 5, planning the theft. No, said Worth, he had not. Exasperated by the series of denials, Beltjens was forced to conclude his case on an anticlimax.

PROSECUTOR: "But you do admit breaking into the trunk?"
WORTH: "Yes."

The prosecution rested, and it was the turn of Théodore de Corswarem, the investigating magistrate, to give evidence. Corswarem briefly outlined "a series of crimes that the English police have attributed to Adam Worth, without furnishing any evidence or proof"—for the simple reason that if Shore of the Yard had had any, Worth would have been in English rather than Belgian handcuffs.

Worth leapt to his feet to protest at the admission of mere hearsay and vehemently declared his innocence. He was unceremoniously told to shut up and sit down. Corswarem then offered a glimpse into the wealthy world of Henry Raymond: "He lived at the time in Piccadilly, where he pursued a life of great luxury. He maintained a crew on a riverboat on the Thames and a yacht at Southampton.

"When interrogated on the origin of his wealth," the magistrate testified, "he replied that he had gambled and won 1,500 francs a week. He doesn't seem to be in dire financial straits. He receives a lot of letters from England and New York, but these are written in such a way that it is impossible for us to know what they meant. One letter was signed Turquoise, which is the name of a woman in New York who just recently sent him $50."

Worth's lawyer chose this moment to make an interjection, his first of the trial and one which Worth could have done without. "That's Mrs. Bullard," he piped up, unhelpfully. The magistrate agreed that Turquoise and the former Mrs. Bullard were one and the same, and noted that the accused had "said he knew her, but denied that they had ever been lovers."

Despite Worth's mounting irritation at this unwarranted speculation into his love life, he kept his composure. The magistrate was still elaborating on Worth's lavish life-style. "He had some very fine furniture in London. The police in London say that he has been convicted in America. I have written for confirmation, but have not yet received a reply"—and never would, thanks to Pinkerton's reticence. At this point Corswarem abruptly terminated his testimony with the bald statement: "He told me he had been stealing for the last two years."

Two more witnesses then described how they helped to arrest the robber, followed by Janssens, a railway worker, who claimed that he had seen Worth following the mail van one month before the robbery. Sensing what was coming, Worth again attempted a denial, but his protestations were growing feeble with repetition.

Beltjens summed up, calling on the jury to award the maximum possible penalty to this "bold and dangerous" miscreant.

Now, finally, it was Jules Janson's turn to present the defense. Perhaps he was overwhelmed by the occasion or by the wealth of evidence against his client, or was simply a bad lawyer, but his performance was distinctly lackluster.

"The importance of the defendant and his circumstances has been completely exaggerated," Janson began. "Mr. Worth had made some admissions, but his situation must be taken into account. He must be seen as the perpetrator of a single crime." As *La Meuse* reported: "Mr. Janson said the information furnished by the English police was the merest calumny, which should never have been allowed into proceedings and which had crossed the sea in order to discredit a man who had never had the slightest conviction for anything." Just as he appeared to be warming to his theme, Janson ground to an abrupt halt. "Worth has never been convicted!" he spluttered, before what sounded suspiciously like a complete abdication: "The jury should be lenient for the sake of the defendant's wife and children." He tailed off and sat down.

The jury had now heard five hours of riveting, if confusing, testimony, but it took them just a few minutes to reach a verdict. Worth was found guilty of robbery as charged and sentenced to seven years solitary confinement with hard labor. At 5 p.m. the court rose, and Worth, trying to demonstrate what little remained of his dignity, was led away to begin his sentence at the notorious Prison de Louvain.

TWENTY-ONE

Gentleman in Chains

Prison life was hard on Worth, who had grown soft from his years of luxurious living in London, but it was made doubly so by the fact that Charley Bullard was not there to keep him company but Max Shinburn was. The authorities had agreed to reduce the Baron's sentence in return for betraying Worth, but he still had another year to serve at the Prison de Louvain. As a convict of some eight years' standing, Shinburn was a power to be reckoned with in the Liège jail, and he set about making Worth's life a misery with that inhuman cruelty some prisoners reserve for their fellow inmates. According to the Pinkertons, Shinburn "had managed to curry favor with the prison officials, held a petty position over other prisoners, was overbearing and tyrannical, and did everything in his power to inflict punishment on his old friend and was the cause of numerous punishments being inflicted on Worth." Before long, Worth was apprised of the Baron's treachery. He had never liked Shinburn, but now his hatred blew white-hot.

"He was a constant give-away on every prisoner in the prison," Worth later ranted. "He was pigeon for the keepers." Even the wardens were wary of him, for he was adept at "getting the keepers into trouble" by reporting on their activities to the head warden. In later years Worth would start frothing at the mere mention of Shinburn's name. "Of all the dirty, despicable scoundrels that ever took up thieving as a profession, Max Shinburn was the worst of them all. He was the most thorough-going, thorough-paced scoundrel I ever knew in my life; he was without the rudiments of manhood in him," Worth told Pinkerton, manhood, or rather gentlemanhood, being the quality he held most dear. "There was nothing from murder down that Shinburn would not do . . . he was the most despicable, low-bred scoundrel that ever lived . . . an over-bearing Dutch pig." Worth finished this tirade by saying that he would "never get over" what his former associate had done to him, and this would "result sometime in his killing Shinburn if he ever got an opportunity."

Worth lapsed into the darkest depression, which deepened when news reached him from England of the fate of his family. Johnny Curtin, proving himself the bounder described by Sophie Lyons, repaid Worth's loyalty with a stunning betrayal. Mrs. Raymond had learned from the newspapers that her husband, the respectable Henry Raymond, was in fact Adam Worth, a man who had committed virtually every crime imaginable and was now serving seven years' hard labor in a Belgian jail. Left with two young children and suddenly abandoned by respectable society, Mrs. Raymond was more than unhappy, she was hysterical. The only person prepared to help her, it seemed, was Johnny Curtin, her husband's dashing "business partner," who, true to his deal with Worth, had rushed to her side. Over many months Curtin comforted the distraught woman, plied her with drink and laudanum, took over the running of the Clapham mansion and, finally, seduced her.

Sophie Lyons was probably the source through which "rumors reached Worth of the undue intimacy of his wife and Curtin. He investigated the reports and found them true," a discovery that left him "raging with indignation at his wife's weakness and his friend's treachery." Unmasked, imprisoned, and now cuckolded, Worth was powerless to stop the events taking place in London. Curtin had usurped Worth's place in the marital bed and now he set about transferring the rest of his assets. Mrs. Raymond was no more capable of defending her money than her virtue, it seems, for she made no objection when Curtin pocketed the cash as he sold off the racehorses, the Brighton house, the Clapham mansion, and finally *The Shamrock,* which was purchased by the aristocrat Lord Lonsdale, who "entertained the Kaiser in the very cabin in which the stolen picture had formerly been hidden." Then, just as suddenly as he had appeared in her life, Curtin vanished, taking with him every penny Worth owned.

The strain was too much for Mrs. Raymond, by now an advanced and semicoherent alcoholic, penniless, homeless, and cast adrift for the second time in one year. Her "mind gave way under its weight of remorse" and she was taken, babbling, to a lunatic asylum, from which she never reemerged. The two children, a boy of six and a girl of three, were sent to live with John Worth and his wife in Brooklyn, where, Lyons claimed, "they grew to manhood and womanhood in ignorance of the truth about their father."

When word reached him of the tragedy, Worth exploded in despair and rage. Years later he was still "very bitter" about the role played in his life by Curtin, and prayed he "would never have a day's luck" all the rest of his life. Mulling his misfortune and tormented by Shinburn, Worth sank ever more deeply into despair. Deprived of the ability to control events, Worth began to deteriorate. "The prison treatment in Belgium was brutal," he later told Pinkerton. He was racked by pain from catarrh, and the ignorant hospital doctor performed a rustic operation on Worth's nose "from the inside," which made matters markedly worse, leaving Worth prey to violent nosebleeds and crippling headaches. "When I fell down with nervous prostration, I was three months in the hospital at one time, and they tried to get me out of the hospital and could not do it, and seared my back with hot irons," he later told Pinkerton. His next nervous collapse consigned him to the prison hospital for another four months.

A brief respite from at least one of the horrors of jail life came when the sadistic Shinburn, his chief tormentor, was finally released. The "document furnished by Max Shinburn to the Belgian government . . . secured the incarceration of Worth and the liberation of its author," the chief prison sneak, who had served only nine years, "considerably less than his full term." The Belgian authorities almost immediately regretted the decision to set Shinburn free. Within a few months an investigating magistrate, fearing, rightly, that Shinburn would at once return to a life of crime, sent out another circular asking "all officers of the police kindly to acquaint him of all details concerning traces of Shoenbein [Shinburn] so that he may be pursued and that one may definitely establish whether this well-known bandit has been recently in Belgium."

A description was provided, suggesting that while Worth deteriorated rapidly in jail, the Baron had survived his prison experience without obvious damage to his soigné airs: "Always well dressed. Has a distinguished appearance because of his polished manners. Speaks very courteously. Always stays at the best hotels." Shinburn, in fact, had left Belgium immediately upon his release, and after an operation to remove the telltale dimple in his chin, and hoping to "blot out his identity by the industrious circulation of a tale of his own death in Belgium," he settled once more in New York.

Shinburn did not enjoy his liberty for long, and no amount of crude surgery could disguise his distinctive manner. Reuniting with the New York criminal fraternity, he began "working on small banks and post offices in order to obtain the necessary capital to carry out his plans for a larger robbery." Two months after $20,000 was extracted from the safe of the First National Bank in Middleburg, New York, Pinkerton's detectives located Shinburn and began tailing him, but it was left to William Pinkerton himself to carry out the arrest, with the greatest possible fanfare. "In his residence was found a complete set of burglar's tools, skeleton keys, lock picks and drills of all kinds; a bottle of nitro-glycerin and a syringe for forcing it into cracks of safe doors; pistols and soft-soled rubber shoes and other articles used by burglars," the detectives reported. "Shinburn has undoubtedly been laying his plans for a big robbery."

"The arrest of Shinburne is undoubtedly the beginning of the end of his career," Pinkerton pronounced. The ancient wound to the Baron's leg had turned septic (he was "now obliged to use a silver tube in order to let out the pus that comes from the open wound," Pinkerton recorded ghoulishly), but at the age of sixty-two, the Baron had lost none of his élan. He was still "a man quiet in manner, of fine address, good appearance, suave, genteel dressed and would pass for a well-to-do foreigner . . . and a fluent talker when he desires to converse on any subject." No amount of talking could help him now, however. He was tried in Middleburg and sentenced to another four years in prison. At the end of that term, he was immediately arrested for another, earlier crime, and he spent the next thirteen years in various American prisons, vigorously protesting his innocence.

Worth, no stranger to Schadenfreude, was delighted to hear of Shinburn's arrest, trial, and imprisonment. He recalled that he was in his cell, "lying sick with nervousness," when one of the wardens, who had also suffered from Shinburn's sadism, came in to give him the "glorious news . . . that Pinkerton had captured the great Shoenbein, alias Shinburn." As Worth later told Pinkerton, "that news had done him more good than all the doctors and all the medicine he ever could take."

The perfidious Curtin also got his comeuppance. Having seduced Worth's wife and taken his money, Curtin had settled in disguise and under a false name in Woburn Place, where, in May, he was arrested by two Scotland Yard detectives for a string of unsolved crimes. "A well-known criminal, named John Curtin, who appeared to be wearing a wig, was charged with failing to report himself under the Prevention of Crimes Act," *The Daily Telegraph* reported. "In a drawer in the prisoner's room they found a six-chambered revolver, fully loaded, and some jewelry"—presumably the remaining property of poor, mad, destitute Mrs. Raymond. Worth eventually came to hear of Curtin's well-deserved fate, but any rise in his spirits was short-lived. Within a year, yet another cruel blow landed. Both the muses who had inspired his black but poetic life were no more.

For years the monumental Marm Mandelbaum, who had taught Worth the essentials of what might be called wing-collar crime, had continued to prosper as the den mother of New York thieves. Much of the property looted during the great Chicago fire of 1871 had found its way into and then out of her warehouses, at a tidy profit. But even the crooked lawyers William Howe and Abraham Hummel had been unable to help her, once District Attorney Peter B. Olney, one of the few honest law-enforcement officials in New York, decided her reign must come to an end. With the help of the Pinkertons, Olney set a trap with some silk he knew Marm had marked out for theft by her cohorts. On raiding her "offices," the Pinkertons found not only the stolen silk but enough evidence to put her away forever. "It did not seem possible that so much wealth could be assembled in one spot," one journalist reported. "There seemed to be enough clothes to supply an army. There were trunks filled with precious gems and silverware. Antique furniture was stacked against a wall and bars of gold from melted jewelry settings were stacked under newspapers. There were scales of every description to weigh diamonds."

Within hours, "the District Attorney procured several indictments charging her with grand larceny and receiving stolen goods," and Marm Mandelbaum's trial was set for December of that year. Released on $21,000 bail, Marm instructed Bill Howe to bribe her out of trouble, but for once the lawyer was pessimistic. Reforming and uncharacteristically honest elements had taken control of New York government and matters looked distinctly gloomy, he explained. So Marm Mandelbaum packed her bags with more than $1 million in cash, it was said, and fled to Canada. The Pinkertons soon tracked her down in Toronto, but she was untouchable under existing extradition laws. The great lady laughed all the way to the bank, particularly after "her bondsman succeeded in transferring the property pledged for her bail to her possession by means of backdated documents."

Early in 1894, after ten years of splendid and opulent exile, the mighty Marm Mandelbaum, now weighing a heroic 350 pounds, finally passed away at the age of seventy-six. Fredericka's mammoth coffin was carried, with considerable difficulty, back to New York, where she was buried with all the pomp worthy of a woman of such astonishing criminal talents. At the funeral, it was reported, several mourners had their pockets picked.

Marm Mandelbaum had been Worth's first inspiration and role model, and her death affected him deeply. Still more crushing was the news that Kitty Flynn, his Turquoise, whom he had not seen for several years, but of whom, if Lyons, the Pinkertons, and every one of his criminal associates are to be believed, he forever cherished fond memories, had died of Bright's disease in New York on March 13, 1894, at the age of forty-one. Hers had been a truly remarkable life, and the New York newspapers had a field day with her obituary. "SHE WAS ONCE A BARMAID," screamed the *New York World*. "Kate Louise Flynn Bullard Terry Dies, Leaving Millions to Her Three Little Daughters. TWO ARE A BURGLAR'S CHILDREN. The History of a Pretty Girl's Adventurous Life and Final Marriage to a Wealthy Sugar Planter."

Kitty had been ailing for several weeks and quietly passed away in her home at 102 West 74th Street. Her daughters, who were staying in Paris with their uncles, Emilio and Francisco Terry, were summoned by her physician, Dr. Clark Wright, but were "on the ocean" when Kitty breathed her last. Eight-year-old Juanita Theresa, Juan Pedro's daughter, was now the heiress to some $5 million of his money, while "the older daughters, children of the bigamous burglar . . . will inherit something like $1,000,000," *The World* estimated.

When Kitty's will was examined, however, matters turned out to be rather different. Juanita, as Kitty pointed out in her will, "was already well provided for." And the entire estate to be divided between her elder daughters, after debts had been taken into consideration, amounted to just $5,000. Kitty had managed to spend more than one million dollars in less than eight years, and died almost as poor as she had started out. Her taste for prolonged litigation was surely part of the explanation. According to one source, the rest of her fortune was "squandered . . . on finery and whims." The dissipation of the Juan Pedro Terry legacy was a magnificent, and entirely typical, act of profligacy by the self-made Grande Dame, of which both her late husband and her former lover would have entirely approved. Despite being left almost nothing, her elder daughters did not go hungry. Lucy Adeleine, now twenty-three years old, was appointed Juanita's guardian by the surrogate court, and in time both she and Katherine Louise would make excellent marriages, becoming the society women their mother had always aspired to be.

Kitty's determination to invent and reinvent herself (and to be reinvented by others) had first endeared her to Worth, a community of spirit that lay at the core of the only human love affair he had ever known. Together they had emerged from nowhere to become persons of substance; Kitty, like Worth, had carved herself a place in the world with other people's money. Kitty married her money; Worth stole his; but they were in many ways birds of a feather, co-conspirators in the great fraud of Victorian morality and appearances.

Yet there was an integrity to Kitty which Worth, in common with so many Victorians, signally lacked. Worth had managed to convince everyone, including himself, that his vast wealth made him a better person, a morally superior being, even though his means to that end were resolutely dishonest. Kitty had been equally steely-eyed in her determination to reach the top by using her manifest talents; yet, while this had led her into some dubious company, she had not lied, cheated, or stolen to get there. Kitty, like Georgiana, Duchess of Devonshire, had remained faithful to her rumbustious character and gave not a fig that the world knew it. Such personal honesty was beyond Worth's grasp, which was perhaps why he loved her, and envied her, to the death, and beyond.

Kitty Flynn, the girl from the Dublin slums, was buried in the Terry family mausoleum in Green-Wood Cemetery, Brooklyn, the most exclusive graveyard in New York, with an imperious view over New York harbor to the skyline of Manhattan. "It is the ambition of the New Yorker to live upon the Fifth Avenue, to take his airing in the Park, and to sleep with his fathers in Green-Wood," *The New York Times* once noted. Kitty would have been delighted at her final resting place; she never disguised her desire for distinction, or her willingness to do whatever it took to get there. She had chaffed with seamen in Liverpool, danced with shysters and crooks in Paris, flirted with the rich bachelors of Manhattan, and ended up an enchanting, litigious queen of society, the richest of the rich, consort of princes, magnates, and tycoons, but always the same woman at heart. And now she lay in Green-Wood, the Irish colleen with the merry eyes, laughing at them all. Her final neighbors were illustrious ones. Not far away lies Lola Montez, another famed consort whose lovers included Franz Liszt, King Ludwig I of Bavaria, and Alexandre Dumas, and one of her nearest neighbors in the vast cemetery is Henry J. Raymond, founder of *The New York Times* and pillar of the Establishment, whose good name had been stolen by her bad lover in perpetuity.

"She had lived enough history to make most women old before their youth," pronounced the *New York Herald,* but she had remained young.

Many years before she died, Adam Worth had lost his onetime lover and spiritual partner in their strange dance, and although she spurned him, he had perhaps retained something of her in the fascinating Gainsborough portrait that bore her willful, wileful gaze. Now, with her mortal passing, the last gossamer link was gone. His wife was mad, his lover and his friends were dead, his children across an ocean. The horses, yachts, books, furniture, shooting parties, and respectable acquaintances had all gone, too, along with his health and strength, and all Worth had to show, or not to show, was a gorgeous painting gathering dust in a distant warehouse vault, as completely incarcerated as he was himself.

Worth would eventually attain literary immortality as Professor Moriarty in the Sherlock Holmes stories, and his partner gained her own niche in popular culture. The story of how Kitty Flynn posthumously made it to Hollywood is almost as peculiar as her own picaresque life story. The year 1945, one half century after

Katherine Louise Flynn Bullard Terry was laid to rest, saw the publication of *Kitty*, the latest romantic novel by Rosamund de Zeer Marshall, author of such bodice-ripping romps as *The General's Wench, Rogue Cavalier,* and *Laird's Choice.*

Kitty is a very odd book. Ms. Marshall appears to have absorbed many of the elements of the story of the theft of Gainsborough's *Duchess of Devonshire,* allowed them to swill around in her head, and finally come up with a fictionalized story of her own—a hybrid, or perhaps a mongrel, of the truth. Marshall's *Kitty* is written in the first person and comes complete with heaving breasts, ripped silk, tight corsets, showers of kisses, and, in obedience to some immutable rule of romantic writing, euphemism-laden sexual congress at least once every fifteen pages.

Cheerful, kindly Thomas Gainsborough encounters the eponymous Kitty, a waif and harlot of London's East End, in Pall Mall sometime around 1785. Gainsborough paints her, and through the painter she meets "handsome, devilish, Hugh Marcy," a cad who immediately beds her and continues to do so, at intervals, for the next two hundred pages. Sir Hugh (for he is a baronet) vows to make his street urchin into a duchess, and under his direction she learns to comport herself like a lady, whereupon he immediately falls in love with her.

Kitty first marries a rich ironmonger, who conveniently dies, and then the elderly and grossly landed Roy Fitz-Alen, Marquis of Ruthyn, Count of Lonmore, Baron of Harden, and, most important, 23rd Duke of Malminster—who dies even more conveniently, leaving Kitty as the staggeringly wealthy Duchess of Malminster and reigning queen of aristocratic society. Marriage to a duke does nothing to impede her activities with Sir Hugh, partly because the old duke has no lead left in his pencil, but mostly because she likes it, as does Ms. Marshall, evidently: "The velvet caress of his kiss was like a million lips on my naked body . . . he parted the deep folds and gazed at me and slowly traced one finger breast to navel . . ." And so on.

Kitty becomes involved in politics as a Whig reformer and is painted by Thomas "Just call me Tom" Gainsborough again, this time as a duchess. "You are by far the most magnificent of my subjects," he tells her. All London, including the Prince of Wales, is agog at the beautiful duchess and her portrait.

"What an ascent for Kitty," mocks jealous Sir Hugh, "from gutter to Royal ante-chamber." Just in case we haven't got the point, the author has Kitty's French dresser explain, with Ms. Marshall's inimitable ear for dialect, "Zere iss only wan ozzer beauty who can compare wis Miss Gordon [Kitty's unmarried alias] . . . she's zee Duchess of Devonshire."

Kitty finally falls in love with one Brett, Lord Mountford, who as a youth, we are told, sat for Gainsborough's portrait *The Blue Boy.* Sir Hugh successfully blackmails her and disappears to Constantinople, and Kitty marries Brett, who is, needless to say, "all man."

"I doffed my night robe," Kitty tells us, "and slipped into the pale wisp of green, the déshabille for the nuptial night."

And that, mercifully, is that.

Published in the closing months of the war, *Kitty* helped to keep the home fires (and, presumably, loins) burning and went through an astonishing eight printings. This novel is, arguably, one of the worst works of fiction ever written in any language, but Ms. Marshall's steamy effort gave birth to a film of the same name that remains a classic. *Kitty,* made by Paramount Pictures and directed by Mitchell Leisen, launched the career of Paulette Goddard, in the title role, into the big time. As Goddard's biographer notes, "a lot of effort went into the conversion of Paulette from Kitty as eighteenth century Cockney street urchin to a Duchess," and the American actress was required to "speak only in a Cockney accent from breakfast to bedtime." In the hands of scriptwriters Darrell Ware and Karl Tunberg, Ms. Marshall's bodice-ripper became cleaner, funnier, and a good deal more subtle. Ray Milland plays an attractive and despicable Sir Hugh, and Cecil Kellaway, as Gainsborough, is considerably less excruciating than one might expect. The film was a successful rival to *Forever Amber* from 20th Century Fox, and earned a massive "$3.5 million in domestic gross rentals" when it opened at the Rivoli Theatre on March 31,

1946. The critics were lavish: "Paulette Goddard has worked up a blazing temperament to go with her ravishing beauty in the title role . . . she gives the work the correct touch of wry romanticism." For publicity stills, Paulette Goddard posed in a vast feathered hat, holding a rose in either hand, in a direct parody of Gainsborough's original duchess, yet again proving the strange durability of that image.

The story of Kitty, precursor of *My Fair Lady* and a host of other modern Pygmalion tales, is now a familiar one. Whatever Hollywood and Ms. Marshall's fervid imagination may have done to it in the process, the tale of the poor girl who becomes a great lady through the molding and coaxing of a wicked man she loves is one that the original Kitty would have recognized, and relished.

TWENTY-TWO

Le Brigand International

On July 24, 1893, *The Pall Mall Gazette* announced beneath banner headlines the solution to "A Seventeen years mystery."

"We are able today to throw some light upon the mystery of the century, and to announce news concerning Gainsborough's celebrated picture of Georgiana, Duchess of Devonshire, the beautiful and witty electioneering duchess to whose fascination Walpole and other contemporary writers paid such lavish tributes," the article began, before going on to recount the story of the sensational sale, theft, and disappearance of the painting.

"That was many years ago," the writer continued, "and the fate of the Gainsborough picture threatened to remain for all time as speculative as the identity of the author of the Letters of Junius or the Man in the Iron Mask. But a man in a sackcloth mask has made a revelation about this portrait of the beauteous Georgiana. A prisoner in the Prison de Louvain, wearing the mask which in Belgian gaols is the penal badge, has been interviewed by an emissary of *The Pall Mall Gazette*, to whom the prisoner confessed that it was he who broke into Messrs. Agnew's on that memorable night and stole the picture . . . the name of the scoundrel was Adam Wirth. He was none other than the celebrated thief who has earned for himself the proud title of 'Le Brigand International.' "

There is a certain amount of journalistic license here on the part of the *Gazette*. Worth had not exactly confessed; he had been entrapped. The previous May, "a man named Marsend went to the prison at Louvain armed with an official pass authorising him to see Wirth. The prison authorities took him for a detective." Worth, on the other hand, assumed Marsend was a solicitor who might help him salvage some of his fortune from the traitor Curtin, and believed his visitor was "a man of business, merely come to settle some vexed questions between the convict and his wife, who lives in England." In fact, Marsend appears to have been a freelance journalist of a most dubious kind who had been tipped off to Worth's past and now hoped to trick the convict into admitting his part in the Gainsborough affair. Marsend was at least partially successful. Worth, starved for company, seems to have been uncharacteristically free with his reminiscences about the Gainsborough theft and other details of his life. Even so, it was rather less than a full "mea culpa," and the *Gazette* had to admit when Marsend's story was published that Worth "has confessed with a certain amount of circumstantiality . . . and we are not in a position yet to put his confession to the test."

As Sigismund Cust, M.P., editor of *The Pall Mall Gazette*, later recounted, Marsend and another man had approached him, saying "they had a clue to the whereabouts of the picture" which they were prepared to sell. They claimed to be working "in consort" with Agnew's and also to have obtained the interview with Worth through the Foreign Office. Cust had given the men some money on account and had promised them more "when they produced the picture," as they assured him they could. The editor then took out his pen and set to work, turning the information provided by Marsend and his accomplice into publishable material. As Cust later told Agnew's, "his principal object in going into this thing was to get what he called 'copy' for his journal. But, of course, he would be only too glad if his efforts resulted in our getting back the picture."

The article concluded with a piece of classic journalistic over-statement: "Worth has promised, however, to supplement the in-formation already given with further facts, which may enable us at no distant date to say with some confidence whether or not the confession is a genuine one."

Worth, of course, had promised no such thing, and when the article was published he realized, too late, how he had been snared. The arrest and unmasking of Worth had caused a minor sensation the year before, but the revelation that the man who had posed as Henry Raymond was the man who had stolen the Gainsborough rekindled the story with a vengeance. Mr. Cust of *The Pall Mall Gazette* had done his homework, and while his prose was somewhat overblown, his information was largely accurate, describing in detail most of the crimes perpetrated by Worth over the preceding twenty years, his arrest in Liège, and his current, uncomfortable situation.

"He made his entry into the world of crime with the boldness of an Alexander who meant to reign in the realms of felony, and to conquer every criminal sphere . . . he embarked on a sea of extravagance and gaiety, concealing the Gainsborough picture like the man who locks up unquoted shares. Taking an expensive house in Piccadilly, and furnishing it with the taste he had ac-quired by his frequent visits to the mansions of the wealthy in the practice of his profession as a burglar, he kept his carriage and pair, received much company, and organised nice, cosy little steam launch parties for river picnics, his favourite diversion."

Why, the author wondered, had Worth refused to part with the valuable Gainsborough? He concluded that Worth had been simply unwilling to take the risk. "A picture of this sort, unlike the swag which the melting pot can instantly render unidentifiable, could not be brought to any market without the risk of immediate detection. The thief thus found himself the possessor of a fortune which he could not realise, an Aladdin's lamp which he knew not how to employ, a storehouse of wealth to which he could not get the 'open sesame'!"

Never suspecting that Worth might have other reasons to

keep the picture and knowing he was not likely to be contradicted, the author gave full rein to his imagination: "Every now
and then the picture, buried beneath some heap of rubbish,
would rise up in his memory and cause him severe qualms, for the
possession of it was a standing menace to his safety . . . he tried
to forget the picture's existence, willing to neglect it, yet loath to
destroy anything so potentially valuable."

Not surprisingly, the story prompted what we would now call a
"feeding frenzy," and the *Pall Mall Gazette*'s report was reproduced in newspapers and magazines throughout the country.
Some were doubtful. "Nothing is said in the account of the present whereabouts of the painting," noted *The Daily Telegraph*, and
"until that information is forthcoming there will be sceptics."
The *Bath Herald* agreed: "Messrs. Agnew, no doubt, will believe in
the truth of the story when they have their picture back."

Another writer in the *New York Sun*, cranking up his prose to
near erotic levels, fantasized that Worth had stolen the portrait
"to worship" the sexy duchess in secret. The anonymous writer
was not so wide of the mark, but realizing he might be in danger
of overdoing things, he suddenly concludes, on the basis of no
information whatever, that Worth "had used the dastard knife for
the mere sake of loot. A guerdon of dross, and not the gratifica-
tion of unholy but artistic passion, was to be his reward."

The *Manchester Courier* suggested "the story may or may not
be true but it is not an improbable yarn" and wondered whether
Worth, if he was indeed the thief, was also a romantic "haunted
during sleepless nights in gaol by visions of the lovely face of the
stolen 'Duchess'," who might now "unburden his mind" and re-
lieve his conscience by agreeing to return it. "As the felon has
been a sort of artist in his own line, perhaps he has some respect
for the artistic achievements of nobler men."

Worth *was* both haunted and burdened by the *Duchess*; he *was*
an artist, in a way, but he had absolutely no intention of returning
the painting. Trapped, increasingly infamous, and irritated that
he had been so incautious when dealing with Marsend, Worth
granted only one interview in the wake of the *Pall Mall Gazette*

furor, to a local paper, the *Indépendence Belge,* in which he claimed the whole thing had simply been a joke on his part. Worth insisted that,

> in the course of the interview Marsend began to talk of the famous painting which was stolen 17 years ago, [and] seeing the interest which his visitor took in the affair [he] thought it would be interesting to "green him up" and accordingly told Marsend that he knew the receivers of the picture; and himself possessed in England a reduced copy of it.

He pretended to be vastly amused that Marsend, and *The Pall Mall Gazette,* had believed his story. Indeed, he went into "fits of laughter" for the benefit of the Belgian interviewer, and "his laughter was apparently sincere." It was an elaborate bluff, and the journalist for the *Indépendence Belge* fell for it. "It seems certain," the paper reported, "that the *Pall Mall*'s story is the result of a hoax, pure and simple; that the secret of the famous picture is not at Louvain; and that the art world must renounce its newly awakened hope of seeing again one of the most admirable masterpieces of English painting."

But not everyone was so convinced. "I still retain the belief that Worth has control of the Gainsboro'," Robert Pinkerton wrote to his brother.

The *Gazette,* in true Fleet Street tradition, defended its story in the very next edition. "Certain newspapers, although availing themselves in their news columns of the benefit of our article on Adam Wirth . . . have, nevertheless, discovered in our report indications that the confession is not to be relied on." C. Morland Agnew, William's son, was interviewed and acknowledged that the convict Worth was indeed the prime suspect. "The firm have recently had negotiations with people acting on Wirth's behalf with a view to the restoration of the painting," the *Gazette* recounted, "and those negotiations are still pending." Bending the truth more than a little, the younger Agnew claimed: "We could have had the picture back several times since the theft," but for a high-minded refusal to contemplate getting the portrait without the thief. "The negotiations for the return of the picture never included the delivery of the thief into custody. We could not think, of course, of continuing negotiations of that sort," Morland protested, falsely.

William Agnew himself feigned insouciance when asked about the *Pall Mall Gazette* account, but the entire Gainborough episode still rankled, partly because it was still costing him money. Just a few years earlier, in 1887, he had been forced to make good on his debt of 1,500 guineas to the engraver Samuel Cousins when the latter died, even though the Gainsborough "was never engraved after the painting was stolen."

"There may be some truth in the rumor . . . but personally I know nothing whatever of the matter," he told the *New York Sun*, which then noted that "Mr. Agnew expressed a column with a shrug." After so many false alarms, the art dealer reportedly "heard the news with the calm indifference of a man who sees an old friend in a summer suit." But Messrs. Agnew were neither calm nor indifferent. Indeed, the *Gazette* story and its aftermath had led to a fresh flurry of activity in Old Bond Street and Scotland Yard as a series of more or less shady characters emerged out of the woodwork, some of them former associates of Worth, claiming to be able to broker a deal with the convict. In William's words: "Mysterious men came to me and said, 'We think we can lay our hands upon the painting,' but invariably wound up with a request for £20, or £50, 'just to cover the initial expenses of inquiry.' " Marsend even tried to capitalize on his scoop and once more "made an application to the authorities in Belgium for permission to have an interview with the convict Wirth, but the authorities declined to grant this permission without Mr. Marsend producing to them an authority from Mr. Agnew that such interview was desired by him." Another man, by the name of McLeod, also offered to act as a go-between, for a consideration. This McLeod, Morland Agnew reported back, claimed "he was Wirth's associate and . . . knows all about the picture and is agitating now in order to get money to assist Wirth." McLeod was sent packing.

Throughout 1893, the letters hurtled back and forth between Scotland Yard, Agnew's, and the various lowlifes scenting a scam. They got nowhere; Worth categorically refused to discuss the matter. Sticking to his story that the whole thing had been a misunderstood prank on his part, he refused to be interviewed by Marsend, McLeod, the Belgian authorities, Sir George Lewis, "or by anybody else"—a position he resolutely adhered to for the remainder of his sentence. "Nothing could be done by anyone," an Agnew's official complained.

Late that summer, Superintendent Shore came to visit Morland Agnew at the Piccadilly gallery, in a somber mood. "Undoubtedly the picture was about and might be recovered," he told the dealer, but not without cooperation from Worth himself. "He said that the authorities had known for some time that the man Worth, now in prison, was the thief," Agnew wrote, "but that it was quite impossible for the police to bring any real proof, nor could the police proceed against anybody who was in possession of the picture as being in possession of stolen goods. The robbery was some 17 years ago and it would be quite impossible to proceed against anybody."

Worth could not be forced to surrender the painting, only persuaded, Shore explained. "There was nothing to be done."

For the Victorian press and public, the image of a master criminal at bay refusing to surrender his last remaining symbol of wicked power was a piquant and powerful one. The *Duchess* had come to represent many of the values of that often self-satisfied society, the artistic reflection of wealth, position, and power. That she could still be held hostage by a jailed international bandit subtly undermined such complacency. Threats, inducements, and punishment had all failed to loosen Worth's tongue, or his grip on his only possession, and so, as the years of imprisonment crawled by, he continued to wage the strange campaign of defiance he could never win but refused to lose.

TWENTY-THREE

Alias Moriarty

In December 1893, just five months after Worth's crimes were revealed, Professor James Moriarty, one of the most memorable antiheroes in literature, came into the world.

The English reading public found the *Pall Mall Gazette* account of Worth's crimes at once terrifying and irresistible. Here was a crook so skilled that he could move in high society undetected, who could travel the world as a man of substance while coordinating his criminal empire, yet always managed to slip "through the fingers of the police." The notion had added piquancy at a time when the duality of man's nature, thanks to Darwin, was a matter of hot debate. Just as the criminal lurked beneath the cloak of respectability, so too did the deliciously sinful, bestial side of human nature coexist with man's finer, civilized instincts. Adam Worth, le Brigand International, was a creature straight out of Victorian fiction, and that, indeed, was where he was now headed. *The Pall Mall Gazette* had made Worth notorious; Sir Arthur Conan Doyle would make that notoriety eternal.

There is no doubt that Conan Doyle based his portrait of Professor Moriarty, the evil genius and bitter foe of Sherlock Holmes, principally on the career of Adam Worth, although aspects of Moriarty's character were doubtless drawn from various sources: his mathematical ability was apparently a reference to

Robert Pinkerton, William's younger brother and head of the Pinkerton's Detective Agency New York office

William Pinkerton in 1876, the year of the Gainsborough theft

An adept burglar and blackmailer of rat-like cunning, "Little" Joe Elliott was distinguished by his love of women in general, and actresses in particular

Kate Castleton, the pretty English-born actress and star of the American comic stage who had the singular misfortune to marry Joe Elliott twice

The "widow" Kitty Flynn, around the time she was being wooed by Cuban sugar millionaire Juan Pedro Terry. The marriage would transform her from a gangster's moll into one of the richest and most litigious women in New York high society [Courtesy: Katharine Sanford]

Alonzo Henne, alias "Dutch Alonzo," a small-time bank thief with "a great reputation for being a staunch fellow," recruited by Worth in the 1880s

"Piano" Charley Bullard at the time of his arrest in 1884, after years of dissipation had taken their toll, leaving him a "grim cipher of the once-glamorous rake"

Adam Worth, alias Henry Judson Raymond. A rogues' gallery photograph taken by Belgian police after his arrest in Liège in 1892

Maximilian Shinburn, alias "the Baron," bogus aristocrat, safecracker, and Worth's nemesis

Patrick Sheedy, a dubious gambler and "sporting man known throughout the world," who acted as the go-between in negotiations between Worth and the Pinkertons over the stolen Gainsborough

J. Pierpont Morgan, fabulously wealthy American financier and art collector, who vowed to get his hands on Gainsborough's *Duchess of Devonshire*, and did

Professor James Moriarty as drawn by Sidney Paget in *The Strand* magazine, Dec. 1893. "He is extremely tall and thin, his forehead domes out in a white curve and his two eyes are deeply sunken in his head . . . his face protrudes forward and is forever oscillating from side to side in a curiously reptilian fashion"

"A personal contest between the two men ended . . . in their reeling over, locked in each other's arms . . . the most dangerous criminal and the foremost champion of the law of their generation." Sidney Paget's illustration for *The Strand*, Dec. 1893

one of Doyle's friends, Major General Drayson; some claim the criminal "abstract philosopher" is a reference to Friedrich Nietzsche, based on the misreading of that philosopher as the architect of racist totalitarianism and thus the root of all evil. Conan Doyle's choice of name for his arch-criminal is believed to refer to one George Moriarty, a crook who featured briefly in the London papers in 1874; the author himself specifically compares Moriarty to Jonathan Wilde, an eighteenth-century crook.

But Adam Worth was Conan Doyle's primary inspiration and Conan Doyle told others as much. "The original of Moriarty was Adam Worth, who stole the famous Gainsborough, in 1876, and hid it for a quarter century, but even that master criminal might have taken lessons from the Moriarty of Holmes and Watson, a figure of colossal resource and malevolence," observed Vincent Starrett, one of the earliest and most reliable of Sherlock Holmes scholars. In a footnote Starrett adds: "This was revealed by Sir Arthur in conversation with Dr. Gray Chandler Briggs [a close friend of the author] some years ago."

Holmes's depiction of Moriarty describes precisely Worth's position at the height of his prowess in London during the 1880s. "The man pervades London, and no one has heard of him," the detective tells his long-suffering sidekick. "He is the Napoleon of crime, Watson. He is the organizer of half that is evil and of nearly all that is undetected in this great city. He is a genius, a philosopher, an abstract thinker."

When Sir Robert Anderson, head of the Criminal Investigation Department at Scotland Yard, was asked "who, in his estimation, was the cleverest and most resourceful criminal he had ever met," he employed nearly the same words. " 'Adam Worth!' he rapped out, without a moment's hesitation. 'He was the Napoleon of the criminal world. None other could hold a candle to him.' "

It is impossible to know whether Conan Doyle was echoing Anderson or the other way around, or neither: everyone who had achieved distinction in Victorian times became, by cliché, the Napoleon of Something. Certainly Conan Doyle knew and relied on Sir Robert Anderson for some of his background material, and the latter's admiration for Worth's criminal talents is well documented. "Fancy the long sustained excitement of planning and executing crimes like Raymond's," he once remarked. "In comparison with such sport, hunting wild game is sport for savages; salmon shooting and grouse shooting for lunatics and idiots."

The Moriarty described by Conan Doyle is physically very different from the man on whom he was modeled: "He is extremely tall and thin, his forehead domes out in a white curve and his two eyes are deeply sunken in his head. He is clean shaven, pale, ascetic-looking, retaining something of the professor in his features. His shoulders are rounded from much study, and his face protrudes forward, and is for ever slowly oscillating from side to side in a curiously reptilian fashion"—a far cry from the diminutive, mustachioed Worth. Moriarty is held responsible for "cases of the most varying sorts—forgery cases, robberies, murders." Worth, as we know, was a master practitioner of the first two, but shunned violence.

Conan Doyle next wrote about the evil professor in *The Valley of Fear*, a novel-length tale which was serialized in *The Strand Magazine* starting in September 1914. By this time, Worth's criminal network and involvement in the Gainsborough theft had been fully established and widely reported, and it is more apparent than ever that Conan Doyle's portrayal of Moriarty is firmly based on Worth, for he leaves numerous clues behind. The writer, like every other educated Victorian, had clearly followed the story of the theft of Gainsborough's *Duchess* over the years. In 1891 he referred to the Duchess of Devonshire fashion in *A Case of Identity*, while *The Red Headed League*, published the same year, describes a robbery remarkably similar to Worth's celebrated break-in at Boston's Boylston Bank fifteen years earlier. But in *The Valley of Fear* (1914) there is, so to speak, physical evidence linking Worth to Moriarty. At the start of that tale, Holmes interrogates Inspector McDonald of Scotland Yard, who has interviewed Professor Moriarty and found him to be, despite Holmes's warnings, "a very respectable, learned and talented sort of man." To prove how misguided is that impression, Holmes asks the policeman whether, during his conversation with Moriarty, he observed a picture hanging on the wall of the professor's study.

"Yes, I saw the picture—a young woman with her head on her hands keeking at you sideways."

Holmes, in a didactic mood, explains that the painting is by Jean-Baptiste Greuze, the eighteenth-century French painter, adding "the trivial fact that in the year 1865 a picture by Greuze, entitled 'La Jeune Fille à l'agneau,' fetched not less than four thousand pounds—at the Portalis sale."

McDonald still does not get the point, so Holmes elaborates. "It shows him [Moriarty] to be a very wealthy man. How did he acquire wealth? He is unmarried . . . His chair is worth seven hundred a year. And he owns a Greuze? . . . Surely the inference is plain."

"You mean he has a great income, and that he must earn it in an illegal fashion?"

"Exactly."

The other logical possibility, left hanging in the air, is that Moriarty, an art connoisseur as well as a felon, has simply stolen the Greuze.

In the original manuscript, Conan Doyle reported that Greuze's *La Jeune Fille à l'agneau* sold for "one million and two hundred thousand francs—more than forty thousand pounds." He was surely thinking of the record-breaking sale of *The Duchess of Devonshire* when he alludes to such an astronomical figure. There is one more, irresistible clue: the title of the imaginary painting itself. *Jeune Fille à l'agneau* means "Young girl with lamb," but the reader is actually being offered one of Conan Doyle's most delicious puns. Would McDonald, for all his "good Aberdeen upbringing," have known the meaning of the word "agneau"? Probably not. He might, in fact, translate the title "The Young Woman from Agneau," and the young woman from Agnew's was none other than the celebrated Duchess of Devonshire, stolen from Agnew's art gallery in 1876. Conan Doyle adored wordplay and must have expected that at least some of his readers would spot this elaborate in-joke.

The Agnew/Agneau pun was current at the time. The origin of Conan Doyle's punning title, *Jeune Fille à l'agneau,* and his choice of Greuze rather than Gainsborough as the artist, seems to lie in a piece of satirical writing which appeared in *The World* in April 1877, less than a year after the original theft. "It is said that Messrs. L'Agneau [Agnew's], the great picture dealers of Paris, purchased at the Hotel Drouot a magnificent portrait by Greuze for the prodigious sum of £10,500," the anonymous satirist wrote, before going on to relate an alleged feud between "the head of the house of Agneau [Sir William Agnew] and "the Marquis of Studely" [Lord Dudley]. The painting is duly stolen but will shortly be "miraculously discovered in America" by Messrs. L'Agneau, the writer predicts, in a truly dreadful piece of writing that might have been summed up in three words: Agnew stole it.

There is one more convincing link tying the person of Adam Worth to that of the fictional Professor Moriarty: William Pinkerton. The great American detective met the celebrated English author just once, during a transatlantic crossing, and, not surprisingly, found they had much in common. The precise date of the encounter is unknown, although one source cites, without corroboration, that it took place "shortly after the turn of the century." During the voyage, the sociable American regaled his companion with tales of the Pinkertons' exploits.

We know for a fact that Pinkerton inspired Conan Doyle with the extraordinary story of the Molly Maguires, the terrorist underground organization which emerged in the Pennsylvania coalfields in the 1870s and which was successfully infiltrated and brought to justice by the Pinkertons' agent, James McParland. It is entirely possible that, in the course of the voyage, William Pinkerton also expatiated on the character of Adam Worth, about whom he knew more than any man alive and whom Conan Doyle had already written about as Professor Moriarty in "The Final Problem."

That shipboard conversation with Pinkerton set Conan Doyle on a new scent, and when he came to write *The Valley of Fear* in 1914 he relied heavily, and without attribution, on an account of

McParland's adventures written by Allan Pinkerton. *The Molly Maguires and the Detectives* was first published in 1877 and then released in an enlarged edition in 1886. The second half of *The Valley of Fear* is, in the words of one scholar, "almost a paraphrase of the actual story" told by Allan Pinkerton in prose and William Pinkerton in conversation. But the first half of the novella, in which Professor Moriarty is reintroduced, appears to have sprung from a similar source. Here again, Conan Doyle did not have to rely simply on his memory of the transatlantic conversation with Pinkerton. For in January 1904 the Pinkertons had published a pamphlet *Adam Worth—alias "Little Adam,"* written principally by William Pinkerton, which told the story of the art-loving criminal mastermind in detail.

Conan Doyle certainly appropriated the story of James McParland, and in part that of Adam Worth as well, for his own literary purposes. It was a dangerous tactic and one that laid him open to charges of plagiarism. One person was in no doubt on the matter. William Pinkerton "raised the roof when he saw the book," according to his general manager, Ralph Dudley. "At first he talked of bringing suit against Doyle but then dropped that after he had cooled off. What made him angry was the fact that even if Doyle was fictionalizing the story, he didn't have the courtesy to ask his permission to use a confidential discussion for his work. They had been good friends before but from that day on their relationship was strained. Mr. Doyle sent several notes trying to soothe things over and while W.A.P. sent him courteous replies he never regarded Mr. Doyle with the same warmth."

Pinkerton was overreacting. Conan Doyle did not base his story simply on their "confidential discussion," but also on other, published sources. Like every writer of fiction, Conan Doyle used real characters, in this case McParland and Worth, but he endowed them with their own unique fictional flavor. More likely, Pinkerton was simply piqued that his own literary effort and that of his father were being overshadowed by Conan Doyle's best-selling works. Pinkerton spent his life dealing with con men and robbers, but the spat over the sources for *The Valley of Fear* must have brought home to him another eternal verity: if there is no honor among thieves, there is precious little among authors either.

As late as 1924, Conan Doyle still appears to have been pondering the life and crimes of Adam Worth. "The Adventure of the Illustrious Client," published by *Collier's Weekly* in 1924 and in *The Strand Magazine* the following spring, describes another master criminal à la Worth. He has a new alias: Adelbert Gruner, the Austrian baron and criminal cad. In an argument more ingenious than persuasive, it has been suggested that the names are linked. "The Worth family name in the homeland was spelled W-I-R-T-H . . . pronounced VIRT. It was simply a matter for Watson to change the German-American ADAM VIRT into the Austrian Adelbert. Watson also noted that the German WIRTH is pronounced much the same as the French VERT, which means green. So Watson tacked on the last name of Gruner, which also means green, not in French, but in German." This may be an example of what happens when one spends too long staring at a page of Conan Doyle, but the tale of Adelbert Gruner does bear some marked similarities to the Worth saga. Holmes's reference to "Charlie Peace," a "great criminal" and "violin virtuoso," would seem to recall Piano Charley Bullard. The "very dangerous villain" turned underworld informer, Shinwell Johnson, who provides Holmes with information on Gruner, may well be a "portmanteau" of the names Max Shinburn and the Bidwell brothers, former habitués of the American Bar in Paris. And certainly the description of Shinwell Johnson as a turncoat and "agent in the huge criminal underworld" reminds one of Shinburn's treatment of Worth in Louvain jail. Kitty Winter, Gruner's former lover, who conspires with Holmes to expose the wicked seducer, may well be another fictionalized version of Kitty Flynn, "a slim, flame-like woman with a pale, intense face, youthful, and yet so worked with sin and sorrow that one read the terrible years which had left their leprous mark upon her."

Adelbert Gruner, the dandy, is uncommonly similar to Adam Worth, right down to his "lucent top hat, his dark frock coat, indeed, every detail, from the pearl tie pin in the black satin cravat to the lavender spats over the varnished shoes." Gruner is possibly even "more dangerous than the late Professor Moriarty," Holmes avers, with his seductive talents and veneer of culture. "He has expensive tastes. He is a horse fancier . . . He collects books and pictures. He is a man with a considerable artistic side to his nature."

Again this recalls Worth, while Holmes's description of Gruner as a man "who collects women, and takes pride in his collection, as some men collect moths or butterflies," is even more strongly reminiscent of the man who, quite literally, "collected" at least one woman for his own private exhibition. Reflecting the duality Victorians saw in all great criminals, Gruner is a "beast-man," a gentleman on the surface, a monster beneath it, and, like Worth, "a real aristocrat of crime."

Worth aspired to Victorian respectability and criminal greatness, but Conan Doyle gave him something more enduring: a literary persona that has spawned myriad imitators, a name that is a byword for criminal cunning, and a game where blindfolded children cosh each other with rolled-up newspapers, having first tried to locate their opponent's head by shouting, "Are you there, Moriarty?"

Adam Worth's impact on popular culture did not end there. In 1939, T. S. Eliot published his delightful *Old Possum's Book of Practical Cats*, not the least memorable of whom is Macavity, the Mystery Cat.

Compare T. S. Eliot's description of the feline felon with Conan Doyle's description of Moriarty, and it is evident where the poet found his inspiration: Here, metamorphosed into feline form, is Adam Worth himself. Conan Doyle took his inspiration from Worth's life, and T. S. Eliot took his from Conan Doyle. To complete the trail, the composer Sir Andrew Lloyd Webber based *Cats*, one of the most popular musicals of all time, on T. S. Eliot's *Practical Cats*. Kitty ended up posthumously in Hollywood and Adam Worth made it, via two more aliases, all the way to Broadway.

Macavity, Macavity, there's no one like Macavity,
There never was a Cat of such deceitfulness and suavity.
He always has an alibi, and one or two to spare:
At whatever time the deed took place—MACAVITY WASN'T THERE!
And they say that all the Cats whose wicked deeds are widely known
(I might mention Mungojerrie, I might mention Griddlebone)
Are nothing more than agents for the Cat who all the time
Just controls their operations: the Napoleon of Crime!

TWENTY-FOUR

Atonement

The Belgian prison authorities finally released Worth in 1897, two years early, for "good behavior," which was another way of saying that he had endured without evident rebellion five long years of prison beatings and barbaric medical treatment, and the taunts, the depression, and the stupefying boredom of imprisonment. Worth had become a docile prisoner, growing more tractable as his body weakened and his spirit began to gutter. There was no one at the gates of the Prison de Louvain to greet the emerging felon, now fifty-three years old. Bullard and Kitty were dead, his wife was as good as dead, quite mad in an English insane asylum; his children knew little or nothing of his situation. Even the journalists who had peppered him with questions about the Gainsborough portrait had temporarily abandoned the chase for new quarry. Professor Moriarty was a household name, but his own name, or names, were all but forgotten by the world. Even if there had been a reception party when he staggered into liberty, it is doubtful that many would have recognized the swaggering, blustering crook of 1892 in this emaciated, shattered old man with the watery eyes and the drooping mustaches. The attentions of the ham-fisted prison doctor had left him with damaged nasal membranes, prey to cascading and unpredictable nosebleeds. At night he would wake in a feverish, screeching sweat, furiously hacking blood from his lungs as the budding symptoms of tuberculosis took hold. The bouts of "nervous prostration" that had struck him in the early part of his imprisonment had gradually lapsed into depressed resignation, for a vital part of Worth had died in his Belgian jail cell. Pinkerton later described him as "broken in health and financially a wreck," but something more vital had been destroyed than his body, wealth, or self-invented reputation. In prison Worth had discovered remorse: not for his crimes, for which he felt nothing but a residual pride, but for those whose lives he had damaged or destroyed. His young wife was beyond help. The two daughters of Kitty Flynn, which he believed to be his own, were now rich society belles who did not need and would certainly not have welcomed the attentions of an aging criminal. But his two younger children, a boy of nine and a girl of six, who lived with John Worth in Brooklyn, were another matter. John Worth had proved a dismal crook but was scarcely more successful as an honest man, and the family lived in crushing poverty and domestic disharmony. In spite of Worth's generosity over the years, or perhaps because of it, John's wife, a fiercely religious and domineering woman, had little but contempt for her felonious brother-in-law, and nothing but scorn for her fatuous husband. In his years behind bars Worth had come to a decision: he would reclaim his children and provide for them, by hook or by crook, fair means or foul.

Since he *was* a crook, and knew no other way, he decided to take the foul option.

Back in London, Worth rented a small room at 63, Piccadilly, a far cry from his former grand residence in the same street, and began making amends. His first act was a sad pilgrimage to visit the woman whose life and mind he had helped to ruin. His wife, according to Pinkerton, was now "a mental and physical wreck," and their meeting was so harrowing that it apparently caused Worth to break a lifelong habit of sobriety. "This is one of the causes that drove Raymond [Worth] to drink as hard as he did," Pinkerton concluded. Like Bullard before him, Worth crawled inside a bottle and stayed there for about a month. He emerged from this terrifying bender thinner and more sickly than ever, but the self-destructive demon inside him appeared to have been sated, at least for the moment. The need to see and provide for his children was by now almost pathological, and since he was fast drinking what little money he had—and his brother and sister-in-law seemed disinclined to send him the cash for the transatlantic fare—he set about planning a fresh set of crimes that would set him, or more accurately his progeny, back on the road to prosperity.

He did not have to search far afield for his first target. When Smith's, London's largest diamond merchants, was robbed late in 1897, the raid had all of Worth's hallmarks. "The thieves entered the place by cleanly cutting the steel bolts which fastened the gate and prying the gate open," one newspaper reported, after some £15,000 worth of jewelry was reported stolen from Smith's. "The shop was considered to be one of the most carefully guarded and secure establishments in London and was practically encased in steel," the *London News* added. "The men—for there were evidently two, and perhaps three, engaged on the job—had, it is apparent, laid the most careful plans for the carrying out of their work . . . the manner in which the place was entered, as well as the discretion shown in selecting everything most valuable upon which hands could be laid, leads the police to believe that the robbery is the work of a party of the most experienced cracksmen." The premises of Smith & Co., it should be noted, stood at 68, Piccadilly, almost directly opposite where Worth had taken lodgings.

Pinkerton had been tipped off by an underworld sneak called Charley Fisher to the fact that Worth was again recruiting men for criminal work in Europe, as well as to his current abode. "Fisher did not say positively that Adam Worth committed this robbery, but intimated that he might have committed it," according to a confidential memo in Pinkerton's archives. Pinkerton, oddly enough, decided not to pass this information on to Scotland Yard.

Despite the conviction in absentia hanging over him in France, Worth selected Paris for his next theft. As one contemporary observed: "He had lost some of the old touch of hand and brain, but he was still formidable." After careful calculation, he worked out the precise timing of the security express van's passing in and out of the Gare du Nord, and the following year, with two accomplices, he broke into the van and escaped with over one million francs in securities and jewelry. The robbery was the talk of Paris, but as Worth ruefully explained sometime later, the takings were less impressive than they appeared. "The French had begun to get wise," he complained with hindsight. "When they used to have the old ink stamp [on the securities] all we did was to clean the ink off the coupon and put it through the market, and there was no trouble about it at all, but now it was different . . . they recently have got to clipping a little bit out of the coupon, thus showing that it had been through the hands of a banker and was not negotiable."

Worth was in a hurry to get to Brooklyn, and prepared to sell the haul back to its owners, through intermediaries in the time-honored tradition, for a fraction of its full value. "The stuff," he later told Pinkerton, "was negotiated back for £12,000, or 60,000 francs, about 25% of the face value of the property." When the proceeds were divided with his accomplices, Worth's share came to some £4,000, rather less than he had hoped for, but enough, when combined with the takings from Smith's, to get him to the United States and to set up a fund for his children. When they found Worth was back in business, his brother and sister-in-law began dunning him for money again and threatened to abandon the two children unless Worth sent cash immediately. It had taken Worth more than two years to steal what he considered a sufficient sum of money.

On his arrival in New York, Worth hurried to his brother's home, handed over a wad of notes to his relatives, and embraced the two children he had not seen for seven years, who now barely remembered him. It was a brief reunion, for Worth had one more piece of business to transact before he could reclaim his kin. He spent just a few days in Brooklyn, under the shrewish and disapproving eye of his sister-in-law, before announcing that he had to meet a lady friend and a business contact in the Midwest. The lady was the *Duchess of Devonshire*, and the business contact was William Pinkerton. He bid farewell to his children once more, with the announcement that when he returned they would all be rich again. As for his greedy relatives, Worth told them he had just one more job in mind, a big one, after which he would finally become a father to his children. In the meantime, he would send sufficient money for their upkeep, and more besides. Grudgingly, Mrs. John Worth agreed. But it would be more than two years before Worth was able to make good on his promise to himself and to his children.

Gainsborough's *Duchess of Devonshire*, which he now retrieved from the warehouse, had been Worth's psychological companion for nearly two decades. It had also proved a heavy obligation. For years the portrait had held him back from, perhaps even deprived him of, human affection. Had he been prepared to surrender the object, and with it his own self-image, he might have gained his liberty years earlier and the family life he craved. Once the painting had obliquely represented his life, a corrupt chimera of love; now the *Duchess* was like some aging mistress, once beautiful, increasingly demanding, holding him in a guilt-edged trap. The deep ambivalence of his feelings was reflected in the long time he took to sever his link with it. The *Duchess* had framed his life, the embodiment of his crimes against society. Now she would be the vehicle for his salvation, his opportunity to atone and a chance, perhaps, to take a place, however humble, in a genuine human world.

Several months earlier, Worth had begun sounding out William Pinkerton, partly impelled by his profound respect, mixed with gratitude for what he regarded as the American detective's forbearance at the time of his arrest in Liège. As an intermediary he selected a former associate, one Patrick Sheedy, "a sporting man known throughout the world." Sheedy was a sharp adventurer and an inveterate gambler, who "made a living by the exercise of his wits, a broad knowledge of human nature, and a vast deal of experience," and who, if not actively crooked, was far from overburdened with moral scruples. He had the additional advantage of being known to both Worth and Pinkerton, for whom he had often acted as a conduit to the criminal underworld.

Worth had met up with Sheedy in Paris while preparing for the Gare du Nord robbery, and the latter appears to have furnished the older man with "financial assistance" of some sort—possibly even capital for his first theft after he left prison. In the course of a conversation one night in a Paris café, Sheedy recalled an exchange he had had with William Pinkerton some years before, during which the detective voiced his suspicion that Worth "controlled the Gainsborough portrait, and asked him if he ever could assist in the matter, whether he would like to bring about a plan for the restoration of the picture." Sheedy was fishing and Worth knew it, but he seems to have trusted the Irish gambler and decided to use him as a messenger.

In the summer of 1898, Sheedy arrived at Pinkerton's Chicago headquarters and outlined a proposition. Worth did indeed have the painting, Sheedy explained, and would be willing to return it to Agnew's, but only if Pinkerton himself acted as the intermediary—the American detective was "the only man he would entrust it with," Sheedy explained, adding that "he thought that a large reward . . . would be paid for the return of the picture," to be divided among the various parties.

Pinkerton, feigning outrage at the mere suggestion, said he would have nothing to do with any such underhand dealing: "under no circumstances would we attempt to handle anything of the kind; that we could not do it in justice to ourselves or in fairness to our relations with the Department of Police in London; that it would be a bad thing for anybody to attempt to handle, and that we could not and would not do it." Sheedy continued to wheedle. He passed on Worth's high opinion of Pinkerton, insisting, as the recipient later wrote, "that I was a nice fellow and a lot of flattering talk of that kind."

"He felt sure that there might be some way that we could see our way clear to take hold of this thing," William wrote to Robert, "but I told him there was none."

This was, of course, a bluff on the part of Pinkerton, who relished the chance to play a role in solving one of the great robberies of the age. To indicate as much, however, was simply to invite Sheedy and Worth to increase their demands. Pinkerton was not about to show his hand this early in the game. Sheedy the gambler was equally aware of the rules. He reported back to Worth: Pinkerton, while he might proclaim otherwise, had taken the bait and negotiations could now begin in earnest.

As the century, and the Victorian era, headed to a close, William Pinkerton was beginning to feel his years. The agency was profitable and renowned across the world, and at the age of fifty-four William was rich and distinguished, a huge, sonorous figure with the vast mustaches and reactionary political opinions to match his repute as "America's leading detective." But he was also a lonely man. His wife, Margaret Ashland, had died in 1895, and their two daughters had left home after marrying men of distinction in Chicago society. The great detective now lived alone in the grand Pinkerton family mansion, with only a single servant and a motley collection of dogs for company. Pinkerton had seen much of the darker side of human nature, hence his "fondness for animals to a marked degree." Toward his family he was kind but rigidly formal—a legacy from his cold, domineering father. His brother was never addressed more warmly than "Sir"; William's letters were always signed with a distant "sincerely." He usually avoided high society and was more likely to be seen at the racetrack, mixing with the colorful and dubious characters of the turf. The revered detective gave speeches on the techniques of law enforcement and spent long hours coordinating his crime-fighting empire, but he was happiest sharing memories of sleuthing with his detectives and, in many cases, with the objects of those campaigns themselves. Criminals were, perhaps, the only people he understood, or who understood him and the strange and violent battle of wits they had waged for so many years. "I am too good a hater," he wrote, when the question of parole for the Younger brothers came up in 1897. But in reality his feelings toward such men were often the reverse of hatred, and as he grew older he seemed to need them more and more. The rogues' gallery of the great criminals he had pursued was on display around his office, symbols of his self-worth, mementos from his old and intimate enemies.

On January 10, 1899, William Pinkerton left his home in suburban Chicago and set out for the Pinkerton office as usual. There he found a telegram with the cryptic message: "Letter awaiting you at house; send for it." The missive was signed "Roy."

"As I knew nobody named Roy the thing was a mystery to me," Pinkerton later recalled. He telephoned his home and was told by his daughter, who happened to be staying, that moments after he left the house "a strange man had called and left a letter, stating that it was important, and requesting that it be delivered to Mr. Pinkerton personally, and to nobody else." The letter was duly sent for.

It read:

Dear Sir,
Presuming upon our friendship in London, I have come to see you about a matter that might be to our mutual benefit in the event of your entertaining it. I have sufficient knowledge of and confidence in your character to know that if I have your word that no advantage will be taken of my position, and that no use will ever be made of any information you may acquire in regard to the matter upon which I wish to consult you. I can safely rely upon it. I am compelled to ask you to give me this assurance, owing to the peculiar complications that might exist (and do occur) in a business such as yours when interests are so directly opposed, as between your firm and a person in my position.

Now I will put it this way: should there be nothing in your business interests to clash and prevent your giving me the assurances I ask for, please insert in the Chicago "Daily News" under personal notice column, the following advertisement: "ASSURANCE GIVEN—W.A.P." and I will make an appointment to see you as soon as possible after I see the advertisement. Should it

not appear say within two days I shall understand that there is
some obstacle and that you have good and sufficient reasons in
a business way that prevent you from giving me your word, and
the matter will be at an end, and I must leave here without
seeing you, which I assure you, I shall do most regretfully.

I shall leave this at your house to avoid accidents as it might
be opened in your absence by your representative at the office. I
shall, of course make certain that you are in town before leaving
my note.

Trusting to hear favourably, I remain,

Yours sincerely,

H. Raymond

(late) London

"I recognised at once that this letter was written by Adam
Worth, alias Henry J. Raymond, and it was undoubtedly written on
account of the proposition which was made to me by Priestone
[the Pinkertons' code name for Sheedy] last summer."

Pinkerton immediately placed the advertisement in the Chicago evening newspaper. "On the 12th I received a personal call
over the telephone that Robert Ray wanted to see me," Pinkerton
recounted. "I knew nobody of that name, but on going to the
telephone somebody with a very pronounced English accent
asked if that was William Pinkerton. I said yes. 'Mr. William Pinkerton,' he repeated again. I told him yes. He said, 'This is the
gentleman from London.' I then replied that I knew who he was
. . . I asked where he was and he said nearly opposite our office. I
told him why not walk over, come in and ask for me personally,
and there would be nobody pay any attention as no one would
know him. He said he would do so."

If Worth's approach was cautious in the extreme, Pinkerton
was also taking no chances. He at once dispatched detectives to
positions "where they could see the man when he came in and
when he went out."

"I wanted him spotted to as many people in the office as
possible so in case in the future they might see him that they

would know him again. In a few minutes Robert Ray was announced . . ."

They knew one another's business intimately, but William Pinkerton had not seen Adam Worth for nearly two decades. The two old adversaries shook hands slowly as, with a practiced eye, the detective appraised the remarkable figure who now stood in his office.

"With the exception of being grey and aged considerable I saw very little difference in him after a period of over twenty years. He seemed to me to be shorter and a little inclined to be stooped, and his hair and mustache, which was black when I knew him, was now an iron gray. I should judge that he weighed 130 to 135 pounds . . . very dapper in his dress; about five feet five inches high; small build; speaks with a very pronounced English accent . . . he is about the last man that would be picked up as the dangerous professional crook that he is. He is undersized and small." The detective also noted that Worth "had indications of a man who drank pretty heavily . . . something that he never did when I knew him."

To judge from Pinkerton's notes, Worth had evidently spruced himself up to prepare for this momentous meeting, summoning up what remained of his former brio: "I weighed him up carefully for the purpose of making an accurate description of him . . . his eyebrows are quite heavy and evidently blacked up; face thin; eyes brown, nose prominent; large ears; rather long arms and hands; genteel; dressed neatly in dark clothes all the way through; frock coat, wears a modest gold chain, in England called an Albert chain, with a cameo charm; in scarf small pearl, pear shape, and sat bolt upright."

Worth greeted his old enemy warmly, and Pinkerton in turn invited him to sit down and "have a chat."

"What brings you here?" Pinkerton asked, for want of a better opening gambit.

"Well, I came to see you," Worth replied. "I told you a great many years ago that if I ever came to America I would look you up; now I have been over a number of times and I never have looked you up, but this time I looked you up of my own accord; I wanted to see you; I have thought a great deal of you of late; I know what your institution has done and I know that you had the opportunity of knocking me at the time I was in Belgium years ago during my trouble in Liège, for which I stayed in college five years, in other words prison . . . Now I am placing myself entirely in your hands; I have never done it with a human being before, but I have implicit confidence in your word that you and yours will not take advantage of what I say.''

TWENTY-FIVE

Moriarty Confesses
to Holmes

Worth had come to Chicago with the sole intention of opening negotiations for the return of the Gainsborough, which was now safely hidden in the old Saratoga trunk in McCoy's Hotel. But while the two men talked, a confessional bond seemed to grow between the burly detective and the visibly aging thief. As Worth candidly admitted, he had never placed himself "in the hands" of another human being; his entire life had been devoted to controlling others. But now he did so utterly, to the man who should have arrested him on the spot. Instinct drew them together, for they had long inhabited the same universe, even if they traveled from opposite directions: the crook who was a man of honor; the man of principle who was now bending the law to its limit. It was a strange meeting of minds.

Their "chat" lasted the rest of the day, and then long into the evening. They met again at Pinkerton's office the next day, and the next. Instead of getting down to business, Worth found himself unburdening his past, partly out of vanity but partly, it seems, out of a need to explain and justify the strange, crooked paths his life had taken. He summoned up the extraordinary rogues' gallery that was his acquaintance of the last forty years: Kitty Flynn, Piano Charley Bullard, the Scratch, Old Junka, and the loathed

Shinburn, laying before Pinkerton "in gossiping frame of mind" a picaresque roster of the international criminal underworld, and his own distinguished role in it. Worth talked of his Civil War days, his experience of Sing Sing, his thievery in New York, Boston, London, and Paris, the robbery of the diamond convoy in South Africa, and, most crucially, the theft of Gainsborough's *Duchess of Devonshire,* which he had jealously guarded for more than two decades but which now must be returned, to end the chapter. He was ill, he explained, perhaps dying. His words echoed his pathetic reverence for the object to which he had mortgaged his life and liberty: "The Lady should return home."

At the end of their three-day interview, Pinkerton was exhausted, exhilarated, and staggered by the sheer range of Worth's exploits, and the strange combination of pride and melancholy with which he had recounted them. "I consider this man the most remarkable criminal of his day," Pinkerton wrote after Worth had departed. "This was a most extraordinary meeting . . . We talked very freely about matters in Europe for the last twenty years, and without hesitation spoke of numerous robberies in which he had been engaged . . . he talked in a general way about almost every big robbery which had taken place in Europe, and his conversation was very interesting indeed." In addition to his large heart, Pinkerton was blessed with a prodigious memory. When Worth slipped out of his office and vanished once more, Pinkerton sat down and committed to paper, sixteen sheets of it, the bizarre interview that had just taken place.

Worth began his confession with some complimentary reminiscences, according to Pinkerton, saying "he had always fancied me and found that I was a man who kept his own counsel and that he had always felt a kindly feeling towards me. How much flattery there was in this I am not prepared to say." There was some, certainly, but also genuine admiration. Worth recalled how he had tried to give the detective a number of presents, but these had always been turned down. In particular he remembered "a very handsome snuff box, a unique thing," which he had wanted to send the detective "as a memento of old times," but he had finally thought better of it, since it was "something that was so unique that it might attract attention." It was also almost certainly stolen. Pinkerton maintained an incorruptible mien. "I told him I was glad he did not do it; that I did not want him to send me any presents."

"Were you afraid that I was trying to job [bribe] you?" Worth laughed.

As Worth relaxed, he began to describe, in no particular order, his many crimes. The Boylston Bank robbery, he reckoned, was so long ago that he was probably safe. "Of course you cannot tell," he added nonchalantly. "I wouldn't want to be tried on it, although thirty years have elapsed." He described how he had sprung the members of his gang from the Turkish jail, how he and Bullard had set up the American Bar only to see it raided and closed on Pinkerton's instigation. He shrugged and added, by way of no hard feelings, "I was beginning to recognize the fact that the American Bar would not be a success in the way I wanted."

From there Worth moved on to minute descriptions of the diamond convoy robbery, the Ostend train robbery, his narrow escape from the Montreal police, and the debacle in Liège. His memories were spiced with vitriol as he recalled the treachery of Junka Phillips and Little Joe Elliott, the cruelty of Shinburn, and what he perceived to be his hounding "like a human tiger" by John Shore of Scotland Yard. The ferocity that simmered in Worth erupted as he recalled the times he had been betrayed, and his solitary belief in his own virtue. "He is quite a roast in his way on most everybody," Pinkerton observed.

When the conversation turned to his own family, Worth grew mournful. Again he blamed others, and fate, describing how his former accomplice, Johnny Curtin, had seduced his wife, introduced her to drink and drugs, and stolen every penny she had. "I asked him where she was now," Pinkerton wrote, "and he said with tears in his eyes that the poor little soul was in the insane asylum, crazy, and would never come out . . . he was very bitter." With the talk of his family, Worth's poise seemed to deflate.

The "brutal" prison treatment in Belgium had left him a physical wreck, he explained. Every day he suffered from "hemorrhages in the head," and he was rapidly losing weight.

"He said he is going into the hands of a specialist as quick as he could to stop the hemorrhages; that if he does not have a hemorrhage every day he has terrific headaches; he blames it on the prison fare he got in Belgium. He said that he bled nearly half a pint of blood on Saturday morning," Pinkerton told his brother.

With a quick piece of mental arithmetic Pinkerton worked out that the melancholy fellow before him by his own account had stolen more than four million dollars in the preceding thirty years. Where had all the money gone? "He said that he had lived recklessly, speculated, gambled, dissipated, and had ran through it, but he remarked to me that if he ever got hold of a couple hundred thousand dollars again that nobody would get it away from him: that he would come back, buy a home and settle down with his children."

Now thoroughly sorry for himself, Worth heaved a sigh. "I realize I am getting to be an old man, but there are one or two things I have yet to do that will get me sufficient money to provide for my family. That is all I have left to do. Then I shall quit."

Finally, after several hours of nostalgia, riveting for Pinkerton and therapeutic for himself, Worth had arrived at the crux: the matter of the Gainsborough. Yes, he admitted, he had stolen the painting and kept it all these years. It had been a spur-of-the-moment decision intended to wangle his brother's release from prison, but in the end it had changed his life. Worth was no longer reminiscing now, but haggling in earnest.

"Of course I want to get some money out of it and I want you to get some money," he went on. "I know you are an honorable man and that you will not make it any other way excepting legitimately, but I think it would be legitimate for you to make the money by restoring this picture to its owner," he declared, and then sat back to observe the effects of this speech on the detective.

But Pinkerton was not to be drawn into a deal so easily. "I

told him . . . that under no circumstances could we undertake anything of the kind; that it would be against everything we ever did and against every principle on which our business was conducted."

Worth tried again with a little oblique flattery. "The great Supt. Byrnes would have given his finger nails to have the opportunity to do what I am offering you but who could trust that kind of swine; nobody will trust them."

Now Pinkerton gave some ground. "There might be other people in our business that would gladly attempt to do anything of that kind," he conceded.

For a while they discussed various possible intermediaries. Worth said his sister Harriet had married a legal man named Lefens, "a sort of office lawyer [who] drew up deeds and documents and things of that kind," but he doubted his "brother-in-law had weight enough to do it." Who would Pinkerton recommend? he countered cannily.

"I told him there were plenty of people who did have weight enough to do it . . . that I would not advise Howe or Hummel or people of that kind who were liable to keep the whole proceeds of the matter or possibly tip him off to the police."

Worth abruptly changed tack, pretending to abandon the whole idea of returning the Gainsborough. "He said he was sorry that we could not see our way clear to take hold of the thing but that he thought I was right in the premises: that it might make a stir and place us in a bad light with the London police." Now it was Pinkerton's turn to make a move in the delicate minuet. "What condition is the painting in?" he asked, with as blasé a manner as he could muster. Worth replied, with equal insouciance, that "he was satisfied the picture was intact." And what, continued the detective, of the stories that he "had recently heard of a picture being discovered in some lodgings which was moss-eaten and mildewed and which was supposed to be the picture of the Duchess of Devonshire?" Worth responded that he, too, had read such accounts and could not explain it except to say that "somebody was faking a painting and trying to put it off for the genuine one."

Deliberately wandering from the subject, Worth suddenly began talking of a burglar-alarm system he was currently working on. "He said sometime he would give me the result of something he is studying up in the way of burglar protection by electricity: it is unique and unheard of," Pinkerton reported. If the detective found it unusual to be discussing the latest burglary-prevention devices with one of the world's most wanted felons, his notes do not betray him.

Again Pinkerton dragged Worth back, indirectly, to the matter of the Gainsborough, by offering to lend him cash. "I asked him how he was fixed and if he needed any money. He said not at all. I told him not to be backward; that if he did need some money I would be willing to advance it to him. He said I was very kind indeed; that I was the first policeman who had ever offered to do anything of that kind, but he did not need the money." To reinforce the point, he pulled out a wallet and asked Pinkerton to change a $100 bill, making sure the detective spotted seven or eight such notes in his billfold.

After a little more badinage, Worth raised the subject of the Gainsborough again. "He said he would think over what attorneys to get and he would probably adopt my suggestion of returning to the Agnews the picture of the Duchess of Devonshire." Worth disingenuously added that "he would gladly give it up without cost of any kind but there were other people interested to whom he had advanced money from time to time for the purpose of keeping them quiet. He did not say who they were, but led me to infer that they were Englishmen."

It was a most subtle exchange between two veteran poker players. Pinkerton was determined to show Worth that he was not about to be manipulated, but he also made it clear that if Worth could find some reliable intermediary or negotiate an exchange in such a way that the Pinkertons' reputation would not be sullied, then they had the basis for a deal. In Pinkerton's own words, "under no circumstances would he do anything that the authorities at Scotland Yard did not acquiesce in." But if the English police were agreeable, that was another matter. Worth made it clear that he, and only he, had control of the painting; that any treachery on Pinkerton's part would mean the deal was off; with his wallet full of cash, he was not about to settle for a cut-price transaction. The two men understood each other perfectly. It only remained to set a symbolic seal on this tentative deal, and it came, oddly enough, in the shape of a small dog.

"I got talking to him about dogs," reported Pinkerton, the avid dog fancier, "and he said he was very anxious to get a fox-terrier pup for his little boy and girl. I told him I would give him one in a couple of weeks from now, that he could leave me his address and I would send it to him."

With this pledge of Pinkerton's good intentions and a promise to be in touch, either in person or through Sheedy, Worth finally rose to take his leave.

"Before going away I asked him for an address where I would send the pup to and he said he would drop me a line and let me know. In parting with him he said if he could ever do me any favor on earth, outside of going right out and being a policeman, he wanted me to call on him. He said I had been very nice indeed, and he appreciated my kindness."

The two men, now firm friends and soon to be partners in a most unlikely and shady business, shook hands warmly and Adam Worth wandered off into the Chicago night. He said he was taking the 9:20 train for New York that evening, but Pinkerton did not even trouble to have him tailed. "He seemed in good faith in everything he was doing, and if he thought I had broken faith with him, I would only scare him away."

An agreement, albeit unspoken, had been struck. William immediately wrote to his brother, outlining his extraordinary conversation with Worth. "Now, I do not know whether we will have any business with this man in the future or not . . . but I make this request, not to give him up to anybody or to allow anybody to know that we are aware he is in the country. I would not have him fall into the hands of the police or anybody else after he has acted in the way he has to me for anything in the world, and I want whoever reads this letter to be especially instructed that nothing must be said of this man and no search made for him." Once his hunter, Pinkerton had become Worth's protector.

"I really and truly think I can handle this man," Pinkerton told his brother—scenting, perhaps, the immense public-relations possibilities should he pull off the return of the great Gainsborough. "I believe I can make this man useful to us at some time."

The next day a cable arrived at Pinkerton's office, bearing salutations from Henry J. Raymond from an address in Brooklyn. A fortnight after that, two young children were astonished and delighted when a fox-terrier puppy arrived, from an anonymous benefactor, on their uncle's doorstep in Brooklyn.

TWENTY-SIX

The Bellboy's Burden

With so many intermediaries involved, the negotiations throughout 1899 over the return of the Gainsborough to Agnew's were necessarily protracted. The Pinkertons lost no time in contacting Superintendent Donald Swanson of the Criminal Investigation Department at Scotland Yard, who passed the information on to Inspector of Detectives Frank C. Froest—John Shore having left the force, to "chase chippies" in retirement down at peg-leg Nelly Coffey's brothel. As Pinkerton noted: "New Scotland Yard had been working on the case for a great many years [and] had practically got the same information which we had, but without the proof, or without the means of effecting a conviction of the thieves."

True to his word, Pinkerton left out any mention of Worth or Sheedy in his communications with the English police, although Scotland Yard was well aware of whom they were dealing with, albeit at an elaborate distance. Inspector Froest contacted Agnew's solicitor, Sir George Lewis, and laid out the version of the facts Pinkerton had chosen to relay to him. A reliable individual had approached Mr. Pinkerton, the English policeman explained. This man had been contacted by "a rich American," mortally ill, who knew where the stolen painting was and wanted to help return it before he died. The intermediary "suggests that the matter should be placed in the hands of Messrs. Pinkerton . . . although he does not desire to receive the reward he suggests it is believed that the reward may have to be paid to someone," Froest reported.

The intermediary, needless to say, was Patrick Sheedy acting on Worth's behalf, and the partial information supplied to Scotland Yard was intended to achieve several objectives simultaneously: to suggest that the thief was dead; to allow Pinkerton to negotiate with Agnew's for the return of the painting without appearing to compromise his principles; to insist that any exchange take place in America; and, above all, to ensure that no one was prosecuted. Both Sheedy and Worth were adamant on this point. The former framed this as a matter of artistic principle, insisting that "there should be nobody punished or injured . . . in order that the lost art treasure might be restored."

In Pinkerton's words: "Sheedy took the position that the restoration of the picture to the art world was of great importance, and that it could only be done in the manner suggested, and that if anybody was to be punished, the picture would never be restored as far as he was concerned." Such talk was probably a reflection of Worth's views. Just months after the theft, he had congratulated himself on "advertising" the painting to a wider audience; only someone as self-flattering as Worth could have believed he was doing the world of art a favor by returning a masterpiece that he alone had seen for more than twenty years.

In a letter dated June 26, 1899, Sir George Lewis advised the newly knighted Sir William Agnew of Scotland Yard's opinion of the offer. "Inspector Froest thinks there really is substance in the communication which he has received . . . he suggests that Messrs. Pinkerton should be communicated with before incurring any expense. I naturally place the matter before you." The art dealer was understandably cautious. His residual concern about appearing to condone a crime troubled him less than the suspicion that he might be about to pay dearly a second time for something that was technically his. Agnew's monetary qualms were clearly more acute than his moral ones.

As one cynic wryly observed later: "Would not a man offering to sell a coat which had been stolen be at once arrested by the first policeman who heard of the matter? They do things differently where a picture worth a small fortune is concerned."

"For the time being the matter hung fire," according to Pinkerton, "on account of the amount involved for the return of the picture, and the attorneys (Lewis & Lewis) claiming that this must be a ruse on the part of some sharp American to best the Agnews." The American detective was also guarded: "We must have a distinct understanding of how far you want us to go before we undertake to do anything at all," he warned Agnew's, who in turn had doubts about the honesty of "honest" Pat Sheedy, despite Pinkerton's assurances that "he is not in any sense of the word a 'crook' but is a heavy betting man and undoubtedly knows many of the swell criminals. I believe he is sincere in what he says."

The two sides circled one another, with Worth and Sheedy on one side of the bargaining table, Agnew's and Scotland Yard on the other, and the Pinkertons somewhere in the middle. Worth was the first to try to break the deadlock. Through Sheedy, he offered to return the picture for nothing if Agnew's "would allow him the privilege of putting the picture on exhibition for four months." Sheedy would garner the profits and then pass Worth the lion's share. This was a ludicrous suggestion—and a measure of Worth's chutzpah that he thought he could steal a valuable painting and then exhibit it—which was summarily rejected by Agnew's. A month later Worth and Sheedy were back with another, equally bizarre idea: "If the Agnews would allow Sheedy to make a steel engraving of the picture, and let him control the plate . . . the picture would be restored." As history had shown, the *Duchess* was an extraordinarily lucrative marketing tool and whoever controlled her image would own a most valuable investment. Again, Agnew's rejected the offer, but the proposition had at least convinced the art dealer that he was in touch with someone who genuinely controlled the famous painting.

To pass the time as negotiations dragged on, Worth put his

mind to "laying down" a little criminal work for some colleagues. Early in 1900, Worth arranged for three notorious American crooks—Kid Macmanus, Brooklyn Johnny, and Fairy McGuire—to "cross the ocean" to London, bringing with them the latest safe-blowing techniques. "They may be the men using nitroglycerine and dynamite as published in the NY journal a short while ago in connection with a burglary," reported one Pinkerton detective, but as usual nothing could be traced directly to Worth.

Later that year Worth packed up the painting and headed back to London himself, in a last bid to speed up negotiations. After another bout of subtle nudging between Pinkerton in Chicago and Worth in London, the detective finally believed he had brokered a deal with the English authorities. Then on January 16, 1901, Pinkerton reported, two years to the day after Worth had first approached him, "the Pinkertons received a cablegram from Supt. Swanson, Scotland Yard, instructing them to take up the matter of the stolen picture, and bring about its return, and the terms asked for by Worth would be accepted, providing it was the genuine picture, and an identifying witness would come forward immediately from England." Precisely what Worth's terms amounted to is unknown; all the parties were careful never to commit to paper the details of this dubious deal. The exchange was to take place in America. A lump payment in cash was clearly agreed upon, to be followed by the balance after delivery, as well as a guarantee of immunity from prosecution for all the parties involved. One contemporary said Worth "insisted that he should get at least £5,000 . . . and Pat Sheedy was to get for his efforts as negotiator a matter of £2,000." According to Sheedy, Worth was paid $25,000 in cash. Agnew's merely decided to accept the convenient fiction that the thief was dead.

After months of haggling, events suddenly began to move at high speed. "Mr. Pinkerton at once communicated with Mr. Sheedy to locate Worth, and have him come to America." Sheedy promptly sent messages to "one or two points" in London where he knew Worth could be found. "On receipt of the letter, Worth cabled Sheedy that he would come over on the first steamer," using a false name and bringing, of course, the false-bottomed trunk and its precious cargo. "When it was known he had sailed, the Pinkertons cabled to London to have the identifying witness come to the United States."

The man selected for the crucial task of identifying the long-lost portrait was none other than C. Morland Agnew, Sir William Agnew's son, who boarded the SS *Etruria* from Liverpool to New York on March 16, 1901, amid conditions of the utmost stealth. "It was a secret known only to the three partners in the firm": Morland, his brother George, and his cousin, W. Lockett Agnew. Even old Sir William, who had purchased the painting back in 1876 and luckily happened to be cruising the Greek isles in his yacht, was not informed of the plan, "for fear, in his excitement, he should give it away."

"I have news compelling me to sail for New York," Morland noted obliquely in his diary. He took his wife along, but even she seems to have been kept ignorant of the reason for the journey until it was under way. The trip was not a pleasant one. Just a day out of harbor, the *Etruria* was struck by a gale which flooded the stateroom, damaged many of the lifeboats, and so terrified the passengers that one committed suicide and another went berserk and had to be forcibly restrained. The state of Mrs. Agnew, as recorded by her husband, gives an accurate impression of the voyage: "Mother was rather nervous" (Day one). "Mother should not have come" (Day three). "I don't think Mother likes it. She begins to wish we were home again" (Day five). "Mother is, unfortunately, very nervous" (Day six).

Mother, as it happened, was extravagantly seasick throughout the voyage, a fact which does not seem to have prevented this stoical creature from eating every meal before promptly dispensing with it over the side of the vessel. "Here's a nice business. What is to be done about Mother," Morland wondered to his diary. Like every sensible British husband, he did nothing, and confined himself to complaining that he could get no exercise and had forgotten to bring his tobacco pouch. He passed the time by jotting down snobbish remarks about the dining habits of his fellow passengers: "These Yankees do eat like pigs—at lunch to-day a woman was eating a sort of cream tart and pickled onions with it! No wonder she has been ill most of the voyage." But even Morland later admitted: "I spent an exceedingly anxious time."

After a hideous, fog-bound nine-day voyage, they arrived in New York to be met by Robert Pinkerton, who told the Agnews that the handing over of the painting, if its authenticity was veri-fied, would take place in Chicago. Despite this "damper to all the hopes I had raised when on board the *Etruria*," the couple made the best of it by spending the night at the Waldorf. The next day they boarded the Lake Shore Express, finally arriving in Chicago on the afternoon of March 27. William Pinkerton, ruddy, spruced up, and thoroughly overexcited, met them at the station, and this "fine, well-set up man," as Agnew described him, accompanied the exhausted, gray-faced couple to the Auditorium Hotel. Every-thing had gone according to plan, he assured them, and the ex-change would take place the following day. "You will have the Duchess in the morning," he announced over a large lunch, be-fore offering to show them around the windy city in his carriage and pair. Agnew was already windy enough, at the prospect of what was about to take place. "Personally, I was too anxious about the morrow to think of doing any sight-seeing in Chicago," he later said.

At 9:30 on the morning of March 28, Morland made his way to Pinkerton's office and the two men set out for Chicago's First National Bank to cash the all-important check for $3,000, presum-ably the first installment of the ransom. "That's a lot of money to carry around in Chicago," piped up the impertinent bank clerk when Morland handed over his check. Morland pointed to the hefty detective standing behind him, one of the most instantly recognizable people in the city. A thief would have to be foolish indeed, or blind, to rob a man under the personal protection of the Eye. "Oh, I guess you'll be all right then," said the cashier.

By ten o'clock the cash, in used bills, had been deposited in Pinkerton's safe, on the understanding that it would not be handed over unless or until Morland Agnew had the painting in his hand. The two men then returned to the Auditorium Hotel, rejoined "Mother," whose seasickness had now been replaced by nervous sickness, and waited.

"As the hour approached at which it was stated that the picture would be returned I noticed Mr. Pinkerton became more and more nervous, even more nervous than I was myself," Morland recalled. Pinkerton's reputation was on the line. Had Worth had second thoughts? Was this some elaborate ploy to humiliate the detectives? Was the ingenious crook even now persuading the staff back at his office to hand over the money, before vanishing with the painting again?

"About a quarter of an hour before the time appointed," Agnew wrote in his diary, "Mr. Pinkerton, myself and Mrs. Agnew adjourned to the room upstairs where it had been agreed that the picture would be delivered. The few minutes we spent behind that closed door were just a trifle nerve-shattering, I can assure you. I smoked a cigar to help the time along." The conversation died. Pinkerton stared at his watch. Morland puffed to conceal his agitation. Mrs. Agnew retched quietly.

"By and by there came a knock at the door," Agnew recalled. " 'Come in,' said Mr. Pinkerton, and the door opened on the instant. An adult messenger was standing in the doorway, carrying a brown paper roll in his arm. 'Mr. Agnew?' he queried. 'Yes,' I replied, and held out my hand. The messenger handed me the roll in silence, and, as if he had been charged to deliver the most commonplace message in the world, at once turned on his heel and left the room, closing the door quietly behind him."

The "adult messenger" was almost certainly Adam Worth himself in heavy disguise and brazen to the last, playing his last great role. If Pinkerton recognized him, and there is no direct evidence that he did, the detective successfully masked his surprise.

Worth slipped back to his rooms at the Briggs House hotel.

"When he had gone," wrote Morland, "I took out my knife, cut the string with which the paper was tied and there, lightly wrapped in cotton-wool, lay the long-lost Gainsborough. Two minutes sufficed to convince me that it was the Duchess."

Her travels had not dimmed the *Duchess*'s radiance, although Morland noted the jagged edge of the canvas where Worth had snipped out pieces to prove his theft so many years earlier. "The face, which is of wonderful beauty, is unhurt and, mutilated as it is, the picture is still of immense value and the highest interest."

Pinkerton "watched his features closely, and saw his eyes fill up for a moment."

"I looked up at detective Pinkerton and told him of the picture's authenticity. Instantly he shook my hand and congratulated me heartily. Until that moment he himself had not been sure that the picture which it had been arranged would be returned to me in his presence was the identical one stolen from our gallery a quarter of a century ago."

"Mrs. Agnew was equally grateful," Pinkerton recorded courteously, but he urged the expert "to make no mistake," telling him "he must use every possible test, measurement, etc. on the picture before he decided the matter . . . he then applied the different tests which are made use of to tell genuine pictures," before turning again to the practical policeman.

"I am positive the picture is the original one stolen from my father's gallery," he said.

"Well, I am glad it is alright," the detective responded. "I had made up my mind if it turned out a fake to burn the thing and wash my hands of the whole business."

After this strangely moving moment, the two men were all bustle once more. Agnew at once dispatched a cable to his partners, obliquely announcing: "Have Secured A Gainsborough," so that they could insure the painting. His use of the indefinite article was quite intentional. The method by which the portrait had been recovered was irregular, to say the least, and Morland had no intention of tipping off the authorities to what had taken place until the Gainsborough was safely back in Old Bond Street.

"Then we went to a shop close by the hotel, where Mr. Pinkerton purchased some waterproof paper and two light boards. With these I made the picture up into a flat parcel and handed it over to the great detective."

Relieved and elated, Pinkerton took the Agnews for the promised tour of the city before loading them, and the wrapped picture, on the 5:30 p.m. Limited Express to New York after another exchange of thanks and congratulations. "Must lose no time getting out of the country," Morland wrote in his diary.

The art dealer, by his own admission, "took no special precautions to safeguard the canvas."

"I hung it up on a peg in the compartment and when leaving it to go to the dining car for dinner simply told the Negro attendant to keep an eye on our things," he wrote. Although the painting was now in the proper hands, Pinkerton was aware that the hands that had stolen it were still at large, and he was taking no risks. The attendant was in the pay of the detectives, with instructions to guard the door to the Agnews' cabin with his life. A Pinkerton detective was stationed at the other end of the carriage, just in case Worth changed his mind and decided to steal the painting back.

"On arriving in New York we were met by two of Pinkerton's men, to them I entrusted the precious parcel and was informed that they would sleep in the same room with it that night and bring it aboard the *Etruria* the next morning. We put up at the Holland House that night and next day boarded the *Etruria* just before the advertised sailing time. In my state cabin I received the Gainsborough from Pinkerton's men. There was a cupboard in the cabin which I first padded with pillows to make a soft resting place for the Gainsborough. That cupboard was my only safe during the voyage."

Bursting with his news though pledged to silence, Agnew wrote to his daughter from the steamer on March 31, telling her the entire strange story. "Some 25 years ago a very beautiful picture by Gainsborough—a portrait of the Duchess of Devonshire—was sold in London and bought by my father for a great price. It was stolen, and the justices have been after it more or less ever since. We never expected to get the picture back, but when its recovery is known, it will of course create a great sensation and we shall have all the world wanting to see it. We dared not even tell Grandpa [Sir William] what I was coming after, lest he should let out the secret and upset the whole business. How excited he will be when he hears!" Pinkerton had kept his word not to reveal Worth's existence. "The thieves are dead," Morland wrote, "and there is no chance of getting anyone punished now."

He also wrote to Pinkerton, expressing "our grateful acknowledgement for the splendid services you have rendered to the world in general and to ourselves in particular in the recovery of this long lost work of art." Pinkerton would later claim $593.35 for his trouble.

A few days into the voyage, Morland could keep his secret no longer. "I told the Purser what I had with me and later on I revealed the secret to the Captain. They and a well-known Catholic prelate were the only people aboard the *Etruria* who knew what I had with me. They all had a look at the picture." One reason for the elaborate secrecy was the lingering fear "that the picture might be stolen" again, but Morland had additional motives for keeping the story out of the newspapers for the time being: "If the customs officers wanted to be disagreeable they could have demanded that duty be paid on the picture and while they probably would not have forced collection, it might have caused a great deal of unnecessary trouble and delay." In the space of a week Gainsborough's *Duchess of Devonshire* had been secretly smuggled into America and then smuggled out again. It was to be her last transatlantic crossing for many years.

The Agnews' return journey was calmer, but Mrs. Agnew's nerves had still not recovered from the outward voyage. "Mother and some of the ladies are singing hymns," Agnew noted, while continuing to point out the social deficiencies of his fellow travelers. "There are not many nice people on board, but many Yankees of a very common sort. The way they talk is horrible, especially the girls, and they have not an idea of behaving."

It might have impaired Morland Agnew's humor somewhat, as he sat in a self-congratulatory mood at the captain's table, to discover that there was one other person on board the *Etruria*, in addition to his wife, the purser, the captain, and the "well-known Catholic prelate," who knew exactly what the art dealer had hidden away in his padded cupboard. Fellow passengers would later describe this man as "a decayed millionaire who crossed by the same boat," a small, polite English gentleman who drank heavily, tipped the staff lavishly, and coughed horribly. Had he worn, for example, the attire of a messenger at Chicago's Auditorium Hotel, then he would probably have caused the febrile Mrs. Agnew to have a heart attack, but the little man with the frock coat, gold chain, and pearl tie pin simply blended into the throng, notable only, perhaps, for the odd intensity with which he observed the art dealer and his wife.

Pinkerton later assured Agnew that he had "arranged through our New York office to look the passengers on the steamer over on which you sailed to see that no American professional thieves were amongst them," and out of offended pride he blasted as "positively untrue" the many subsequent reports stating that Adam Worth had boarded the *Etruria* to return to England in the company of the portrait he had just relinquished. But this was almost certainly the case. The painting portrayed, not just a grand duchess, but Worth's grand hoax, his arrogant success, and his abject failure. Now, a fading shadow, he followed it home.

TWENTY-SEVEN

Pierpont Morgan,
the Napoleon of Wall Street

W hile Adam Worth was accompanying the Gainsborough home for the last time, "going back to England as quietly as he arrived," another ardent suitor for the lovely *Duchess* was in hot pursuit, a man who had more in common with Worth than he would ever have cared to admit.

J. Pierpont Morgan, the Goliath of U.S. finance and perhaps the most powerful man in America, had long ago set his sights on the *Duchess of Devonshire*. A quarter-century earlier his father, Junius Spencer Morgan, had been prevented from purchasing the painting for his son when Worth "eloped" with it. Pierpont Morgan was determined to prevent the *Duchess* from slipping through his family's hands a second time.

In the intervening years, the wealth of the House of Morgan had swelled from enormous to immeasurable. According to one estimate, the combined fortune of the Morgan empire and its associated companies would soon be worth more "than the assessed value of all the property in the 22 states and territories west of the Mississippi." In 1895 Morgan had organized a syndicate to support the U.S. gold reserve, thus stabilizing the American economy; he had forged America's railways into a 33,000-mile network from coast to coast; he ran a company with 341 directorships in

112 corporations. In the same year that the *Duchess* was recovered, he had set up the U.S. Steel Corporation, the world's largest financial conglomerate. There was nothing Morgan money could not do, and nothing Morgan money could not buy. Like a Renaissance prince, Morgan had crowned his stupendous fortune with an art collection beyond compare. From Paris to London to Luxor, he collected works of art like a magpie Ozymandias, buying up what ever caught his fancy, with barely a thought to the expense. The higher-brow cognoscenti whispered that his collecting was indiscriminate, the work of a barbarian with a bottomless bank account, but it would eventually become a hoard more magnificent and eclectic than any on earth.

Before leaving New York with the *Duchess* on the *Etruria,* Morland Agnew had sent a message to the Morgan mansion asking if the millionaire was in the market for the painting his father had once tried to purchase. But the tycoon was away on business. Morgan's friend Bishop William Lawrence of Massachusetts described Morgan's reaction on returning to New York and learning that the *Duchess* was available once again.

"His butler said that a representative of the Messrs. Agnew had called and that he had 'The Duchess of Devonshire' with him.

" 'Where is he?' asked Mr. Morgan. 'I want to see him.'

" 'He is just going to sail for home and is gone,' the butler replied."

Morgan was not the sort to let the Atlantic stand in the way of his desires. "I was determined to have that picture and I took the next ship for England," Morgan recalled.

As he was rushing to disembark from New York, a cheeky young reporter spotted the financier and asked: "Going to London, Mr. Morgan, to teach the English how to invest their money?"

"My boy," Morgan replied, "the English know very well how to invest their money. It's likely they'll get some of mine before I come home." Morgan had resolved to crown his collection with Gainsborough's Duchess of Devonshire, whatever the price. Obtaining it would be a publicity coup of immense proportions, and thoroughly satisfy his dynastic pride.

"The Napoleon of Wall Street," as Morgan was dubbed by *The Economist*, was a direct contrast in physique to "The Napoleon of crime." While Worth was small and sleek, Morgan was vast and corpulent, the financial mogul par excellence, with the eyes of a shark and a nose, afflicted with "acne rosacia," which grew to the size and texture of an inflated raspberry. No organ in modern times has inspired crueller mockery than Morgan's nose, with its changing crenellations. It was the sign to lesser beings that, for all his amassed power, Morgan was fallible. The tycoon, a sensitive and vain man, had his nose airbrushed to more discreet proportions in every photograph he could get his hands on.

But, in other respects, Morgan and Worth were birds of a Victorian feather. Both for a time stood at the center of a vast network of men and resources: one purely criminal, the other financial; and both were less than scrupulous in how they obtained their money—wealth being, for each, an end in itself and a powerful narcotic. They never met, but their lives were eerie echoes of each other, one played out boldly on the stage of international finance, the other conducted in the hidden recesses of the underworld.

Like Worth, Morgan had viewed the American Civil War as an opportunity not for glory but for financial gain. The crook had faked his own death at the Battle of Bull Run, apparently by substitution, and Morgan had executed a similar maneuver. When he was drafted after the Battle of Gettysburg, Morgan, like many of his class, simply paid a proxy $300 to take his place, afterwards referring to him as "the other Pierpont Morgan." The other Adam Worth, in all probability, was buried in a Washington cemetery. Where Worth had made money from the war by "bounty jumping," Morgan did so by underwriting a highly dubious deal to buy some five thousand Hall carbine rifles at $3.50 apiece, which were resold to the government at six times their original price. Even the banker's most objective biographer admits that

Morgan, like Worth, "saw the Civil War as an opportunity for profit, not service."

The Hall carbine affair was by no means the last in which Morgan's ethical approach to business would be questioned, but in the era of the robber barons, he was not alone in voicing one set of moral principles and following another. As one historian has written: "This was a day of corruption on a grand scale. It was a time when the Drews, Vanderbilts, and Goulds could use a railroad as a toy and rob it of money . . . when members of Congress and legislators could be bought, not once, but again and again."

Morgan and Worth reflected their times, in different arenas, but with similar philosophies, for both were pirates in the old tradition. Indeed, Morgan might be descended from the aristocratic Spencers, but he also claimed the bloodthirsty Elizabethan pirate Sir Henry Morgan as one of his ancestors. It was only appropriate that he should name his succession of vast sailing yachts the *Corsair,* for that is precisely what he was himself.

Both men were Anglophiles, generous to a fault, with a similar business philosophy: increase profits by centralizing, rationalizing, and cutting out unnecessary and debilitating competition. Morgan and Worth shared another trait peculiar to their time—a firm and well-founded belief that great wealth could buy the veneration of their fellow men. Both bought respect with "other people's money," to use Adam Smith's phrase. Both purchased large houses with every luxury, and sleek sailing ships—those badges of wealth that once caused Morgan to observe pompously that "anybody who even has to think about the cost had better not get one." Even in his heyday, Worth could never match the opulence of Morgan's life-style, yet his instincts were the same: so to dazzle the beholder with affluence that the soul of the man within passed unquestioned.

One Morgan biographer, Frederick Lewis Allen, caught Worth's aspirations perfectly when he described, in reference to his subject, what made the average Victorian multimillionaire tick: "The man who had accumulated great wealth sought both to establish or secure his place among the elect by indulging in those forms of 'conspicuous waste' which found favor among the privileged, and to enrich his own life according to whatever tastes he possessed or could acquire. He tended, in Western civilization, to want to have his womenfolk admirably attired and outfitted; to want to have a fine house full of luxurious appointments and rare and lovely things; and to want to give magnificent parties . . . he might even add a yacht, the very symbol of luxury . . . If his tastes were sporting, he could now engage in those forms of sport which traditionally required the most retainers, such as grouse shooting, or were expensively speculative, as was the maintenance of a racing stable. But none of these exercises of wealth quite satisfied his sensibilities, if he had any; were there not in life finer qualities than these? There were the arts . . . He could collect the well certified art of the European past, thus simultaneously exercising the talent for acquisition that had made him rich, stimulating and satisfying his appetite for beauty . . . and appeasing his own sense of financial prudence . . . and if he were an American, he could have as well the added inner satisfaction of bringing to American shores a treasure trove."

Morgan had no alias to hide behind, but the contrast between his pronouncements and his actions was fairly remarkable. Just as there were two Worths, "there were two Pierponts," in the words of one historian, "the proper banker and the sensualist—yoked together under extreme pressure."

Both men were given to fits of sanctimony, and like Worth, Morgan considered himself a creature of the highest righteousness, the only man of honor among a rabble of thieves. In fact, again like Worth, he was greedy, vain, touched by megalomania, and blissfully unaware of, or at least unwilling to face, these facts. His father once gave Morgan this advice: "Never under any circumstances do an action which could be called in question if known to the world." Morgan's principle, and that of Worth, was closer to: "Do whatever you want, and so long as you maintain a consistent front, the world remains in ignorance."

In addition to having the ear of kings and potentates the world over, Pierpont Morgan assumed a direct communication with God. His will begins with a passage of lordly self-commendation that sounds suspiciously like a direct order to the Almighty to arrange admission to heaven forthwith: "I commit my soul into the hands of my Saviour, in full confidence that having redeemed it and washed it in His most precious blood He will present it faultless before my Heavenly Father; and I entreat my children to maintain and defend, at all hazard and at any cost of personal sacrifice, the blessed doctrine of the complete atonement for sin through the blood of Jesus Christ, once offered, and through that alone."

To all outward appearances, Pierpont Morgan was a pillar of the church, a dedicated family man, and a self-appointed guardian of public morality. As a member of the board of New York's Metropolitan Opera, he was instrumental in helping to cancel a performance of Richard Strauss's *Salome* on the grounds that the plot was too racy for general consumption. In 1873 he helped to found the Society for the Suppression of Vice, to root out depravity, gambling, and other moral evils among the lower orders. Under the moral crusader Anthony Comstock, the Society set about reforming public morality with a vengeance, covering up nude statues, wrecking the New Orleans lottery, and trying to ban the plays of George Bernard Shaw.

Privately, if not always discreetly, Morgan philandered like a priapic goat and "generally behaved himself in a way that would have drawn writs and summonses from the vice-baiting Anthony Comstock." The steadfastly married man of virtue who so arrogantly presented his eternal soul to Heaven was sexually incontinent to an almost pathological degree, and his taste for and generosity toward actresses inspired at least one good joke against the red-faced Lothario. One actress remarks that she recently got a pearl out of an oyster. "That's nothing," her companion replies. "I got a whole diamond necklace out of a lobster." The original Henry Raymond of *The New York Times* would have recognized the double standard here, as would the man who filched his good name.

However one regards Morgan's morals in business, the stark contrast between his public image and his private behavior is impressive. But there is no evidence that this double life tweaked his conscience any more than Worth's troubled his, for both knew only too well how to "smile, and smile, and be a villain." And while both men existed in a world of moral duality, they were also incurable romantics.

In 1861 Morgan, then aged twenty-four, fell in love with one Amelia Sturgis, "a high-minded young girl of good New England ancestry . . . with beautiful teeth." No sooner had their courtship started than Mimi, as she was called, began to display all the symptoms of advanced consumption. Morgan had to carry his fiancée downstairs and prop her up during a marriage service that was moving and tragic. She died in Nice four months later. When Morgan returned home after burying his young wife, one of his first acts was to buy an oil painting, the first of thousands, which depicted "a young and delicate looking woman" by George F. Baker. This touching "reminiscence of Mimi" hung in Morgan's library until his death. Worth stole his *Duchess* and Morgan built his stupendous collection on a similar foundation of failed love and emotional deprivation.

Many years and countless paintings later, Morgan resolved to add Georgiana to his vast collection. Perhaps, as in Worth's case, the act of ownership had become an end in itself, more important than any other consideration, as "is true of all collecting," John Fowles once observed. "It extinguishes the moral instinct. The object finally possesses the possessor."

Gainsborough's *Duchess* held a special attraction for Pierpont Morgan. His determination to own the painting Junius Morgan had wanted to buy for him may well have been "a deeply sentimental homage to his father." But he also seems to have been personally touched, as so many had been, by the ravishing looks of the sitter. For a man who knew a fair bit about amorous conquests, buying the image widely considered one of the most beautiful in the world was the ultimate challenge, a gallant conquest. Gainsborough's Georgiana, moreover, was blowsy, flirtatious, and had that unmistakable "come-hither" glint in her eye. The Duchess was Morgan's sort of woman.

TWENTY-EIGHT

Return of the
Prodigal Duchess

On the afternoon of April 8, 1901, Morland Agnew arrived in Liverpool with the *Duchess,* and so did Adam Worth, with Pierpont Morgan bringing up the rear in his own craft just a few hours later. The London papers had been tipped off to the story, and a few enterprising reporters even hired small boats in an unsuccessful effort to get to the art dealer and extract a quote from him before he made land. "Down the gangway from the *Etruria* came Mr. Morland Agnew, with a lady by his side, a flat, sealed parcel in his arm, an anxious look on his face." He announced that he had "nothing to say," and did likewise at Euston.

That evening the London newspapers carried a telegram announcing the return of the painting. *The Daily Express* reported both the recovery of the Duchess and the arrival of Pierpont Morgan on its front page, with drawings of both the beauty and the beast, but making no connection between the two. "Mr J. Pierpont Morgan, the great American trust maker, who arrives in England today, is certainly not the sort of man to take a trip across the Atlantic for mere pleasure; and speedy developments may be looked for," the press promised. In its fawning profile, the *Express* did note Morgan's "fondness and keen appreciation of art" and concluded "Mr Morgan's vaulting ambition is tempered with a certain nobleness, for he aims at the betterment of the race . . . always using money as an instrument and not as an aim. It is a goal worthy of a great mind." The arrival of Adam Worth—another great mind whose acquisitiveness was also tempered by a certain nobility—passed unnoticed.

The portrait was dispatched under guard to Agnew's London bank, where it was inspected by the firm's experts in art restoration, who pronounced that "save for the slightest trace of a scar on the rim of the hat, the picture is perfect; the face, hands and body of the portrait are absolutely untouched." *The Times* declared it to be "in a beautiful state of preservation." Old Sir William Agnew, who had been kept in ignorance of the negotiations lest he blab, was still on the Aegean when he heard the news. Although he had retired from active dealing in 1895, Sir William at once turned his boat around and headed for London to view the prize he had bought and lost a quarter century before. "Father telegraphs his delight at the news and that he is coming back," Morland noted.

True to his word, Pinkerton had kept Worth's secret and, although pressed by reporters, would say only, with impressive inaccuracy, "that the thief fought for the North during the rebellion with distinction, and the finish of the struggle found him promoted to a lieutenancy." The Central News Agency reported categorically that "the police in both England and America have the strongest reasons for believing that the actual thieves are dead."

Morland Agnew remained ignorant of how close he had stood to the thief of the Gainsborough. "So far as I know it came from a sick man who was lying ill in one of the Western states. Remorse perhaps suggested restitution. It was a good job we took the matter up, for if the man had died, as they tell me he is likely to, the probabilities are that his children, not knowing the value of the picture, might have destroyed it. I do not think that the man who sent the picture back was the original thief. That individual's name, I am of the opinion, was Worth."

The Daily Telegraph, relying on information from Scotland Yard to frame this "romance as strange as any in fiction," scooped the competition by reporting: "When Mr. Agnew sailed for England on the *Etruria* with the canvas there was also on board the man who stole the picture. His identity has not been made public but it has been ascertained that he has been living quietly in England with a family who are not aware of his past." *The Times* then went one better. Pronouncing "the third sensational chapter in the remarkable history of the portrait," it reported the rumor "that the man who stole the picture is named Adam Worth, or Wirth, and is well known to Scotland Yard." None of the papers made the link with Henry Raymond, disgraced so many years before.

"Its authentic history during the last quarter of a century will probably, and for very obvious reasons, never be disclosed—except by highly imaginative writers," *The Times* declared, which did not stop the more popular newspapers from speculating wildly on how the *Duchess* had made her way home, and quizzing Morland Agnew to the point where the art dealer was thoroughly exasperated. "Papers full of reports of the finding of the lost Duchess . . . make rather much use of my name. Much interviewed again. Am getting sick of the Duchess and feel very tired. Too much excitement lately," he grouched. Agnew became still more peeved when one newspaper wickedly published a cartoon of the art dealer in a tight embrace with "The Dear Old Dutch." Even though the portrait was not yet on display, art connoisseurs and journalists descended on the Bond Street gallery in droves. "We have been literally overwhelmed with callers," Agnew's manager, Mr. Thompson, told reporters, adding, as proof of his long service with the firm, that the painting "looked as fresh and beautiful as on the day it first appeared in these galleries . . . the face is perfect and bears no trace of the adventures that have befallen it."

Conjecture over the worth of the painting was rife. "Her value must have been considerably increased by the hide-and-seek that this winsome lady has played with the detective force of two continents," the *Evening News* averred. But Agnew adamantly refused to say how much had been paid to get the painting back. "You may take my word for it," he tried vainly to convince the inquisitive, "I paid nothing in the way of reward for return of the painting, and do not expect to be asked for any." He was roundly and rightly disbelieved on both sides of the Atlantic. "The newspaper reporters of their own accord stated that the price paid was from $5,000.00 to $25,000.00, some stating one figure and some another," Pinkerton reported to Agnew from Chicago. "As agreed with you, we have never given out a figure."

The painting was once again a style statement: "Now that the stolen duchess has been restored to her rightful owners, will the picture . . . set the fashion again?" wondered one newspaper and, like all the best journalists, immediately supplied the answer, noting that Mrs. Morland Agnew, now recovered from her traumatic journey, and her cousin, Mrs. Lockett Agnew, "have already made up their minds on the matter . . . exact duplicates of the famous Gainsborough hat are to be made for them in celebration of the restoration of the famous picture." The paper concluded that this "would undoubtedly lead to an increased demand for the Gainsborough hat, cartwheel brim, feathers and all. So matinee attenders have plenty of trouble in store for them." Canny seaside entrepreneurs cashed in by setting up lifesize cardboard replicas of the *Duchess,* with the face cut out, so that holiday-goers could peer out for the camera, to pose as "the real Gainsborough," for sixpence each.

As the public pondered the romantic history of the portrait, speculation mounted over its possible future. "It is to be hoped," noted one critic, "that after all the buffeting in dark and secret places which it has undergone, the masterpiece may now find a permanent and secure position in one of our public galleries, to be a lasting memorial to the greatness of one of the most brilliant artists of our race; an enduring representation of the beauty of one of the most charming and notable English women."

Morland Agnew was adamant on one point. "Now that the picture is in our possession once more we are going to take good care that it doesn't go on its travels again before we find a purchaser," he declared loftily, unaware that Pierpont Morgan was closing in, having chased Morland Agnew and the *Duchess* across the ocean.

"My ship was faster than his," Morgan later boasted to Bishop Lawrence. "He arrived in London on Saturday, I on Sunday. I sent word to one of the firm that I must see him on Monday morning before he went down town. He came to Prince's Gate [Morgan's London home] and I said 'You have the Duchess of Devonshire?'

" 'Yes,' he replied.

" 'You remember that my father, on the afternoon before that picture was stolen, was about to buy it, and was going to make his decision the next morning. He wanted it. What my father wanted, I want, and I must have the Duchess.'

" 'Very good,' said the dealer.

" 'What is the price?' asked Mr. Morgan.

" 'That is for you to say, Mr. Morgan.'

" 'No, whatever price your firm thinks is fair, I pay.' "

This was Morgan's habitual, brusque method of doing business. According to one contemporary report, Senator Clerk of Montana also made a bid for the painting, "but Mr. Morgan was given the preference by the sellers because of his many previous purchases."

By April 12, four days before his sixty-fourth birthday, Morgan had struck a deal, "subject to Sir William Agnew approving the purchase." This the old man duly did, although he was plainly disgruntled that his younger relatives had stolen the limelight by selling the *Duchess* before he had a chance to examine her. From Vienna he wrote to Morgan: "I have this morning arrived here and heard by telegram that my people have sold you the Duchess. Well, I am glad, although I did not wish anything done with the picture until I reached London. It is, I hear, in very dirty condition and will require some few weeks cleaning and putting into order. I have been greatly excited about the picture and my first thought, as the picture is my property (or rather was), at a fitting time to offer it to you, for I feel it as no one can and towards your collection I feel too the greatest interest, greater than in any other in the world. I congratulate you in possessing the finest Gainsborough in the world. Pardon me if I write incoherently—for I am much moved."

The American magnate was delighted with his acquisition and the fresh flood of publicity it brought him. By the terms of the deal with Agnew's, Morgan, like his father before him, agreed to let the painting go on display at Agnew's Seventh Annual exhibition in November and December 1901. Just in case history might repeat itself and the portrait vanish once more, Morgan insisted he would pay for the picture only when it was finally delivered. In return, the art dealer agreed not to reveal who had bought the *Duchess*. But Morgan could not contain himself. For days Agnew's refused to divulge the name of the new owner, until, as Morland recalled, "a reporter flatly contradicted our denials with 'Well, all I can say is Mr. Morgan is standing on the steps of the Ritz telling everyone he has bought it!' "

Pierpont Morgan was good copy—"more columns of newspapers in more different countries were filled with stories about Mr. Morgan than about any man in public or private life"—but the conjunction of one of the world's wealthiest men and one of the world's most beautiful women was irresistible. Newspapers broadcast the event far and wide, although the full story of the painting's theft and return remained a piquant mystery.

"This was one of the many cases where he did the thing that men do who seek advertisement to attract attention to themselves or to their business or for political reasons," noted his simpering biographer and son-in-law, Herbert Satterlee. "In whatever field he entered, he bought the highest priced corner lot; he added championship horses to his stable; built the best steam yacht, and purchased the most notable pictures, books and objects of art for his collections . . . he always showed a perfect disregard for the element of investment or 'getting his money's worth,' and yet almost everything that he bought increased in value—'The Duchess of Devonshire' was a good instance of this."

Canny self-publicist that he was, Morgan steadfastly refused to say how much he had paid for the painting. When a clergyman friend pressed him on the matter, Morgan's reply was calculated to keep speculation roiling: "Nobody will ever know. If the truth came out, I might be considered a candidate for the lunatic asylum." In fact, the price he paid—£30,000, or $150,000—was huge but hardly insane, and barely even extravagant by Morgan's standards. Had the truth come out, he might have been considered, not so much mad, as highly fortunate. Morland Agnew later wondered whether he had agreed to part with the picture "rather hastily."

Morgan's characteristically highhanded acquisition of one of Britain's most celebrated art treasures was not greeted with universal approval. If Worth was symbolic of one sort of nightmare for respectable Victorian England—the crook lurking beneath a moral cloak—then Morgan was beginning to represent another: the barbarian multimillionaire denuding the Old World of its valuables with wads of newly created cash. A cartoon in the *New York World* from this year showed Pierpont Morgan arrogantly demanding of John Bull: "What else have you for sale?" and imaginative London street peddlers mocked the mogul's omnipotence by offering a "license to stay on earth," signed by J. Pierpont Morgan, for a penny apiece.

The master dialect humorist Finley Peter Dunne perhaps best encapsulates Europe's insecurity in the face of such stupendous buying power as that wielded by the Colossus of Wall Street: "Pierpont Morgan calls in wan iv his office boys, the president of a naytional bank, an' says he, 'James,' he says, 'take some change out iv th' damper an' r-run out an buy Europe f'r me,' he says. 'Call up the Czar an' th' Pope an' th' Sultan an' th' Impror Willum, an' tell thim we won't need their sarvices afther nex' week,' he says, 'Give thim a year's salary in advance . . .' " Many British art experts were alarmed at the steady drain of Britain's art treasures by "nouveau" American millionaires. Into the fray strode none other than Henry James.

James's last novel, *The Outcry,* was not published until 1911, but in thinly veiled form it is a direct response to the issues raised by Morgan's purchase of the celebrated Gainsborough. In the author's words: "*The Outcry* deals with the question brought home of late to the conscience of English society—that of the degree in which the fortunate owners of precious and hitherto transmitted works of art hold them in trust, as it were, for the nation and may themselves, as lax guardians, be held to account for public opinion." The novel, which ran to four editions, tells the story of Breckenridge Bender, a wealthy American determined to secure the best and most valuable of Britain's artworks, whatever the cost. The acquisitive millionaire and the "lax guardians," Lord Theign and Lady Sandgate, are shamed by a young connoisseur when they consider selling off their ancestral portraits, including the fictitious *Duchess of Waterbridge*, by Sir Joshua Reynolds.

James's descriptions of the "beautiful duchess," painted "down to her knees, with such extraordinarily speaking eyes, such lovely arms and hands, such wonderful flesh tints," "the most beautiful woman of her time," leave little doubt that the *Duchess of Waterbridge* is intended to represent Gainsborough's celebrated *Duchess of Devonshire*. As Adeline R. Tinter observes, the identity of Breckenridge Bender is still more obvious: "the billionaire with the cheque book in hand, who enlivens *The Outcry*, ready to buy only the most expensive pictures, has clearly been modelled on the American financier" J. Pierpont Morgan. Morgan and Bender even have the same blunt way of expressing their desires: "I must have the duchess," said Morgan. "Bender knows what he wants," James writes of his fictionalized Morgan. "He most usually wants what he can't have." Lord Theign's money troubles are the result of his elder daughter's gambling habits, a daughter whose name and extravagant tendencies have a strong though surely coincidental ring: "Kitty wants so many things at once. She always wants money, in quantities, to begin with—and all to throw so horribly away."

James, like Worth, had abandoned his American origins and chosen to identify himself with England and the English; just four years after *The Outcry* was published, the novelist adopted British citizenship. This novel, inspired by one of the most famous art acquisitions of the century, was intended as a warning to the Brit-

ish art world of the looming dangers of rapacious American art
collectors. "The art world is at the mercy of a leak there appears
no means of stopping," one of James's characters laments. "Precious things are going out of our distracted country at a greater
rate than the very quickest—a century and more ago—of their
ever coming in."

Whatever the misgivings of British art connoisseurs, Gainsborough's *Duchess* was now securely the property of Pierpont Morgan,
but she had one more London season to run before disappearing
into the millionaire's maw. On May 23, 1901, one day shy of
twenty-five years since she had left it in the dead of night, Georgiana returned to Agnew's Bond Street gallery. "This time it will be
guarded with the greatest care," one paper noted tartly. "Men
will watch the famous picture night and day, and when closing
time comes each afternoon the gallery will be thoroughly
searched to make sure that no visitor remains in hiding."

Cleaned and relined, Georgiana took the breath away. "She
looks splendid," thought Morland Agnew. In November the painting was again put on display for Agnew's Seventh Annual Exhibition. For two months, thousands of visitors flocked to see the
painting, and once again she worked her peculiar spell. "The
music halls were full of songs," Agnew's official history records,
"the papers of poems about the lost duchess, and Duchess of
Devonshire hats had again become the raging fashion."

And while the crowds milled and fawned on the prodigal
Duchess, in their midst might have been seen a little man with
rheumy eyes and a dagger cough, who knew that enchanting image better than he knew his own face.

TWENTY-NINE

Nemo's Grave

From a cautious distance, Worth had observed the excitement surrounding the return of the *Duchess*. He had read of J. Pierpont Morgan posturing on the steps of the Ritz and wryly noted the fevered speculation over how the painting had come back to London. But with the loss of his prize, he seemed to fold in on himself again. His brio turned to self-pity, his health became even more precarious, and his drinking verged on the suicidal.

What little remaining energy he had was devoted to making a home for the two children he knew he had wronged, who were, as Pinkerton noted, "all in the world he had to care for." With the profits from the return of the Gainsborough, he took accommodations in Camden at 2, Park Village East, a large, rambling house that was as solid and bourgeois as his earlier London accommodations had been flashy and extrovert. How wealthy Worth now was as a result of the Gainsborough deal is unclear: Pat Sheedy later claimed he would not take any part of the $25,000 he said Worth had received from Agnew's, a statement which is surely untrue and may cast doubt on the authenticity of the figure as well. Agnew's calculated it had cost a total of £7,500 to retrieve the painting, but again that figure is open to question, since the partners never specified the amount paid as ransom. Eddie Guerin thought the sum nearer to £1,000, and pronounced it "the worst deal Harry ever made in his life."

If not the worst deal, parting with the Gainsborough was certainly the hardest decision Worth had ever made. With it went his pretensions to aristocratic life and worldly (i.e., criminal) success. The forgery was exposed. But in its place was a feeling perhaps more human than anything he had felt since falling in love with Kitty Flynn: a visceral need to create the family life he had never known, and so find himself. Returning the *Duchess* had released him, but the rupture was agonizing and with each fresh accolade to the lovely portrait that was no longer his to control, Worth dwindled a little more.

"The sudden return to town of Her Grace the Duchess of Devonshire has caused nearly as great a sensation as if the beautiful Georgiana had come back to life, with a fresh lease of beauty and of charm." The recovery had also brought back to life the ancient debate over its authenticity. "Never previously in the history of art and its masters has such intense excitement been aroused over a work . . . as has been awakened by the discovery of the long-lost portrait by Gainsborough of the Duchess of Devonshire," wrote one observer, noting that, in the matter of authenticity, "the critics have advanced every feasible as well as every untenable argument that they can devise." Some again said it depicted not Georgiana but Elizabeth, the other Duchess of Devonshire; others that the work was not by Gainsborough; and still others that there was such a painting, by Gainsborough, but that the "one newly brought to light is a spurious copy."

The Pall Mall Gazette pronounced magisterially that "she is not, after all, the more famous of the two duchesses . . . she is not Georgiana, but Elizabeth," yet with equal conviction insisted that, once the portrait was exhibited, the suggestion that it was by anyone other than Gainsborough "will vanish as the morning mist before the sun. The portrait is typically and thoroughly Gainsborough."

The Times suggested that the matter of authenticity be settled by holding an exhibition of the collected paintings of both Geor-

giana and Elizabeth, and then comparing the likenesses in a sort
of artistic identity parade. "An exhibition in London of as many
of these pictures as could be got together, with the newly-recov-
ered duchess as the 'leading lady' would form a great attraction in
itself, and be useful in settling one or two points about which
there may be some little doubt at this present time."

"Probably all the speculation with which the newspaper columns have teemed will prove creations of . . . impalpable fabric," one jaundiced critic observed, while the *Daily Express* mocked
the experts' furious debating with a doggerel *Ballad of Georgiana*
(with apologies to Tennyson's *Oriana*), which was almost as bad as
some of the odes to the duchess during her lifetime:

> *Our hearts were wasted with our woe—*
> *'Twas five-and-twenty years ago,*
> *You left us in the winter snow,*
> *And didn't even let us know,*
> *The next address to find you—oh,*
> *   Georgiana!*

> *And now, when we have got you back,*
> *We get this very nasty smack,*
> *From folks who surely culture lack,*
> *Or like a silly joke to crack—*
> *That you're no better than a quack—*
> *   Georgiana!*

> *They say that if you are the same*
> *You really sneak another's fame,*
> *In fact, they venture now to claim*
> *The picture stolen from the frame,*
> *Was Lady Hetty What's-her-name,*
> *   Georgiana!*

> *And worse than all, they loudly bawl,*
> *You're not a Gainsborough at all,*

The expert's proof they blandly call,
That black is white, and short is tall,
That Paul is Peter, Peter Paul,
Georgiana!

So if you are not you, 'tis clear,
You're not the party who was here,
And if of Gainsborough's you're a mere
Rough sketch, I think it must appear,
You're neither lost nor found, my dear,
Georgiana!

The return of the Gainsborough had breathed new vigor into the mythology surrounding the Duchess of Devonshire. It had precisely the opposite effect on Adam Worth. Sensing that time was short, he set about reclaiming his children with a determination he had never shown while the painting held him back. Hitherto, Worth's life had been defined by his possessions, but now he struggled to capture something more valuable and intangible: the *Duchess* had symbolized what he aspired to take and own, but his children might finally be a reflection of what he now wanted to be.

His first act on returning to London had been to send money to his brother in Brooklyn with instructions to send over young Harry, now aged fourteen, and his younger sister as soon as possible. But even this was proving elusive. His sister-in-law, sensing that Worth was once again "in the money," flatly refused to release the children to their father without a substantial payment. Worth was livid, and wretched. In June 1901, he wrote to Pinkerton, excoriating "that brother and sister-in-law of mine" for their disloyalty and greed, and suspecting that his children's minds had been poisoned against him.

"I have kept them all my life, and they expect me to continue. She is a dirty, hypocritical cow; she professes to be religious, but as I told her every rag on her body, the house she lives in, are the proceeds of— [he was careful not to use the word "crime," lest the letter should fall into the wrong hands]. She has been cunning enough to get a hold on the children and probably frighten them by hints, so they will not come over here; but that is done for their own selfish interest, not for the children's sake. Three years ago, when I had no money, they wrote me that they could keep them no longer . . . There is only one way to do [it], and that is to starve them out. When no more money is forthcoming, the children will be glad to come over." Worth, ever the "roast," still held to a residual belief in the ultimate controlling power of money.

Lonely, drunken, and plaintive, Worth cut himself off from all human company. Word had reached the underworld of his return to London, and some of his colleagues from the criminal past looked him up for money, as in the old days, or to see whether Worth had anything profitable afoot. He sent them away with a little loose change and the firm impression that the onetime master criminal was now firmly in retirement.

William Pinkerton, once his sworn enemy, was now the only human being in whom Worth placed any trust. He wrote the detective long, distressed letters, usually in cryptic "secret writing" and signed with the alias "Robert R. Bayley." On his better days Worth gossiped about mutual acquaintances in the criminal world, but for the most part his missives were, as Worth admitted, "boozy" rants against his ill fortune, his mercenary relatives, and his failing health. "I am little better on the chest," he wrote of the coughing fits that left him shivering and weak. "Not so much blood but I am afraid it is only temporary, as I have these awful night sweats and cough." Pinkerton wrote back with genuine concern, more like an anxious brother than a world-famous detective to an elite member of the criminal fraternity.

Their relationship had long passed beyond the merely professional. Both were hard men—the Pinkertons' union-busting techniques had made William a hate figure for many working Americans—but both had psychological weaknesses that seemed to find release in their friendship. Perhaps Pinkerton saw in Worth the rebellion against authority that eased some of his resentment against a dour father and a life spent obeying the rules. The detective had risked his professional reputation in the Gainsborough affair, for if Agnew's or Scotland Yard ever learned how closely he was in league with Worth he would have been hard put to defend himself. Worth, conversely, seemed to look on his friendship with the detective as a justification for his past, proof that during their long battle on opposite sides of the law they had played by the same rules of honor and respect—a tribute that meant more to Worth now than all the fake "respectability" he had stolen. The Eye had long protected Worth from prosecution; now he sought to protect him from himself.

"Friend H.," the detective wrote from Chicago. "You have no idea how sad it made me feel to have you write in the despondent manner in which you do . . . the sooner you get out of the atmosphere of London, the better it will be, and would advise that you come at once to this country and go to Colorado, where the altitude is very beneficial for people suffering from pulmonary trouble.

"I want to say to you, Harry, that the excessive use of liquor has a good deal to do with your trouble. I know that you were on one or two big sprees, and they must have considerable to do with the bringing about of your present condition. I find that nobody can drink in sociability without taking liquor to excess, and it is bound to create no end of trouble, therefore I have stopped the use of it entirely."

Pinkerton sent his friend poems cut from the local paper, snippets of underworld news, and the latest racing results. He tried to buck Worth up with news about the *Duchess of Devonshire*, perhaps inadvertently reminding him of his loss. "I have had several nice letters from the client for whom I worked in connection with the picture, and he is very well satisfied with everything that was done for him." So friendly had the correspondence become between the two that William's more cautious brother was alarmed. "I think you write this man too fully," Robert Pinkerton told William. "He is liable to be arrested and his mail gotten hold of. I am aware that it is written in typewriting and signed by an initial and nothing could be proved back, but there are things said in this letter that would enable any shrewd detective to guess who the probable writer is . . . If this letter was to fall into Scotland Yard hands, would they not think that we ought to inform them of any such man being in Europe at the present time and living in London?'' William was contrite. He promised his brother he would "stop this correspondence entirely," and did no such thing. His imprudent loyalty to Worth now far outweighed that to Scotland Yard.

As the letters passed back and forth, the detective and the criminal discussed how Worth could best use his remaining money. "I urged upon him to invest . . . in securities, and leave the same in my care," for the benefit of his children, Pinkerton later recalled in a letter to Worth's son. "I urged upon him at that time to quit Europe and come back here . . . and with the means he had to settle down to some little business . . . he took seriously to the matter and thought he would like to locate at Hot Springs, Ark., and I told him that would be a good idea and to bring yourself and your sister out here and with the means he then had he could easily have started himself in a nice little business in Hot Springs and made a good living for you all, and his health would have been much improved. I feared his return to London among genial companions would be too much for him in the state of health he was then in." The genial companions Pinkerton referred to, of course, came in bottled, not human form.

In a late burst of his old ingenuity, Worth began to discuss again his ideas for making a burglar-proof safe alarm, a gadget he was uniquely qualified to perfect. But as his battle to secure his children dragged on, and crippling headaches beset Worth (Pinkerton ascribed them to a "tumor"), both he and the detective seem to have realized that the talk of moving to Arkansas, of investments and burglar alarms, was mere dreaming. Time was running out, and Worth's need to bring together his family had become desperate. Finally he swallowed his pride and agreed to send his avaricious sister-in-law as much money as she wanted, if only

she would send his children to England. She agreed, but the price
was high. Worth was now virtually penniless once again.

Late in 1901, the children finally arrived in Camden where
their father, according to Pinkerton, "had fitted up a nice home."
For almost the first time in his life, Worth was at the center of a
family. He was determined to prevent his children from finding
out about his crimes, and Pinkerton remained convinced that
they "knew nothing of his past career." But the younger Harry
Raymond was no fool; the teenager may have caught more than
an inkling of his father's unorthodox profession. "He told me
little or nothing about his affairs," the young man later confided
to Pinkerton, but in the same letter he stressed his intention "to
put my shoulder to the wheel and earn an honest living, which
will always be my desire to do." Would a young man take so much
trouble to emphasize his honesty if there was no reason to
doubt it?

Even his children knew Adam Worth as Henry Judson Raymond, and to the end the master crook kept up the façade that
had served him so well for years. If his children suspected he was
other than the respectable if ailing businessman he appeared to
be, they at least had the generosity to grant him this one last
delusion and disguise.

On December 31, 1901, Agnew's Seventh Annual Exhibition came
to an end and was pronounced a rousing success by all. Pierpont
Morgan prepared to take possession of his trophy. Despite being
seriously ill, Worth "would consult no doctor" and insisted on
leaving the house to visit his old friend in Old Bond Street one
last time. When the *Duchess* was finally taken down and out of his
life, Worth's spirit crumbled at last and he took to his bed. Weak,
but in a spirit of liberation, he wrote to Pinkerton for the last
time, enclosing a package—containing what little money he still
possessed after his sister-in-law's final demands had been met—
and thanking the detective for his many acts of kindness. Pinkerton was free to speak about him after his death, but, if possible,
Worth asked him to avoid causing his son and daughter any em-

barrassment. He also told his son to contact Pinkerton when the end came. His family later reported that he seemed oddly elated, his gray cheeks flushed a little, as if some weight had been removed from his emaciated shoulders.

On January 4, Pierpont Morgan, Worth's unencountered soul mate and fellow expert in elegant double standards, transferred to Agnew's the sum of $30,000 and arranged for the *Duchess* to be delivered to 13, Princes Gate, his great five-story neoclassical mansion south of Hyde Park (which would later become the ambassadorial residence for Joseph P. Kennedy and home to the future American President, John F. Kennedy). Morgan would prove just as jealous a protector of the *Duchess* as Worth had been. He declined to exhibit the portrait again, and flatly refused permission for engravings to be made—to the fury of Morland Agnew, who had hoped to give one to Pinkerton as an expression of thanks for his role in its reappearance. "Mr Morgan will not allow the painting to be engraved at all, and we are powerless to do anything," spluttered the enraged art dealer. "I trust he will relent later." But Morgan didn't. He was determined to keep the *Duchess* for his private pleasure.

Morgan brought the same absolutism to picture-hanging that he sought in every other aspect of his life. Some years later King Edward VII came to tea at Prince's Gate and noticed another great portrait, the *Countess of Derby* by Lawrence.

"The ceiling is too low in this room for that picture. Why do you hang it there?" demanded the King.

"Because I like it there, sir," snapped the magnate.

Nobody, monarchs included, told Pierpont Morgan where to put his pictures, and there was no doubt in his mind where the *Duchess of Devonshire* should now reside. The great Gainsborough was hung in pride of place above the mantelpiece, the most prominent position in the house. The *Duchess* was a badge of social prominence and sexual conquest, and a symbol of worldly success, for a second time and for another man.

On January 8, 1902, four days after Morgan finally took possession of the Noble Lady and just a few miles away in Camden, the man who had kept her for twenty-five years lay quietly, his son and daughter near at hand. The pain throughout his body had slowly ebbed, leaving Adam Worth pathetically feeble, but exuberant. "I left his room to go down to my supper and he seemed to be in the best of spirits," young Harry Raymond reported. "When I came back to his room he was, as I thought, sleeping; several hours afterwards the landlady went into the room and came out to me and said that she did not like the looks of my father and requested me to go in, and I did so, but my father had quietly passed away without a struggle."

The death certificate described Henry Judson Raymond as a man of "independent means" whose death, at the age of fifty-six, was the result of heart failure, disease of the liver, and, in the coroner's disapproving phrase, "chronic habits of intemperance."

Harry Raymond, Jr., buried his father in Highgate Cemetery, where he lies still in an unmarked, "common" grave, overgrown by a thicket of brambles, and without headstone or any other marker. The burial register for plot number 34281 is made out in the name of Henry Judson Raymond. Even in death, Adam Worth was someone else, and perhaps it is only right that a man who adopted and shed so many aliases lies forever without a sign to betray his whereabouts.

Young Harry Raymond, still bearing the name his father had filched thirty years before, sold off the furniture in 2, Park Village East, and headed back to America with his younger sister. Two weeks after Worth's death, the Pinkertons received a note, postmarked St. Paul, Minnesota: "I beg to state to you that my father (Harry J. Raymond) passed away on the 8th January between six and seven in the evening," signed H. J. Raymond.

Robert, the more cynical of the Pinkerton brothers, was inclined to suspect another ruse on the part of the arch-counterfeiter, who had, after all, faked his death before. "Do you think it could possibly be a trick on the old fellow's part to deceive us before he went into some other scheme of robbery?" he wrote to his brother. But William was convinced, and immediately penned a reply, making no mention of Worth's past:

> Yours of the 24th informing me of the death of your father, came to me in the light of a shock. I had a letter from your father about the first of the year, telling me he had been quite ill . . . I wrote him stating I hoped he would take good care of himself and get himself fully restored to health.
>
> I have known your father for over 30 years, and though our lives were very different, yet there was always a warm friendship between us. I hope he has left you in some sort of condition to take care of yourselves. I regret your father's death very much. It seems incredible that a few months ago your father was here with me and enjoyed his visit very much . . . Your father used to talk very much about his children, and his whole life seemed centered in you two. Nobody wishes you better luck than myself. In deep sympathy, believe me,
> Sincerely yours,
> W. A. Pinkerton

According to one account, Worth left a will, "proved in the autumn of 1907, [which] showed that he died possessed of about £23,000." There is no evidence to corroborate this, and plenty to suggest that Worth died with nothing. Young Harry soon wrote to Pinkerton again: "My father left little or no money, and after paying the funeral expenses and our passages back to America, we are practically penniless . . . but I am working for the future so that it will enable me to provide both for myself and my sister who is entirely dependent on me for support." Clearly suspecting that there was more to his father's past, the young man pressed the detective for information: "My father often used to speak of you . . . you will no doubt be able to enlighten me to things regarding my father that I do not know and that would interest me greatly."

The detective kept both sides of his bargain with the dead

thief. He sent Worth's final package, which at least ensured that the two young people would not starve, and over the coming years he stood as guardian to each of them. He never directly discussed Worth's criminal past with them, describing Worth only as "a man of great inventive ideas" and stressing his "kindness of heart." His decorous observation to Worth's son that their lives had been "very different" was as far as he was prepared to go.

"I shall always have a kind remembrance of your father, for while we had not met in years up until two years ago, and then again a year ago, still we always had a kindly feeling for each other and I would willingly do anything consistently in my power to aid either you or your sister." It is a tribute to the affection Worth could inspire, and the size of Pinkerton's heart, that the letters betray genuine grief at the loss of his old enemy and friend. "I was very sorry, indeed, to hear of the little fellow's death," he wrote to his brother. "I think we were about the only people he ever trusted. His prolonged sprees undoubtedly helped to shorten his life."

"I feel as you do about Little Adam," Robert replied.

News of Worth's death was filtering through the underworld grapevine, but the detective brothers decided to "keep the matter of his death secret for the present," while agreeing that if the news broke and they were called on to comment, "we should leave his family out entirely." It was only a matter of time, of course, until the press picked up the scent. As far back as 1893, when *The Pall Mall Gazette* had published its "exposé" of the imprisoned thief, Adam Worth alias Henry Raymond had been linked with the theft of Gainsborough's *Duchess of Devonshire*. When the painting reappeared in the hands of Morland Agnew there was again speculation about Worth's role, but by then the thief had gone to ground, and since Morland Agnew did not know, and Pinkerton would not say he was involved, the story had petered out.

On February 5, 1902, the London newspapers published a brief dispatch announcing the death of Adam Worth, alias Henry

Raymond, and within hours journalists on both sides of the Atlantic began to put the pieces together. The Pinkertons were bombarded with requests to confirm or deny that the late criminal was really the Gainsborough thief. "I have a letter from Adam Worth stating I could make use of anything he told me, after he was dead," William Pinkerton recorded, and finally, with evident reluctance, he decided to tell the full story. "I hated to say anything about him after his death, but thought it would be better for us to say something and have the thing right, than have the article given out by some detective, who knew nothing about it." Journalists were an unreliable crew, he noted. "You cannot get a thing right for a newspaper man . . . if you write the facts down for him, he will change them about to suit himself."

On February 6, William Pinkerton summoned the increasingly persistent journalists to his Chicago office and delivered a prepared statement outlining Worth's life, his trail of crime, his theft of the Gainsborough, and the detective's part in its return, although not his close relationship with the late felon. The next morning the story, sensational even by the standards of the time, was published from coast to coast, detailing the events of Worth's remarkable life with considerable accuracy, or, in Pinkerton's words, "about as correct as a newspaper ever gets anything."

Reflecting the ambivalence toward crime that still exists today, the newspapers competed to pay tribute to a man who had robbed, forged, and conned his way through life. The adulatory tone of the obituaries was not so very far removed from that of other "great men," such as the original Henry Raymond, whose breathless valediction had once caught Worth's eye and provided him with the alias he took to his grave. The *New York Sun* called the Gainsborough theft "the most remarkable crime committed in the nineteenth century" and proclaimed that "the memories of the police of two continents do not go back to the time when he was ever an amateur. The authorities seem to be agreed that, in his criminal specialties, Worth had neither superior nor equal and, when he died, he left none worthy of his mantle." The *Eve-*

ning Sun lauded him as "one of the most celebrated thieves in the criminal history of Europe and America." The *New York World,* with peculiar civic pride, called him "one of the most remarkable crooks this city ever produced."

"He was personally very charming, and his charity was proverbial. Thousands of Americans have been helped by him," noted Randolph Hearst's *Chicago American,* while *The Tribune* recalled his title, as did so many others—"The Napoleon of Crime"—and mourned "the last of a really great band of high-grade criminals who operated in America and all the world . . . in all his work [he] aimed only at large game." Even such august publications as *The Times* and *The New York Times* listed his achievements with undisguised awe.

Perhaps the most telling, and certainly the best-informed assessment, came, not surprisingly, from the Pinkertons:

> In the death of Adam Worth there probably departed the most inventive and daring criminal of modern times . . . In all his criminal career, and all the various crimes he committed, he was always proud of the fact that he never committed a robbery where the use of firearms had to be resorted to, nor had he ever escaped, or attempted to escape from custody by force of jeopardizing the life of an officer, claiming that a man with brains had no right to carry firearms, that there was always a way, and a better way, by the quick exercise of the brain. Among all the men Pinkertons have known in a lifetime, this man was the most remarkable criminal of them all.

Worth had spent a lifetime stealing respectability and social elevation. With plundered lucre he made himself into the quintessential Victorian gentleman, complete with thoroughbred racehorses, grand houses, expensive yachts, and the most coveted painting of the age, before his fabulous fabricated existence fell apart. Worth had believed he could steal respect, and he was right, but not the way he had meant it. In death, he garnered the admi-

ration and homage of the world, not for upholding the rules of
Victorian respectability, but for secretly breaking every one.

"Adam Worth is dead," proclaimed *The New York Journal.* "His
demise marks the closing of a singular modern romance."

The Inheritors

Adam Worth's great if dubious talents survived him. In August 1899, Kitty Flynn's three daughters were out driving in the New Jersey countryside when their carriage became stuck on a railway line and was tragically demolished by an express train. Katherine Louise, Kitty's younger daughter, and Juanita Terry, her child by Juan Terry, were both killed. But Lucy Adeleine, almost certainly Worth's oldest child, who had married the eminently respectable Charles Trippe some years before, survived, along with her infant son, Juan.

Juan Trippe, grandson of a career criminal, inherited the Terry fortune and went on to create Pan American Airways, once the most powerful airline in the world. His business methods were not so far removed from those of his grandfather. Gore Vidal, with a nod to Trippe's criminal ancestry, called him "the robber baron of the airways." Juan Trippe's forty thousand employees merely referred to him as the "Great Dissembler."

The other, legitimate branch of the Worth family tree grew completely straight. Harry J. Raymond, Adam Worth's son, started "at the bottom of the ladder" as an "office boy with the American Car & Foundry Co.," on a salary of "only four dollars a week." The teenager was soon rescued by none other than William Pinkerton, in fulfillment of the vow to his old friend. By means of the most benevolent subterfuge, the Eye sent Raymond a check for $700, pretending this was a debt owed by "a man in this city." When the firm published a pamphlet recounting the life of Adam Worth, the proceeds were sent, anonymously, to the thief's children. Nor did Pinkerton's generosity end there. "We ought to be able to place you in a short time in a better position than the one you now hold," the detective promised. A few months later, young Henry Raymond joined the detective firm which had chased his father and sometime namesake around the globe for half a century.

William Pinkerton was deeply and permanently affected by Worth's death. "Professional crime among intelligent men is largely extinct. We have no great burglars or forgers in the United States today," he said sadly a month after the great criminal was buried. Instead of hunting down crooks, William Pinkerton was increasingly their protector and benefactor, sending magazines, money, Thanksgiving turkeys, and even clean underwear to men he had helped land in prison. Many former felons found employment in the Pinkerton Detective Agency. William forever mourned the loss of the old "gentleman thieves" like Adam Worth and blamed Hollywood gangster movies for being "a prime motivation for younger criminals." He died in 1923 at the age of seventy-seven, leaving a fortune estimated at $15 million and prompting one oldtime thief to grumble that it was "quite obvious that he made more money out of crime than any of the people whom he hunted down." The majority of mourners at his vast funeral in Chicago were members of the criminal fraternity, including that veteran thief, Sophie Lyons.

La Dame de Lyons, as she was known to the Paris Sûreté, Sophie Lyons had become a close friend of the Pinkertons as a consequence of her repeated arrests. In 1897, to the surprise of just about everyone who knew her, Lyons declared she was "turning respectable," so she joined the staff of the *New York World* and became America's first society gossip columnist. Her memoirs, published in 1913, were entitled *Why Crime Does Not Pay* but were clearly designed to prove the opposite and became an instant bestseller. Finally her past caught up with her. When she was some seventy years old, "three men called at her Detroit home" and clubbed her to death. The Pinkertons estimated Lyons had amassed more than $1 million from various forms of theft, larceny, extortion, con trickery, journalism, and real estate, the bulk of which she left "in trust for the education of the children of convicts."

Pat Sheedy, the professional gambler who helped negotiate the return of the Gainsborough, cherished Worth's memory and made excellent use of it. In 1905 he suddenly claimed that Worth had given him another stolen painting, *The Magdalen* by Murillo, which had been filched from a Mexican convent forty years earlier. "Worth knew a lot about pictures. He thought this was a finer work than the duchess," the seedy Sheedy claimed. The Pinkertons were not fooled. "There is nothing in this," Robert Pinkerton wrote. But such was Worth's fame that others were prepared to believe the tale. The Murillo was purchased for $15,000 by one John Condon, the former owner of a betting parlor and the proprietor of the Harlem racetrack in Chicago. Condon said that the great Worth had once gambled at his establishment, and he now wished to possess the painting "for reasons of sentiment." He clearly had not bought it for artistic reasons, since Condon was stone-blind.

Charlie the Scratch Becker, the great forger whom police compared to "Michelangelo, Rembrandt and Whistler in artistic talent," was finally nabbed in 1900 for a counterfeiting spree involving some forty banks. In 1903 he emerged from San Quentin prison in a thoroughly cheerful mood, having spent his imprisonment perfecting a new type of forgery-proof paper and ink which he intended to sell to the very banks he had been fleecing for decades. "I am what you call an artist," he told the waiting journalists, adding that he would like to be thought of as America's version of Benvenuto Cellini, the great Renaissance sculptor and goldsmith. Generous as ever, the Pinkertons tried to interest a number of banks and paper firms in Becker's ineradicable ink and tamper-proof paper, but without success. He died in 1916, having spent the intervening years working, quite happily, as a Pinkerton guard, arresting pickpockets at the Chicago race course.

Another recipient of Pinkerton's benevolence was Max Shinburn, the Baron, who spent most of the rest of his life in prison, and all of it claiming to be someone else. In his spare time, which was copious, the mechanically gifted Shinburn worked on a new design for automobile wheels. Pestered by reporters to admit his identity, he snapped, "I don't know the man . . . I'm not Shinburn; but unless they leave me alone I'll tell some things myself that will create a sensation in certain quarters." He was finally released on April 19, 1908, by which time he claimed to have "discovered the secret of perpetual motion [and] planned to spend the rest of his life, perfecting his extraordinary discovery." Instead, like so many of his kind, he found himself dependent on the charity of the Pinkertons. William Pinkerton commissioned him to write a history of safecracking, entitled *Safe Burglary—Its Beginning and Progress,* which remains the definitive disquisition on the Victorian safe-blower's art. "From the early fifties up until the present time the writer witnessed in the most practical manner the evolution of the safe," Shinburn began with dry humor. The work turned out to be "so revealing and instructive to the novice criminal that its publication was forbidden." This remarkable work has never left the Pinkerton archives. Pinkerton eventually found a job for the irascible, duplicitous, but endlessly entertaining rogue as a janitor when he became "absolutely down and out" and resorted to the indignity of selling "a whole lot of ghost stories to the papers" about Adam Worth, simply to survive. Max Shinburn died on February 13, 1916, at the John Howard Home for Reformed Prisoners in Boston, at the age of seventy-seven. Rivals in death, as in life, Max Shinburn, like Worth, finally made it to the Great White Way when his life was adapted for the Broadway stage in *Alias Jimmy Valentine* by Paul Armstrong.

As for Adam Worth's literary afterlife, Sir Arthur Conan Doyle tried to kill off both his hero and his antihero when Sherlock

Holmes and Professor Moriarty met, fought, and fell to their apparent deaths, "locked in each other's arms," over the Reichenbach Falls at the end of "The Final Problem." Holmes came back to life; Moriarty did not. But as Conan Doyle observed, "Everything comes in circles, even Professor Moriarty . . . The old wheel turns and the same spoke comes up. It's all been done before, and it will again."

The art collection of the financier Pierpont Morgan increased exponentially as he grew older and richer. His homes contained "an immense and widening variety of beautiful things, which in due time were to include paintings, bronzes, terra cottas, jades, ivories, enamels, crystals, glass, tapestries, bas-reliefs, miniatures, snuff boxes, watches, Bibles, Church of England rituals, autographs, and of course books and manuscripts." In 1904, at the age of sixty-seven, he became the benefactor, president, and guiding force behind New York's Metropolitan Museum of Art, even though some compared him to a "tipsy dowager with unlimited credit moving down Fifth Avenue on a riotous shopping trip."

He went to church often and opined on moral matters, but was he an enlightened financial genius protecting the capitalist world, or a greedy, self-serving potentate out to protect his own interests and those of his class? In his lifetime Morgan gave away much, and "his gifts were closely connected with his personal loyalties and affections," but one painting for which he clearly felt an enduring personal affection, Gainsborough's *Duchess of Devonshire*, never left his possession. When Morgan died on March 31, 1913, the great portrait was among the first objects claimed when Morgan's children came to divide up his astonishing legacy.

For years afterward, though, the *Duchess of Devonshire* languished in obscurity. In 1960 the *Duchess* was briefly displayed at the Wadsworth Athenaeum in Hartford, Connecticut, but with that exception, the portrait was never again put on display by the Morgan heirs. Out of the public eye, the great Gainsborough slowly faded from memory, although the image lived on in a thousand prints and copies, busts, crumbling music-hall ballads, biscuit tins, and chinaware. Eventually the portrait passed to Mabel Satterlee Ingalls, Morgan's last surviving grandchild. It was hung, periodically, in Mrs. Ingalls's New York apartment, but mostly the *Duchess* was kept in a cupboard. Mrs. Ingalls, it was said, did not think the alluring portrait "quite respectable." Mabel Ingalls died on December 28, 1993, at the age of ninety-two, and her heirs elected to put the painting up for sale at Sotheby's in London.

The auction took place on July 13, 1994. Sotheby's salesroom was packed and buzzing when the portrait was unveiled and placed on the block for the first time since the extraordinary sale at Christie's more than a century earlier. The bidding was brisk. A Mr. Smith sat impassively before the portrait, and despite a number of "sporting bids from the back of the room," he raised his paddle in response to every one. Someone, it was clear, was determined to gain possession of the portrait, regardless of the price. After a few tense minutes, the implacable Mr. Smith raised his arm for the last time and Gainsborough's *Duchess of Devonshire* was knocked down for £265,500.

Far more remarkable than the price was the buyer. With the auction over, flushed and visibly relieved, the bidder revealed himself to be Nicholas Smith of Curry & Co., solicitor and designated proxy for none other than the present Duke of Devonshire.

The Lady, to quote Adam Worth, was returning home.

The return of the *Duchess* to Chatsworth on July 22, 1994, was triumphal. The duke's staff, local pensioners, and their spouses were invited to attend the unveiling and drink a toast to the prodigal duchess.

"It was just such a wonderful, extraordinary story, I felt we had to have the painting here," said the duke, reclining amid the old leather and rare volumes in the study of Chatsworth. Beyond the window, the acres of the ducal estate rolled into the Derbyshire distance, and below, in the grand dining room, Georgiana, Duchess of Devonshire, was holding court once again, as waves of tourists ebbed and flowed around her. With the portrait cleaned and restored, the twinkle in her eye seemed brighter than ever.

"She was a wicked'un, they say," announced a Derbyshire accent, with approbation and authority.

Soon after the sale, the painting was subjected to a barrage of tests by the Tate Gallery, and the results were intriguing. "There is no technical evidence to doubt that the central section is basically by Gainsborough," Rica Jones of the Tate concluded cautiously. X-rays revealed an earlier hat beneath the duchess's ostrich-feather extravaganza, one very similar to the hat in one of Gainsborough's drawings for the *Richmond Water Walk*. Technical research suggested that the visible hat may have been "put in by someone else fairly early in the painting's history," while "the ground, the paint mixtures, the type of lay-in, the layered structure on the remnant strips and, most importantly, the shape of the earlier hat, which relates to a bona fide drawing, all point to an origin in [Gainsborough's] studio."

So as far as science can tell, the painting is most likely by Gainsborough, and probably depicts Georgiana, but there can never be complete certainty. Throughout its checkered history, observers have seen what they want to see in this painting: Adam Worth saw Kitty Flynn, or a man-made symbol of perfect female beauty, or a badge of his own criminal prestige; Pierpont Morgan saw power; some saw Georgiana of Devonshire, others Elizabeth Foster. But it may well be that the subject of the portrait was someone else entirely, a mysterious, unknown woman elevated into a grand duchess.

Her knowing gaze across the great dining room of Chatsworth, amid the sort of opulence that Adam Worth stole and Pierpont Morgan bought, gives nothing away. But perhaps, behind that painted smile, the greatest impostor of them all is laughing still.

Acknowledgments

I must thank many people in several countries for helping me to track down the elusive Adam Worth: Tony Blair, whose indefatigable sleuthing turned up so many gems; Thelen Blum and Derek Andrade, archivists at Pinkerton's Detective Agency; David Wright, archivist of The Pierpont Morgan Library; the Duke of Devonshire and Peter Day, archivist at Chatsworth House; Agnew's art gallery; Margaret Harradine, Port Elizabeth Library, South Africa; William E. Lind, National Archives, Washington, D.C.; staff at the British Library, the New York Public Library, and the National Film Archive, Washington, D.C.; the University of Miami; Andrea Cordani in London and Mark Leonard in Belgium.

I am also grateful for the help and encouragement of the following: my agent Ed Victor; John Glusman at Farrar, Straus and Giroux; Dermot Clinch; Jack Baer; Paul Richard; Blair Worden; Magnus Macintyre; Kate Macintyre; Hugh Belsey; Irving Kamil; Jack Schwartz; Patterson Smith; J. Spencer Beck; Lord Lonsdale; Jean Strouse; William Righter; Susan Bell; Kathy Sanford; Mindy Friedman Horn; Bob Robinson; Marilyn Bender, and my editors and colleagues at The Times.

This book could not have been written without the unwavering support of my mother and the memory of my father—scholar, inspiration, and much-missed friend.

Notes

The following abbreviations denote the principal archives used in this
work:

PA = Pinkerton's Detective Agency Archive, California
AA = Agnew's Archive, London
CHA = Chatsworth House Archives, Derbyshire
NG = National Gallery of Art, Washington, D.C.

EPIGRAPHS
"Adam Worth was the Napoleon"   C. McCluer Stevens, *Famous Crimes
and Criminals* (London, 1907), p. 38.
"He is the Napoleon of crime, Watson"   Sir Arthur Conan Doyle, *The
Final Problem,* in *The Annotated Sherlock Holmes,* Vol. II (New York, 1992),
p. 303 (henceforth, Conan Doyle).
"I hope you have not been"   Oscar Wilde, *The Importance of Being Earnest* (London, 1895), Act II.

ONE
"the amenity and graces"   Nathaniel Wraxall, *Posthumous Memoirs,* Vol.
III, p. 342, quoted in *Pictures in the Collection of J. Pierpont Morgan* (London, privately printed, 1907), Gainsborough section, p. 2.

TWO
"his father was a Russian"   E.A.B., *The Gainsborough Duchess,* p. 25, AA.
This frustratingly undated 30-page pamphlet is highly informed and

appears to have been written shortly after the return of the painting, possibly by a member of Agnew's staff (henceforth, *The Gainsborough Duchess*).

"Had he continued"   *Adam Worth, alias "Little Adam"—Theft and Recovery of Gainsborough's Duchess of Devonshire,* pamphlet privately printed by Pinkerton's Detective Agency and written principally by William Pinkerton (New York, 1904), p. 1 (henceforth, *Adam Worth*).

"born of an excellent"   Sophie Lyons, *Why Crime Does Not Pay* (New York, 1913), p. 38.

"entered school when six years"   *Adam Worth*, p. 1.

"gave him a most"   Max Shinburn, *Life of Adam Worth, alias Henry Raymond,* unpublished document (c. 1894), p. 1, in PA.

"impressing on him"   *Adam Worth*, p. 1.

"From that day"   ibid.

"The Napoleon of"   C. McCluer Stevens, p. 38.

"never in his life"   *The Education of Henry Adams* (1907; 1995 ed.), introduction by Jean Gooder, p. xiii.

"Not a Polish"   ibid., p. xxiv.

"probably no child"   ibid., p. 10.

"ambition"   Cardinal Newman, *Parochial and Plain Sermons,* 8, No. 11, 159 (1836). Quoted in Walter E. Houghton, *The Victorian Frame of Mind* (Oxford, 1957), p. 183.

"Serious poetry"   George Santayana, quoted in Lyndall Gordon, *Eliot's Early Years* (Oxford, 1977), p. 17.

"knelt in self-abasement"   Adams, p. 24.

"So this is dear"   John Collins Bossidy, *Toast at Holy Cross Alumni Dinner,* 1910.

"a nervous, hysterical"   Henry James, *The Bostonians,* cited in Gordon, p. 16.

"The Bostonian could"   Adams, p. 14.

"a vagabond life"   Shinburn, p. 1.

"in one of the"   *Adam Worth*, p. 1.

"bounty of $1,000"   ibid., p. 2. This figure appears far too large to believe, and was doubtless inflated by Pinkerton.

"He became associated"   ibid., p. 1.

"mud hole"   Jacob Roemer, *Reminiscences of the War of the Rebellion* (Flushing, 1897), p. 26.

"All we wanted"   ibid., p. 27.

"Shot and shell flew"   ibid., p. 58.

"Boys, it is no longer" ibid., p. 72.

"Bullets, shot and shell" ibid., p. 79.

"During this battle" ibid., p. 82.

"stationed for a time" *Adam Worth,* p. 2.

"On his third enlistment" Shinburn, p. 1.

"About this time" ibid., p. 1.

"took advantage" ibid., p. 3.

"through the Confederate States" ibid., p. 1.

"gained experience" Foreword by John Shuttleworth to Alan Hynd, *The Pinkertons meet Jimmy Valentine* (New York: Macfadden Publications, 1943).

THREE

"elegant storehouses" William Howe and Abraham Hummel, *In Danger* (1888), quoted in Luc Sante, *Low Life* (New York, 1991), p. 213.

"became required reading" Carl Sifakis, *The Encyclopedia of American Crime* (New York, 1992), p. 352.

"On account of his" *Adam Worth,* p. 2.

"Most of the saloons" Eddie Guerin, *I Was a Bandit* (New York, 1929), p. 49.

"growing from every orifice" Sante, p. 116.

"Sadie [the Goat] acquired" Herbert Asbury, *Gangs of New York* (New York, 1928), p. 64.

"the most notorious" ibid., p. 216.

"Picking pockets has" Edward Winslow Martin, *The Secrets of the Great City—A Work Descriptive of the Virtues and the Vices, the Mysteries, Miseries and Crimes of New York City* (Philadelphia, 1868), p. 366.

"Like myself" Lyons, p. 39.

"it was not" ibid.

"the first manifestation" ibid.

"The Dodger trod" Charles Dickens, *Oliver Twist* (1839).

"plenty of money" Lyons, p. 39.

"I don't believe" Sifakis, p. 450.

"tomb of the living dead" ibid., p. 451.

"never had an idea" 16-page letter from William to Robert Pinkerton, Jan. 16, 1899, PA (henceforth, Worth's Confession), p. 9.

"discharged itself" Shinburn, p. 1.

"he managed to get" ibid.

"had the satisfaction" ibid.

"lonely dock"   ibid.
"He managed"   ibid., p. 2.
"was law with"   Lyons, p. 39.
"He furnished"   ibid.
"restless ambition"   ibid.
"the state of society"   Shinburn, *Safe Burglary—Its Beginnings and Progress,* unpublished document, c. 1905, PA.
"Such operations"   Sante, p. 208.
"instead of the clumsy"   Allan Pinkerton, *The Bankers, the Vaults and the Burglars* (1873). Cited in Patterson Smith, "The Bank Burglar—Real Life Raffles," *Antiquarian Bookseller,* May 8, 1989.
"a successful bank"   Guerin, p. 301.
"It was hard"   Lyons, p. 40.
"itching to get"   ibid.

FOUR

"The greatest crime"   Lyons, p. 187.
"most successful fence"   Asbury, p. 214.
"first put crime"   Sifakis, p. 470.
"She was a huge woman"   Asbury, p. 214.
"without a friend"   Lyons, p. 188.
"her coarse, heavy features"   ibid.
"afflicted with"   ibid.
"Mrs Mandelbaum"   ibid., p. 190.
"plunder from"   Asbury, p. 215.
"handled the loot"   ibid.
"the law made"   ibid., p. 217.
"where small boys"   ibid.
"post-graduate work"   ibid.
"she was scheming"   Sifakis, p. 470.
"were furnished with"   Asbury, pp. 214–15.
"entertained lavishly"   ibid., p. 215.
"I shall never forget"   Lyons, p. 196.
"an especial soft spot"   Asbury, p. 216.
"It just goes"   Sifakis, p. 471.
"The army of enemies"   Lyons, p. 193.
"great disgust"   ibid., p. 41.
"established him"   ibid.

"a master hand"   B. P. Eldridge and Wm. B. Watts, *Our Rival, the Rascal* (Boston, 1893), p. 85.

"Once, after robbing"   ibid.

"a bank burglar"   Asbury, p. 215.

"the judicious"   ibid.

"probably the most expert"   Thomas Byrnes, *Professional Criminals of America* (New York, 1895).

"Speaks English with a"   Circular from Ed. Mechelynck, Juge d'Instruction, Brussels, March 16, 1893, PA.

"small blue penetrating"   George Bangs to William Pinkerton, New York, July 6, 1897, PA.

"on back of left"   ibid.

"a ratchet which"   Edward J. Gallagher, *Robber Baron* (Laconia, New Hampshire, privately printed, 1967), p. 58.

"his ear was so"   Eldridge and Watts, p. 45.

"Shinburn revolutionized"   Sophie Lyons in *Chicago Daily American,* July 1913.

"for some time"   Account of Shinburn's arrest, June 28, 1896, p. 1, PA.

"came into such"   Shinburn, *Safe Burglary,* p. 3, PA.

"The safe I can't open"   Lyons, *Chicago Daily American,* July 1913.

"had a good common"   Eldridge and Watts, p. 53.

"devoted his ability"   *Bullard, the Burglar Prince,* Document #175, PA.

"dissipation and a restless"   Eldridge and Watts, p. 53.

"one of the boldest"   *Bullard, the Burglar Prince.*

"Bullard is a man"   John Cornish to George Bangs, Boston, Nov. 23, 1886, Document #197, PA.

"delicacy of touch"   Eldridge and Watts, p. 53.

"An inveterate gamester"   *Adam Worth,* p. 4.

"The robbers were"   *Bullard, the Burglar Prince.*

"concealed themselves"   ibid.

"as he was returning"   John Cornish to George Bangs, Boston, Nov. 23, 1886.

"Shinburn used to take"   Lyons, p. 78.

FIVE

"made a tour"   Lyons, p. 42.

some two hundred *Boston Post,* Nov. 23, 1869.

"The bottles served"   *Adam Worth,* p. 3.

lining of the vault *Boston Post,* Nov. 23, 1869.

"To cut through this"   ibid.

"The treasure was"   ibid.

"The trunks were"   ibid.

"fairly thunderstruck"   ibid.

"nearly one million"   *Adam Worth,* p. 3.

"a dozen bushels"   *Boston Post,* Nov. 23, 1869.

"Everyone continues to talk"   *Boston Post,* Nov. 26, 1869.

"he gambled, drank"   *Adam Worth,* p. 3.

"an old man, broken down"   ibid.

"Those damned detectives"   Quoted in James D. Horan, *The Pinkertons—The Detective Dynasty That Made History* (New York, 1967), p. 286. While Horan's historical method is open to criticism, his chapter on Worth is invaluable. He had access, in the 1950s and 1960s, to a variety of sources either destroyed since (in the case of Scotland Yard) or lost (in the case of the Pinkerton's archive).

"All [the robbers] need do"   *Boston Sunday Times,* Nov. 28, 1869, p. 1.

"There must be"   ibid.

"an attack of apoplexy"   *New York Times,* June 19, 1869.

"always the true" ibid.

"He was always"   *Evening Mail,* June 18, 1869.

"one of the brightest"   *New York Telegram,* June 18, 1869.

"he was a gentleman"   *Evening Post,* June 18, 1869.

"Contemporary opinion"   *New York Times,* June 20, 1869.

"sat with his family"   *New York Times,* June 19, 1869.

"paying a visit"   Marilyn Bender and Selig Altschul, *The Chosen Instrument—Juan Trippe and Pan Am* (New York, 1982), p. 19.

"She was an unusually"   Lyons, p. 44.

"Bullard and Raymond"   ibid.

"inclined to live fast"   *Adam Worth,* p. 4.

"The race for her favor"   Lyons, p. 44.

"to his credit"   ibid., p. 45.

"He looked around"   *Adam Worth,* p. 4.

SIX

"badness of the"   Lady Amberly, mother of Bertrand Russell, quoted in Alistair Horne, *The Fall of Paris* (London, 1965), p. 17.

"France is an astonishingly"   ibid., p. 420.

"bought up part of"   ibid., p. 421.

"palatial splendor"   *Adam Worth,* p. 4.

"which were, at that time"   ibid.

"Americans were cordially"   ibid.

"her beauty and"   Document #172, PA.

"the headquarters of"   Address by William A. Pinkerton to the Annual Convention of the International Chiefs of Police, at Jamestown, Virginia, 1907. PA.

"Mrs. Wells was a"   *Adam Worth*, p. 4.

affable   John Cornish to George Bangs, Boston, Document #197, PA.

"which the bar-tender"   William to Robert Pinkerton, Feb. 12, 1902, p. 3, PA.

"made two or three"   *Adam Worth*, p. 4.

"astonished by"   ibid.

"masquerading as a"   Eldridge and Watts, p. 46.

"a complete work shop"   Account of the arrest of Max Shinburn, p. 4, PA.

"one of the most"   Eldridge and Watts, p. 46.

"With the money"   Arrest of Shinburn, PA, p. 2.

"nobody cared to dispute"   Eldridge and Watts, p. 48.

"with an open"   ibid.

"overbearing Dutch pig"   Worth's Confession, p. 3.

"I could name a hundred"   Guerin, p. 301.

"but one vice—forgery"   Horan, p. 290.

"the ablest professional"   William to Robert Pinkerton, Feb. 12, 1902, p. 4, PA.

"a great fellow for"   Worth's Confession, p. 7.

"swell Americans who"   Arrest of Shinburn, p. 2.

"but Mr. Sanford"   John Cornish to George Bangs, Boston, Document #197, PA.

"In the gay French capital"   Eldridge and Watts, p. 54.

"waged a ceaseless war"   Shuttleworth.

"It was not unusual"   ibid.

"When Bill Pinkerton went"   Guerin, p. 301.

"We were rather troubled"   Quoted in Horan, p. 293.

"There was no intention"   Worth's Confession, p. 6.

"nearly dropped dead"   ibid., p. 7.

"Old Vinegar went"   ibid.

"entrances were guarded"   ibid.

"Joe made the drop"   ibid.

"two well known American"   Shuttleworth.

"The respectable people"   William to Robert Pinkerton, Feb. 12, 1902, p. 3, PA.

"who insisted on the police"   Harold M. Lloyd, "Confidences of American Frank," *Boston Sunday Herald,* Oct. 7, 1934.

"The robbery startled"   *Adam Worth,* p. 5.

"The place was finally"   ibid.

"The bar-tender was"   William to Robert Pinkerton, Feb. 12, 1902, p. 3, PA.

"Wells [Bullard] and others"   *Adam Worth,* p. 5.

"never again be a success"   Worth's Confession, p. 7.

"English betting man"   William to Robert Pinkerton, Feb. 12, 1902, p. 3, PA.

"the ruction which"   Worth's Confession, p. 7.

"Afterwards when we"   ibid.

"The history of Britain"   T. B. Macaulay, *Critical essays* (1835), 3, 279, cited in Houghton, p. 39.

"We remove mountains"   Carlyle, "Signs of the Times" (1829), *Essays,* 2, 60, cited in Houghton, p. 41.

SEVEN

"then in the bloom"   Allan Cunningham, 1829, chapter on Gainsborough, cited in *Pictures in the Collection of J. Pierpont Morgan.*

"but her dazzling beauty"   ibid.

"Drawing his wet pencil"   ibid.

"giving promise even"   Mrs. Arthur Bell (N. D'Anvers), *Thomas Gainsborough, A Record of His Life* (London, 1897), p. 63.

"greenish"   William T. Whitley, *Artists and Their Friends in England, 1700–1799* (London, 1928), Vol. I, p. 199; also Geoffrey Williamson, *The Ingenious Mr. Gainsborough* (New York, 1972), p. 171.

"More portraits exist"   *Magazine of Art,* June 1901, article by W. Roberts, "Portraits of the two Duchesses of Devonshire," p. 369.

"spoke of it as"   *The Gainsborough Duchess,* p. 15.

"one of which Lady Spencer"   See W. T. Whitley, *Thomas Gainsborough* (London, 1915).

"abandon friends as soon"   Letter from Dr. Sjaak Zonneveld to Peter Day, archivist, Aug. 28, 1994, CHA.

"effects were dispersed"   Ellis Waterhouse, *Portraits by Thomas Gainsborough,* Walpole Society, Vol. XXXIII, No. 3 (1953), p. 28.

"very wooden legs"   Henry James, *The Old Masters at Burlington House*

(1877), cited in Rupert Hart-Davis, *The Painter's Eye* (Wisconsin, 1989), p. 127.

"It was then hanging"   *Times*, April 11, 1901, p. 6.

"Sir, I am obliged"   *The Gainsborough Duchess*, p. 13.

"never had the slightest"   *Times*, April 11, 1901, p. 6.

"The picture remained"   ibid.

"Mr Bentley was the intimate"   ibid.

"haberdasher, hosier and mercer"   *Dictionary of National Biography*, p. 716.

"had an intense dislike"   ibid., p. 717.

"the painting which"   *The Gainsborough Duchess*, p. 14.

"There was"   Robert Kempt, *Pencil and Palette* (London, 1881), p. 97.

"Though a great lover"   *The Gainsborough Duchess*, p. 14.

"watercolour drawings, porcelain"   *Dictionary of National Biography*, p. 717.

EIGHT

"now delights"   John Shore to William Pinkerton, May 21, 1888, PA.

"a big lunk head"   Worth's Confession, p. 4.

"Bullard, alias Wells"   William to Robert Pinkerton, Feb. 12, 1902, PA.

"tennis courts, a shooting gallery"   Lloyd.

for £600 a year   *The Gainsborough Duchess*, p. 25; also *London Evening News*, April 9, 1901, p. 2.

"international clearing house"   Lyons, p. 46.

"the most remarkable"   *Adam Worth*, preface and p. 6.

"Crimes in every corner"   Lyons, p. 47.

"One robbery followed"   *Adam Worth*, p. 6.

"the West End was full"   Guerin, p. 302.

"There were some men"   Worth's Confession, p. 13.

"An unwilling photograph"   *Adam Worth*, facing p. 6.

"a crew of twenty-five"   *London Evening News*, April 9, 1901, p. 2.

"This last exploit"   Lyons, p. 56.

"Inspector Shore agrees with me"   Horan, p. 295.

"To be respectable"   Herbert Spencer, Exeter Hall lectures, 3 (1847–48), 364, cited in Houghton, p. 184.

"Now that a man"   John Ruskin, *Pre-Raphaelitism* (1815), cited in Houghton, p. 187.

"expected to be honest"   J.C.F. Harrison, *Late Victorian Britain, 1875–90* (London, 1990), p. 42.

"It is only shallow people"   Oscar Wilde, *The Picture of Dorian Gray* (1891), Chap. 2.

"costly furniture, bric-a-brac"   Lyons, p. 45.

"he was a man"   George Dilnot, *Master Minds of Crime*, p. 659, AA.

"lived like a prince"   Lyons, p. 56.

"He became a student"   ibid., p. 58.

"ten racehorses"   *London Evening News*, April 9, 1901, p. 2.

"he employed a staff"   ibid.

"When he had money"   *Adam Worth*, p. 23.

"Anybody with whom"   ibid.

"throughout his career"   Milton Esterow, *The Art Stealers* (New York, London, 1960), p. 184.

"It's just as easy"   Charles Kingston, *Remarkable Rogues* (London, 1921), p. 260.

"If you want to get on"   Horan, p. 302.

"They pretended to be"   Houghton, p. 395.

"I hope you have not"   *The Importance of Being Earnest*, Act II.

"A man with brains"   *Adam Worth*, p. 23.

"there was always a way"   ibid.

"It was his almost unbroken"   Lyons, p. 47.

"could thank God Almighty"   Worth's Confession, p. 5.

"What he says is true"   ibid.

"How much flattery"   ibid., p. 7.

"to relentlessly hunt"   Horan, p. 362.

"with an unyielding"   ibid., p. 190.

"uppermost in their"   ibid., p. 403.

"a good mixer"   Frank Morn, *The Eye That Never Sleeps* (Indiana, 1982), p. 131.

"water cure"   Horan, p. 247.

"open war against the"   Cited in Clive Emsley, *Crime and Society in England 1750–1900*, 2nd ed. (London and New York, 1996), p. 168.

"I think my poor"   *Sunday Times*, June 23, 1957.

"victim of the richer"   ibid.

"by support of The Claimant"   Harrison, p. 155.

"I don't care whether"   cited in *Sunday Times*, June 23, 1957.

"maintaining his guise"   Horan, p. 295.

"he would change his"   ibid.

NINE

"the biggest coward" Worth's Confession, p. 12.

"microscopic scrutiny" Horan, p. 300.

"a small black moustache" I. W. Lees to William Pinkerton, San Francisco, Feb. 19, 1886, PA.

"He has a very nervous" ibid.

"Chapman had been trained" Eldridge and Watts, p. 176.

"Bullard was, like all thieves" William Pinkerton in *Illustrated Police News,* Sept. 22, 1888.

"through the principal" Eldridge and Watts, p. 176.

"Jail meant nothing to us" Horan, p. 296.

"I have had but bread" Howard Adams (Sesicovitch's alias) to "My dearest Alima," Jan. 29, 1875. Quoted in Horan, p. 296.

"unwavering loyalty" Lyons, p. 47.

"never forsook a friend" *Adam Worth,* preface.

"in the guise of an American" Kingston, p. 265.

"that it was he who took" Worth's Confession, p. 3.

"while passing through Asia Minor" *Adam Worth,* p. 7.

"The only thing that Reilly" Worth's Confession, p. 3.

"which money 'Little Joe' " *Adam Worth,* p. 7.

"needed money from her" Letter from Robert Pinkerton to Larry Hazen, printed in *New York Tribune,* April 29, 1878.

"was possessed of " ibid.

"a scheme had been" ibid.

"her death at the hands" William to Robert Pinkerton, May 12, 1902, Document #2454, PA.

"the first and second fingers" Pinkerton to Larry Hazen, 1878.

"served his full sentence" *Adam Worth,* p. 7.

"With Raymond's cool" Lyons, p. 46.

" 'How's Kate?' would be" Horan, p. 301.

"an old sweetheart" Guerin, p. 298.

"Had this woman become" Lyons, p. 47.

"He never forgot" ibid., pp. 46–7.

TEN

"natural refinement" Hart-Davis, 1956, p. 127.

"15/20 for Beauty" Cited in *Derbyshire Life,* Sept. 1994, p. 35.

"very handsome" *Magazine of Art,* p. 369.

"her youth, figure"   Walpole, *Letters*, vi, p. 186; see *Pictures in the Collection of J. Pierpont Morgan*, p. 3.

"early disposition to coquetry"   Mrs. Mary Robinson, *Beaux and Belles of England*, p. 298.

"one of the most showy girls"   Whitley (1928), p. 397.

"Hurt not the form"   Peter Pindar, "Petition to Time in favour of the Duchess of Devonshire," *Magazine of Art*, June 1901; also *Pictures in the Collection of J. Pierpont Morgan*.

"I could light my pipe"   Brian Masters, *Georgiana, Duchess of Devonshire* (London, 1982), p. 36; *Pictures in the Collection of J. Pierpont Morgan*, p. 3.

"The slaves of fashion"   Whitley (1928), p. 398.

"Oh Lady, nursed"   *Dictionary of National Biography*, p. 1256.

"he had handed the Duchess"   See *Loan Collection of Pictures*, Art Gallery of the Corporation of London, 1892, No. 92, NG.

"When people of rank"   Masters, p. 123.

"drinking daily since"   Whitley (1928), p. 400.

"irresistible queen"   Bell, p. 64.

"the most brilliant"   ibid.; also *Loan Collection of Pictures*, NG.

"Before you condemn me"   Masters, p. 69.

"Then the best-natured"   ibid., p. 300.

"The beauty of the subject"   Herbert L. Satterlee, *J. Pierpont Morgan— An Intimate Portrait* (New York, 1939), p. 351.

"Her protean beauty"   Esterow, p. 183.

"Artists and connoisseurs"   Robert Kempt, p. 97.

"the handling appeared"   ibid.

"in the voluptuousness of the figure"   ibid.

"originally a sketch"   *History of the Duchess of Devonshire by Gainsborough*, anonymous and undated, AA.

"the head was painted"   *The Gainsborough Duchess*, p. 6.

"who had known both"   Lord Hawkesbury in a letter to *The Times*, quoted in *The Gainsborough Duchess*, p. 15.

"There thus arose constantly"   *Times*, May 8, 1876.

"So much interest has"   ibid.

"the solid surface of"   *Pictures in the Collection of J. Pierpont Morgan*, p. 7.

"this is simply one"   *Times*, Nov. 13, 1901.

"The answer is that"   ibid.

"The Doctors, though they differ"   *Times*, May 8, 1876.

"The majority"   ibid.

"created such a sensation"   ibid.

"the doubters were put to the rout"   Kempt, p. 97.

"The sale will long"   *Times,* May 8, 1876. See also *The Art Amateur,* Vol. XXIX, Sept. 1963, p. 80, for an account of when this record was broken.

ELEVEN

"lived at the rate"   *London Evening News,* April 9, 1901, p. 2.

"a damn fool" Worth's Confession, p. 13.

"He has generally"   I. W. Lees to William Pinkerton, San Francisco, Feb. 19, 1886, PA.

"rose cheeked girl"   Horan, p. 298.

"Joe courted the lady"   Guerin, p. 48.

"they settled down"   Horan, p. 299.

"like a human tiger"   Worth's Confession, p. 4.

"turned on him"   ibid.

"To prevent detection"   Adam Worth, pp. 7–8.

"a man of good position"   Undated account in *Duchess of Devonshire* file, PA.

"the application for bail"   ibid.

"was at this time"   *History of the Duchess of Devonshire,* AA.

"employed another agent"   ibid.

"portrait of the Duchess"   ibid.

"that it was owing"   ibid.

"the interest in the sale"   *Times,* May 19, 1876.

"You remember that landscape"   Oscar Wilde, *The Picture of Dorian Gray,* p. 33.

"Then and there the idea"   Worth's Confession, p. 3.

"would go to an acquaintance"   Adam Worth, p. 9.

"a clumsy thing"   Lyons, p. 49.

"All England was talking"   C. McCluer Stevens, p. 39.

"princely gift"   Ron Chernow, *The House of Morgan—An American Banking Dynasty and the Rise of Modern Finance* (New York, 1990), p. 41.

"the connection was enough" Letter from J. Spencer Beck, printed in *New York Times Magazine,* Aug. 21, 1994.

"Mr. Junius Morgan dropped"   Satterlee, p. 352.

"he had to consent"   ibid.

"absolutely secret"   ibid.

"It is in the nature" Laurence Sterne, *Tristram Shandy*, Book II, Chap.
19.

TWELVE

"double his usual amount" Rodney Engen, *Pre-Raphaelite Prints* (London, 1995), p. 20.

"Being inhabitants of Bond Street" *Times*, May 27, 1876, p. 12.

"is said to have given" *Times*, April 10, 1901, p. 4.

"all over the known" *Adam Worth*, p. 10.

"the hue and cry" *The Gainsborough Duchess*, p. 21.

"in no way answered" Worth's Confession, p. 3.

"an accessory after the fact" Esterow, p. 187.

"had the picture" Worth's Confession, p. 3.

it had been burned *The Art Amateur*, Vol. XXIX, Sept. 1963, p. 80.

"No one who knows the high" ibid.

"wise ones had it that" *The Gainsborough Duchess*, p. 7.

"I have a very good clairvoyant" M. Mortimer to William Agnew, May 28, 1876, AA.

"No doubt you will" Anon. to William Agnew, May 27, 1876, AA.

"Could they not have" Daniel Berman to William Agnew, May 29, 1876, AA.

"I shall not take a fraction" "Australia" to William Agnew, Aug. 6, 1876, AA.

"Now Mr Agnew you must come" ibid.

"A woman will do" ibid.

"Sir, Although unknown to you" Marguerite Antehuester to Messrs. Agnew, Boxhill, May 26, 1876, AA.

"The interest, not to say anxiety" *Midland Daily Telegraph*, July 25, 1893, AA.

"impresarios paid the leading" Esterow, p. 201.

"accomplished a task before" *New York Sun*, July 26, 1893, AA.

"at most of the public ceremonials" *New York Herald*, July 18, 1897, AA.

"the Gainsborough hat" *New York Sun*, May 29, 1894, AA.

"a large curling red feather" Conan Doyle, *Case of Identity*, in Vol. I, p. 407.

THIRTEEN

"furnished rooms on the upper floors" Bender and Altschul, p. 22.

"an influence peddler" ibid.

"dissipated" William to Robert Pinkerton, Feb. 12, 1902, PA.

"a sort of semi-assignation house" ibid.

"at one time considered" ibid.

"Adam told me he always" ibid.

"Gents" "E. Chattrell" to Messrs. Agnew, New York, June 10, 1876, AA.

"does not appear" Robert Pinkerton to Superintendent Williamson, Scotland Yard, New York, July 13, 1876, AA.

"Our impression, on first reading" William Schaus to Messrs. Agnew, New York, July 22, 1876, AA.

"the best managed hotel" Worth's Confession, p. 10.

"which was greatly frequented" ibid., p. 9.

"He felt sure it was one" ibid., p. 11.

"found in the letter box at" Note written by J. M. Worrall, Letter from NEW YORK to Messrs. Agnew, Dec. 15, 1876, AA.

"Gentlemen: We beg to inform you" ibid. Note that this letter as well as the previous letter (signed "Edward Chattrell") both refer to the "advertisement" resulting from the theft, a peculiar expression which strongly suggests the same writer.

"New York, Letter received" *Times,* Jan. 2, 1877.

"a longer piece of the upper" New York to Messrs. Agnew, Jan. 22, 1877, AA.

"in order to facilitate matters" New York to Messrs. Agnew & Son, March 6, 1877, AA.

"The Picture is over here" ibid.

"New York. Am waiting to hear from you" *Times,* March 26, 1877.

"the penalties for the crime" NEW YORK to Agnew's, May 22, 1877, AA.

"I have vainly" NEW YORK to Agnew's, May ?, 1877.

"NEW YORK, No danger to you" *Times,* May 31, 1877.

"Finding that it was impossible" NEW YORK to Agnew's, Aug. 8, 1877, AA.

"I really cannot suggest" NEW YORK to Agnew's, Aug. 21, 1877, AA.

"It seemed evident that he was not" *New York Herald,* July 18, 1897.

"a *fin de siècle* scoundrel" *New York Sun,* July 26, 1893.

"a white elephant" Worth's Confession, p. 5.

"Feasting his eyes on" Lloyd, p. 2.

FOURTEEN

"perfected herself in the arts"   *New York World,* March 21, 1894.

"baptized in the local church"   *Historia de familias Cubanas,* Francisco Xavier de Santa Cruz y Mallen, Vol III (Havana, 1940). See also Arzobispado de la Habana, Sección de Dispensas de Amonestaciones, Legajo 36, Número 106.

"when he heard that his father-in-law"   *New York Herald,* Aug. 25, 1899.

"Every transaction in which"   ibid.

"proved veritable gold mines"   ibid.

slave trade Document #175, PA.

"one of the wealthiest"   *New York Herald,* Aug. 25, 1899.

"The Terrys owned houses"   Bender and Altschul, p. 23.

"with which he went into"   *New York Herald,* Aug. 25, 1899.

"distinguished for his business ability"   ibid.

"Young Terry was infatuated"   Lyons, p. 46.

"She was pretty and fascinating"   *New York World,* March 21, 1894.

"His conduct as a prisoner"   Eldridge and Watts, p. 54.

"insulting postal card"   *Illustrated Police News,* Sept. 22, 1888.

"stating that the Manhattan Bank"   John Cornish to George Bangs, Boston, Nov. 23, 1886, Document #197, PA.

"his ill-gotten gains soon"   Eldridge and Watts, p. 54.

"fingers so sensitive"   John Cornish to George Bangs, Boston, Nov. 23, 1886, Document #197, PA.

"while pennyweighting"   William to Robert Pinkerton, Feb. 12, 1902, PA, p. 3.

was arrested and sent   *Illustrated Police News,* Sept. 22, 1888.

"greatly to the consternation"   *New York World,* March 21, 1894.

"exceedingly happy marriage"   Lyons, p. 46.

"who had grown up"   William to Robert Pinkerton, Feb. 12, 1902, PA, p. 3.

"permitted Kate's daughters"   Bender and Altschul, p. 23.

"Returning from a shopping tour"   *New York Times,* June 15, 1888.

"the tone of which indicated"   *New York World,* March 21, 1894.

"She wrote a reply"   ibid.

"sitting smoking and drinking"   *New York Times,* June 15, 1888.

"Mrs. Terry, as soon as she entered"   ibid.

"in the course of which"   ibid.

"complaining that Mrs. Terry"   ibid.

"a person of bad character"   ibid.

"a similar cross-examination"   ibid.

"Her marriage to Bullard"   ibid.

"The court experience"   *New York World,* March 21, 1894.

"afterwards went South"   *New York Times,* May 7, 1891.

FIFTEEN

"being the perpetrator"   *Adam Worth,* p. 11.

"While in prison he sent"   ibid.

"could not control it"   ibid.

"Gradually certain facts leaked out"   ibid., p. 10.

"back at the old stand"   John Shore to William Pinkerton, in Horan, p. 308.

"He became such a 'bugaboo' "   *Adam Worth,* p. 11.

"to get even with him"   Worth's Confession, p. 4.

"Shore was in the habit"   ibid.

"keeping a brothel"   ibid.

"called the Rising Sun"   ibid.

"He said they had gotten"   ibid.

"he had got tired of waiting"   ibid.

"had Supt. Shore treated him"   ibid., pp. 3–4.

"I told him I thought"   ibid., pp. 4–5.

"would never have amounted"   ibid., p. 3.

"This robbery was perpetrated"   *Adam Worth,* p. 16.

"From time to time"   ibid., p. 10.

"for a bagatelle"   Horan, p. 305.

"not out of the vaults"   Worth's Confession, p. 12.

"refused to have anything"   ibid.

"Phillips demanded that the picture"   *Adam Worth,* p. 10.

"suspecting treachery"   ibid.

"a fighting man"   Worth's Confession, p. 13.

"commenced to abuse him"   ibid.

"He jumped up and struck"   ibid.

pulled off   ibid.

"denounced him for striking"   ibid.

"looked to him like Junka"   ibid.

"they never met again"   *Adam Worth,* p. 11.

SIXTEEN

"a combination of the artist" Bank of England statement, March 11, 1880, quoted in Horan, p. 308.

"be on his guard when dealing" Worth's Confession, p. 12.

"On account of his tendency" ibid.

"He might have lived" Eldridge and Watts, p. 48.

"came to London" Worth's Confession, p. 3.

"number of dynamite explosions" *Adam Worth*, p. 12.

"the very best of the lot" Quoted in Horan, p. 306.

"he feared to leave it" Lyons, p. 53.

"thirty or so paintings" Jules Verne, *Twenty Thousand Leagues Under the Sea* (1870), Chap. 11.

"I'm not what you would" Verne, Chap. 10.

"partly on business, partly on pleasure" Chief Inspector J. G. Littlechild, *Cassel's Sunday Journal*, Nov. 22, 1893.

"a noted English crook" *Adam Worth*, p. 13.

"crystallized romance" Cited in Stefan Kanfer, *The Last Empire: De Beers, Diamonds, and the World* (New York, 1993), p. 30.

"Rabbis, rebels, rogues" Cited in Kanfer, p. 34.

"large ostrich feathers" Kanfer, p. 37.

"As there were no restrictions" *Standard Encyclopedia of Southern Africa* (Pretoria, 1971), Vol. III, p. 487. See: "Crimes, Non-violent."

"He opened an office" Horan, p. 308.

"While looking about" *Adam Worth*, p. 13.

"looked the situation over" ibid.

"an American sea captain" ibid.

capture the driver ibid., p. 14.

"the horses were thrown" ibid.

"created quite a sensation" ibid.

"game fellow" William to Robert Pinkerton, Feb. 12, 1902, p. 4, PA.

"had weakened and got scared off" Worth's Confession, p. 6.

"decided to remain to have" *Adam Worth*, p. 14.

"£200 immediately" Worth's Confession, p. 6.

"His intention" ibid.

"an old gentleman" *Adam Worth*, p. 14.

"took three parcels out" ibid.

"pleaded that it was of" ibid.

"there was a deep stream" ibid.

"The next night" ibid.

"The swag"   Worth's Confession, p. 6.

"he had been embezzling"   *Adam Worth,* p. 15.

"experts from England"   Littlechild.

"Knowing that anyone who"   *Adam Worth,* p. 15.

"seeing the thing in the papers"   Worth's Confession, p. 6.

"some article which he had"   ibid.

"more for the"   ibid.

"He said that John"   ibid., p. 13.

"clever, educated fellow"   *Adam Worth,* p. 15.

"married to a lady"   Shinburn, p. 8.

"By putting their goods"   *Adam Worth,* p. 15.

"If I had ever possessed"   Dilnot, p. 657.

"It has been 'discovered' "   *Times,* April 10, 1901, p. 4.

"I believe I have found"   Anonymous letter, May 5, 1884, AA.

"while a gang of men were engaged"   *Pall Mall Gazette,* undated clipping, AA.

"seen the thief"   Anonymous, undated letter in AA.

"custodians of this article"   Meiklejohn & Son to G. Lewis, Feb. 16, 1887, AA.

"racing frauds"   Worth's Confession, p. 4.

"Negotiations can be opened"   *New York Herald,* cited in Esterow, p. 193.

"New York.—If the present owner"   ibid.

"What his precise"   *New York Sun,* May 29, Vol. XLV, no. 271, otherwise undated, AA.

SEVENTEEN

"as the first gentleman"   Harrison, p. 34.

"a pair of the finest"   Lloyd, p. 2.

"even his heavy losses at"   Lyons, p. 56.

"a very fine house"   Lloyd, p. 2.

"About five o'clock on the"   C. McCluer Stevens, p. 40.

"down the steps leading to the basement"   ibid.

"the office was plunged"   ibid.

"Worth, the moment the gas failed"   ibid.

"had the effect of causing"   *Midland Daily Telegraph,* July 25, 1893, AA.

"I made an average"   Lloyd, p. 2.

"If ever a man in this"   Guerin, p. 76.

"he loved . . . to pit his skill"   C. McCluer Stevens, p. 38.

"Raymond loved his work"   ibid.
"From year to year the safemakers"   Shinburn, *Safe Burglary*, p. 3, PA.
"the burglar kept pace"   ibid.
"one of the cleverest framers-up"   Guerin, p. 297.
"It is an odd thing"   Oscar Wilde, *The Picture of Dorian Gray*, Chap. 18.
"a mob of all round crooks"   I. W. Lees to William Pinkerton, San Francisco, Feb. 19, 1886, PA.
"It was a clean job"   ibid.
"He is still dead"   ibid.
"grew worse than ever"   Guerin, p. 48.
"slugged one of"   ibid.
"It was surely the irony"   ibid.
"dispute with the baggage man"   I. W. Lees to William Pinkerton, San Francisco, Feb. 19, 1886, PA.
"twisted the lock off"   Worth's Confession, p. 6.
widow who lived with   Lyons, p. 58.
"He became, in time"   ibid.
"She was a beautiful woman"   ibid.
"one of the little girls"   Worth's Confession, p. 8.
"devotedly attached"   William to Robert Pinkerton, Feb. 12, 1902, PA.
"standing in fine grounds"   *The Gainsborough Duchess*, p. 28.
"under the roof of a summer"   Lloyd, p. 3.
"he hid it in the chartroom"   ibid.
"the proceeds from the big"   Worth's Confession, p. 9.
"he made a great bluff"   ibid.
"scared them out of"   ibid.
"after his liberation"   *Adam Worth*, p. 13.
"would have given him"   Worth's Confession, p. 9.
"several thousand dollars' worth"   ibid.
"At a small cost of a few"   Horan, p. 311.
"one occasion he walked out"   C. McCluer Stevens, p. 43.
"Sophie Lyons was a"   Guerin, p. 119.
"I was walking down"   ibid., p. 120.
"noted American bank sneak"   William Pinkerton to George Bangs, Chicago, April 27, 1913, PA.
"We went to have a drink"   Guerin, p. 120.
"that dinner might have"   ibid.
"I didn't say anything"   ibid., p. 121.
"Thieves came to him"   Kingston, pp. 264-5.

"Adam Worth" *New York World,* Sept. 2, 1888.

enmity between Worth's Confession, p. 6.

"A friend of mine who" Dilnot, p. 662.

"who has been known to me" John Shore to William Pinkerton, May 21, 1888, PA.

"have fitted up the place" ibid.

EIGHTEEN

"It was nip and tuck" Shinburn, *Safe Burglary,* p. 2.

"The guns leave the Big Man's" Quoted in Morn, p. 121.

"the Pinkertons did more" Guerin, p. 301.

"the practice of" Horan, p. 356.

"principally constituted" Morn, p. 148.

"There are few" Cited in Horan, p. 389.

"instinctive altruism" Morn, p. 138.

"didn't like" Horan, p. 369.

"Crooks Club" Morn, p. 131.

"the Canadian government looks" ibid., p. 121.

"he had looked about this country" Worth's Confession, p. 9.

"plays sad havoc" Guerin, p. 301.

"fidgety over the" John Shore to Pinkerton's, Aug. 4, 1888, Document #744, PA.

"for uttering spurious" *Police News,* Aug. 10, 1895.

"The urge to speculate" Gallagher, p. 72.

"gambling and extortion" ibid.

"with resources sadly depleted" ibid.

"Max and Charlie [sic] after" *New York Herald,* July 18, 1897.

"tired of supporting his old" ibid.

"hoped to realize at least" Gallagher, p. 75.

"They planned to rob the bank" ibid., p. 74.

"To save time rather than" ibid., p. 76.

"fired a pistol at one" ibid.

"one of the experts requested" ibid.

"identified them as notorious" *New York Herald,* July 18, 1897.

"to reunite with the" Bullard, *Prince of Burglars,* Document #176, PA.

NINETEEN

"Worth was living" *Adam Worth,* p. 11.

"One would have thought" ibid., p. 16.

"the boy would be sent" Worth's Confession, p. 8.

"one of the most" *New York Jeweler's Review,* March 16, 1889.

"make a tour of the continent" ibid.

"Alonzo, in spite of the fact" Worth's Confession, p. 9.

"jumped on the seat" ibid.

"in less time than this" *Meuse,* Oct. 6, 1892.

"Alonzo was to be on the lookout" Worth's Confession, p. 8.

"got off the van" ibid.

"Monsieur Decorty, a railway employee" *Meuse,* Oct. 6, 1892.

"seeing the" ibid.

"he too set off after" *Gazette de Liège,* Oct. 6, 1892.

"The fugitive already had" ibid.

"hastened to rid himself" *Meuse,* Oct. 6, 1892.

"two blocks away" Worth's Confession, p. 8.

"an audacious coup" *Gazette de Liège,* Oct. 6, 1892.

"he was dressed in gentlemanly" *Soir,* Oct. 7, 1892.

"conventional attire" *Meuse,* Oct. 6, 1892.

"the extremely solid 'Pince Monsieur' " ibid.

"There is evidence to suggest" *Gazette de Liège,* Oct. 7, 1892.

"If you knew the truth" *Gazette de Liège,* March 21, 1893.

"He refuses to disclose" ibid.

"With the loyalty for which" Lyons, p. 59.

"this individual had" *Meuse,* Oct. 6, 1892.

"a million francs or $200,000" Worth's Confession, p. 8.

"valuable state papers" ibid.

"The official value of the papers" *Meuse,* Oct. 6, 1892.

"continued to maintain" *Gazette de Liège,* Oct. 10, 1892.

"This fellow speaks and writes" Belgian legal circular, Oct. 10, 1892, issued by Juge d'Instruction Théodore de Corswarem, Liège, p. 2, PA.

"neither the police nor the detectives" *New York Herald,* July 18, 1897.

"Interrogated on the subject" *Meuse,* Oct. 10, 1892.

"Investigations have been made" ibid.

"had got hold of the newspaper" *New York Herald,* July 18, 1897.

"had never passed out of Worth's hands" Shinburn, p. 6.

"lives in extravagant style" ibid.

"His policy is to deal" ibid.

"known Worth, alias Raymond" ibid.

"rather Jewish" ibid.

"very fond of wearing" ibid.

"It may be said with truth"   ibid.

"Shore blistered me"   Worth's Confession, p. 8.

"he expected every day"   ibid.

"we were not called on"   ibid.

"To tell the truth he has changed"   William Pinkerton to John Shore, Denver, Colorado, Nov. 3, 1892, PA.

"I will write to the Judge"   Robert Pinkerton to John Shore, misdated Oct. 1, 1892, PA.

"I know what your institution"   Worth's Confession, p. 2.

"a debt of gratitude"   ibid.

TWENTY

"Session of 20 and 21st March"   *Gazette de Liège,* March 20, 1893.

"Henry Raymond, a well known sporting"   *World,* November 7, 1892.

"the man Wirth"   *Daily Telegraph,* March 22, 1893.

"claimed to represent"   *Adam Worth,* p. 17.

"declined to have anything"   ibid.

"English authorities"   ibid.

"word from the"   ibid.

"admit to his own lawyer"   ibid.

"eager to see the defendant"   *Gazette de Liège,* March 21, 1893.

"lost much of his gentlemanly"   ibid.

"deprived of the magnificent whiskers"   *Meuse,* March 21, 1893.

"This is no longer the gentleman"   ibid.

The condensed account of Worth's trial is translated from *La Gazette de Liège,* March 21, 1893. The *Gazette's* reporter misheard Worth's alias as "Rau," thus, no doubt, further confusing matters.

TWENTY-ONE

"had managed to curry"   *Adam Worth,* pp. 17–18.

"He was a constant give-away"   Worth's Confession, p. 2.

"He was pigeon for the"   ibid.

"Of all the dirty"   ibid.

"There was nothing from"   ibid.

"never get over"   ibid.

"result sometime in his"   ibid.

"rumors reached Worth"   Lyons, p. 59.

"entertained the Kaiser"   *The Gainsborough Duchess,* p. 26.

"mind gave way under"   Lyons, p. 60.

"they grew to manhood"   ibid.

"very bitter"   Worth's Confession, p. 8.

"would never have"   ibid.

"The prison treatment"   ibid., p. 10.

"from the inside"   ibid.

"When I fell down"   ibid.

"document furnished by"   *New York Herald,* July 18, 1897.

"considerably less than his"   ibid.

"all officers of the police"   Gallagher, p. 73.

"Always well dressed"   ibid.

"working on small banks"   Arrest of Shinburn, p. 11, PA.

"In his residence was found"   ibid.

"The arrest of Shinburne is undoubtedly"   ibid.

"now obliged to use"   ibid.

"a man quiet in manner"   ibid.

"lying sick with nervousness"   Worth's Confession, p. 2.

"glorious news"   ibid.

"that news had done"   ibid.

"A well-known criminal"   *Daily Telegraph,* May 11, 1893.

"In a drawer in the prisoner's"   ibid.

"It did not seem possible"   Sifakis, p. 471.

"procured several"   Asbury, p. 217.

"succeeded in transferring"   Sante, p. 211.

"SHE WAS ONCE A BARMAID"   *World,* March 21, 1894.

"the older daughters"   ibid.

"was already well provided"   Bender and Altschul, p. 24.

"squandered . . . on finery and whims"   ibid.

"It is the ambition of the New Yorker"   ibid.

"She had lived enough history"   *New York Herald,* Aug. 25, 1899.

"handsome, devilish, Hugh Marcy"   Rosamund de Zeer Marshall, *Kitty*
    (London, 1945), p. 180.

"The velvet caress"   ibid., p. 175.

"Just call me Tom"   ibid., p. 3.

"You are by far the most"   ibid., p. 260.

"Zere iss only wan"   ibid., p. 132.

"all man"   ibid., p. 302.

"I doffed my night robe"   ibid., p. 304.

"a lot of effort went"   Julie Gilbert, *Opposite Attraction* (New York,
    1995), p. 299.

"speak only in Cockney" ibid.

"$3.5 million in domestic" ibid., p. 301.

"Paulette Goddard has worked up" *New York Herald Tribune,* April 1, 1946, quoted in Gilbert, p. 301.

TWENTY-TWO

"A Seventeen years mystery" *Pall Mall Gazette,* July 24, 1893.

"a man named Marsend" *Globe,* July 28, 1893.

"a man of business" ibid.

"has confessed with" *Pall Mall Gazette,* July 24, 1893.

"they had a clue to the" Undated memo from "McGeorge," c. July 26, 1893, AA.

"in consort" ibid.

had given the men ibid.

"his principal object" ibid.

"Worth has promised" *Pall Mall Gazette,* July 24, 1893.

"He made his entry" ibid.

"Nothing is said in the account" *Midland Daily Telegraph,* July 25, 1893.

"Messrs. Agnew, no doubt" *Bath Herald,* July 26, 1893.

"to worship" *Sun,* July 26, 1893.

"had used the dastard knife" ibid.

"the story may or may not" *Manchester Courier,* July 25, 1893.

"haunted during sleepless nights" ibid.

"unburden his mind" ibid.

"As the felon has been" ibid.

"in the course of the interview" *Globe,* July 28, 1893.

"fits of laughter" ibid.

"It seems certain" ibid.

"I still retain the belief" Robert to William Pinkerton, undated letter, PA.

"Certain newspapers" *Pall Mall Gazette,* July 26, 1893.

"The firm have recently" ibid.

"We could have had the picture" ibid.

"The negotiations for the return" ibid.

"was never engraved" Engen, p. 20.

"There may be some truth" *Sun,* July 26, 1893.

"heard the news with the calm" ibid.

"Mysterious men came to me" ibid.

"made an application to" M. Worrall, memo, Aug. 25, 1893, AA.

"he was Wirth's associate"   Morland Agnew, memo, Aug. 2, 1893, AA.
"or by anybody else"   ibid.
"Nothing could be done"   M. Worrall, memo, Aug. 25, 1893, AA.
"Undoubtedly the picture"   Morland Agnew, memo, Aug. 2, 1893, AA.
"There was nothing to be"   ibid.

TWENTY-THREE

"through the fingers of the"   *Pall Mall Gazette,* July 24, 1893.

Even before he definitively introduced Moriarty in "The Final Problem," the Sherlock Holmes story published in *The Strand Magazine* and *McLure's Magazine* in December 1893, Conan Doyle appears to have been aware of some of Worth's exploits. "The Resident Patient," published in August of that year, refers to the "Worthingdon Bank Gang."

"The original of Moriarty"   Vincent Starrett, *The Private Life of Sherlock Holmes* (London, 1933), pp. 141–42.

Dr. Briggs, a well-known physician from St. Louis, was a close friend of Conan Doyle. His quest for the factual origins of Conan Doyle's writing led him to establish the "real" premises of 221B Baker Street.

"The man pervades London"   Conan Doyle, "The Final Problem," in Vol. II, p. 303.

"who, in his estimation"   C. McCluer Stevens, p. 38.

"Fancy the long sustained"   Quoted in Dilnot, p. 657; also McCluer Stevens, p. 39.

"He is extremely tall and thin"   Conan Doyle, "The Final Problem," in Vol. II, p. 304.

"cases of the most varying"   ibid., p. 303.

"a very respectable"   Conan Doyle, *The Valley of Fear,* in Vol. I, p. 478.

"one million and two hundred"   ibid., p. 479.

A painting of a little girl with a lamb attributed to Greuze does exist, but it is titled *Innocence.* A painting of this name was sold at the Paris Pourtales Gallery of Art (Holmes corrupts this to "Portalis") in 1865 for 100,200 francs, or £4,000. In 1918 it was shown to be a copy of the original *Innocence* by Greuze, now in the Wallace Collection in London. In fact, as *The Times Literary Supplement* noted on July 1, 1960, "the sale room price of a Greuze has never exceeded the 129,000 francs given for 'Les Oeufs Cassées' at the Demidoff sale in 1870."

"young girl with lamb"   I am indebted to Charles Higham, who notes this clue in his book *The Adventures of Conan Doyle* (New York, 1976), p. 114.

"It is said that" "The Story of a Picture," *World,* April 11, 1877.

"shortly after the turn" Wayne G. Broehl, *The Molly Maguires* (Cambridge, Mass., 1964), vi, p. 409.

"almost a paraphrase of " ibid.

"raised the roof when" Interview with Ralph Dudley, 1948, by James Horan, quoted in Horan, p. 499.

"At first he talked" ibid.

"The Worth family name" Bob Robinson, *The Illustrious Convert,* unpublished address to South Carolina Sherlockian group, The Handsome Wheels.

"great criminal" Conan Doyle, *The Adventure of the Illustrious Client,* in Vol. II, p. 675.

"violin virtuoso" ibid.

"very dangerous villain" ibid.

"agent in the huge criminal" ibid.

"a slim, flame-like woman" ibid., p. 677.

"lucent top hat" ibid., p. 672.

"more dangerous than" ibid.

"He has expensive tastes" ibid., p. 675.

"who collects women" ibid., p. 678.

"beast-man" ibid., p. 680.

"a real aristocrat" ibid., p. 676.

TWENTY-FOUR

"broken in health and" *Adam Worth,* p. 18.

"a mental and physical wreck" William to Robert Pinkerton, Feb. 12, 1902, PA.

"This is one of the causes" ibid.

"The thieves entered the place" *New York Evening Journal,* Nov. 1, 1897.

"The shop was considered" *London News,* Nov. 2, 1897.

"Fisher did not say" Memo, PA.

"He had lost some" Dilnot, p. 661.

"The French had begun to" Worth's Confession, p. 12.

"The stuff " ibid.

"a sporting man known" *Adam Worth,* p. 18.

"made a living by the" Dilnot, p. 662.

"controlled the Gainsborough" *Adam Worth,* p. 18.

"the only man he would" Worth's Confession, p. 1.

"under no circumstances" ibid.

"that I was a nice fellow"   ibid.
"He felt sure that there"   ibid.
"America's leading"   *Chicago Observer,* cited in Horan, p. 456.
"fondness for animals"   *Chicago Tribune,* cited in ibid.
"I am too good"   ibid., p. 482.
"Letter awaiting you"   Worth's Confession, p. 1.
"a strange man had called"   *Adam Worth,* p. 18.
"Dear Sir,"   Quoted in Esterow, pp. 196–97.
"I recognised at once"   Worth's Confession, p. 1.
"On the 12th I received"   ibid.
"I wanted him spotted"   ibid.
"With the exception"   ibid., p. 2.
"had indications of a man"   ibid., p. 5.
"I weighed him up carefully"   ibid., p. 13.
"Well, I came to see you"   ibid., p. 3.

TWENTY-FIVE
"in gossiping frame of mind"   Worth's Confession, p. 6.
"The Lady should"   Horan, p. 316.
"I consider this man"   ibid., p. 2.
"he had always fancied"   ibid., p. 7.
"a very handsome"   ibid., p. 10.
"Of course you cannot tell"   ibid.
"and he said with tears"   ibid., p. 8.
"He said that he had"   ibid., p. 13.
"Of course I want to get"   ibid.
"The great Supt. Byrnes"   ibid., p. 5.
"somebody was faking"   ibid., p. 9.
"I asked him how"   ibid., p. 12.
"he would gladly give"   ibid., p. 14.
"under no circumstances"   *Adam Worth,* p. 19.
"I got talking to him"   Worth's Confession, p. 11.
"Before going away"   ibid., p. 14.
"He seemed in good faith"   Quoted in Horan, p. 316.
"Now, I do not know whether"   Worth's Confession, p. 10.
"I believe I can make"   ibid., p. 13.

TWENTY-SIX

"New Scotland Yard had been"   *Adam Worth*, p. 19.

"a rich American"   *History of Agnew's, 1817–1967* (London, privately printed, 1967), Appendix III, p. 81 (henceforth, Agnew's history).

"suggests that the matter"   ibid., p. 82.

"there should be"   *Adam Worth*, p. 19.

"Sheedy took the position"   ibid.

"Inspector Froest"   Agnew's history, p. 81.

"Would not a man offering"   *The Gainsborough Duchess*, p. 23.

"For the time being"   *Adam Worth*, p. 20.

"We must have a distinct"   William Pinkerton to Messrs Lewis and Lewis, solicitors, Chicago, July 10, 1899, PA.

"he is not in any sense"   ibid.

"would allow him"   *Adam Worth*, p. 20.

"If the Agnews would"   ibid.

"cross the ocean"   George Bangs to Robert Pinkerton, Jan. 16, 1900, PA.

"They may be the men using"   ibid.

"the Pinkertons received"   *Adam Worth*, p. 20.

"insisted that he should"   Dilnot, p. 662.

"Mr. Pinkerton at once"   *Adam Worth*, p. 20.

"When it was known"   ibid.

"It was a secret known"   *London Evening News*, April 11, 1901.

"for fear, in his excitement"   Agnew's history, p. 82.

"I have news compelling"   Morland Agnew, diary, quoted in Agnew's history.

"Mother was rather nervous"   ibid.

"These Yankees do eat"   Morland Agnew to Daisy Agnew, March 17, 1901, AA.

"I spent an exceedingly"   *London Evening News*, April 10, 1901, p. 2.

"damper to all the hopes"   ibid.

"fine, well-set up man"   ibid.

"You will have the Duchess"   Esterow, p. 200.

"Personally, I was too"   *London Evening News*, April 10, 1901, p. 2.

"That's a lot of money"   Agnew's history, p. 82.

"As the hour approached"   ibid.; also *London Evening News*, April 10, 1901, p. 2.

"About a quarter of an hour"   ibid.

"By and by there came"   Agnew's history, p. 83.

"adult messenger"   ibid. Agnew's emphasis on the distinctive age, insouciance, and silence of the messenger all suggest strongly that this was Adam Worth and that the art dealer, for all his later claims, knew it. Pinkerton's subsequent refusal to identify Worth's whereabouts during this transaction, when he was so free with all other details, is further evidence that the elderly bellboy was Worth himself.

"When he had gone"   ibid.

"watched his features"   *Adam Worth,* p. 21.

"I looked up at detective"   Agnew's history, p. 83.

"I am positive the picture"   *Adam Worth,* p. 21.

"Well, I am glad it is"   *London Evening News,* April 10, 1901, p. 2.

"Then we went to a shop"   Agnew's history, p. 83.

"I hung it up on a peg"   ibid.

"On arriving in New York"   ibid.

"Some 25 years ago a very"   Morland Agnew to Daisy Agnew, March 31, 1901, AA.

"our grateful acknowledgement"   Morland Agnew to William Pinkerton, March 31, 1901, AA.

"I told the Purser"   Agnew's history, p. 83.

"If the customs officers"   *Adam Worth,* p. 21.

"Mother and some of the ladies"   Morland Agnew to Daisy Agnew, March 31, 1901, AA.

"a decayed millionaire"   *Daily Express,* April 9, 1901, p. 5.

"arranged through our"   William Pinkerton to Moreland Agnew, Chicago, April 8, 1901, AA.

"positively untrue"   *Evening Standard,* April 10, 1901, p. 1.

TWENTY-SEVEN

"going back to England"   *Adam Worth,* p. 22.

"than the assessed value"   Howard Zinn, *A People's History of the United States* (New York, 1990), p. 316.

"His butler said that"   Bishop Lawrence, quoted in Cass Canfield, *The Incredible Pierpont Morgan* (New York, 1974), p. 114.

"I was determined"   ibid.

"Going to London"   Delos Avery, *Kidnapping Done in Oil,* article in PA.

"The Napoleon of Wall Street"   Jonathan Hughes, *The Vital Few* (Boston, 1966), p. 404.

"saw the Civil War"   Chernow, p. 22.

"This was a day of corruption"　George Wheeler, *Pierpont Morgan and Friends—The Anatomy of a Myth* (Englewood Cliffs, N.J., 1973), p. 131.

"anybody who even has" Frederick Lewis Allen, *The Great Pierpont Morgan* (New York, 1949), p. 154.

"The man who had accumulated"　ibid., pp. 111–12.

"there were two Pierponts"　Chernow, p. 35.

"Never under any circumstances"　ibid., p. 26.

"I commit my soul"　Allen, p. 13.

"generally behaved himself"　Wheeler, p. 132.

"That's nothing"　Chernow, p. 115.

"smile, and smile"　William Shakespeare, *Hamlet*, I:v, 105.

"a high-minded young girl"　Wheeler, p. 82.

"a young and delicate"　ibid., p. 83.

"reminiscence of Mimi"　ibid., p. 84.

"is true of all"　John Fowles, *The Magus* (London, 1977), p. 178.

"a deeply sentimental"　Chernow, p. 42.

TWENTY-EIGHT

"Down the gangway"　*Daily Express*, April 9, 1901, p. 5.

"Mr. J. Pierpont Morgan"　*Daily Express*, April 10, 1901.

"fondness and keen"　ibid.

"Mr Morgan's vaulting"　ibid.

"save for the slightest"　*London Evening News*, April 10, 1901, p. 2.

"in a beautiful"　*Times*, April 9, 1901, p. 8.

"Father telegraphs his delight"　Agnew's history, p. 84.

"that the thief fought"　*Evening Standard*, April 10, 1901, p. 1.

"the police in both England"　ibid.

"So far as I know it"　Agnew's history, p. 84; also *London Evening News*, April 10, 1901, p. 2.

"romance as strange as"　*Daily Telegraph*, April 9, 1901.

"the third sensational"　*Times*, April 10, 1901, p. 4.

"that the man who stole"　*Times*, April 9, 1901, p. 8.

"Its authentic history"　*Times*, April 10, 1901, p. 4.

"Papers full of reports"　Agnew's history, p. 84.

"The Dear Old Dutch"　*London Evening News*, Thurs., April 11, 1901.

"We have been literally"　*Evening Standard*, April 10, 1901, p. 1.

"Her value must have"　*London Evening News*, April 9, 1901, p. 2.

"You may take my word"　*London Evening News*, April 10, 1901, p. 2.

"The newspaper reporters" William Pinkerton to C. Morland Agnew, Chicago, April 8, 1901, AA.

"Now that the 'stolen duchess' " *London Evening News,* April 9, 1901, p. 2.

"the real Gainsborough" Photograph in AA.

"It is to be hoped" *The Gainsborough Duchess,* p. 29.

"Now that the picture" *London Evening News,* April 10, 1901, p. 2.

"My ship was faster" Canfield, p. 114.

"but Mr Morgan was given" *New York Herald,* Feb. 7, 1902.

"subject to Sir William" Thos. Agnew & Sons to J. Pierpont Morgan, April 12, 1901, AA; also Agnew's history, p. 84.

"I have this morning" Agnew's history, pp. 84–85.

"a reporter flatly" ibid., p. 84.

"more columns of newspapers" Satterlee, p. 352.

"This was one of the many" ibid.

"Nobody will ever know" ibid., p. 353.

"rather hastily" Morland Agnew to William Pinkerton, Nov. 19, 1902, PA.

"What else have you for sale?" *New York Times,* Aug. 11, 1963, cited in Chernow, p. 100.

"license to stay on earth" Allen, p. 179.

"Pierpont Morgan calls in" Wheeler, p. 203.

"The Outcry deals with" Henry James, *The Outcry* (London, 1911), jacket blurb for first edition.

"beautiful duchess" ibid., p. 22.

"the most beautiful" ibid., p. 30.

"the billionaire with" Adeline R. Tinter, "Henry James: *The Outcry* and the art drain of 1908–9," *Apollo,* Feb. 1981, p. 110.

"Bender knows what" James, p. 21.

"Kitty wants so many" ibid.

"The art world is at" ibid., p. 52.

"Precious things are going" ibid.

"This time it will" *London Evening News,* April 9, 1901, p. 2.

"She looks splendid" Agnew's history, p. 86.

"The music halls were" ibid., p. 84.

TWENTY-NINE

"all in the world" *Adam Worth,* p. 22.

would not take any *Pittsburgh Leader,* March 3, 1905.

"the worst deal Harry"   Guerin, p. 298.

"The sudden return"   *Magazine of Art,* June 1901, p. 368.

"Never previously in the history"   *The Gainsborough Duchess,* p. 5.

"one newly brought"   ibid., p. 6.

"she is not, after all"   *Pall Mall Gazette,* April 9, 1901, p. 1.

"will vanish as the"   ibid.

"An exhibition in London"   *Times,* April 10, 1901, p. 4.

"Probably all the speculation"   *The Gainsborough Duchess,* p. 6.

"Our hearts were wasted"   *Daily Express,* April 10, 1901, p. 4.

"that brother and"   Adam Worth (alias Robt. R. Bayley) to William Pinkerton, June 22, 1901, PA.

"I am little better"   ibid.

"Friend H."   William Pinkerton (B.) to Friend H. (Adam Worth), June 30, 1901, PA.

"I have had several"   ibid.

"I think you write"   Robert to William Pinkerton, July 3, 1901, PA.

"stop this correspondence"   William to Robert Pinkerton, July 5, 1901, PA.

"I urged upon"   William Pinkerton to Harry L. Raymond, Feb. 21, 1902, PA.

"tumor"   ibid.

"had fitted up a nice home"   *Adam Worth,* p. 22.

"knew nothing of his past"   ibid.

"He told me little or nothing"   Henry L. Raymond to William Pinkerton, undated, PA.

"would consult no"   ibid.

"Mr Morgan will not"   Morland Agnew to William Pinkerton, telegram, Nov. 19, 1902, PA.

"The ceiling is too low"   Wheeler, p. 203.

"I left his room to go"   Henry L. Raymond to William Pinkerton, undated, PA.

"independent means"   Death certificate (Jan. 8, 1902) in St. Catherine's House, London.

"I beg to state to you"   H. L. Raymond to William Pinkerton, Jan. 24, 1902, PA.

"Do you think it could"   Robert to William Pinkerton, Feb. 6, 1902, PA.

"Yours of the 24th informing"   William Pinkerton to H. L. Raymond, Feb. 2, 1902, PA.

"proved in the autumn"   C. McCluer Stevens, p. 44.

"My father left little" Henry L. Raymond to William Pinkerton, undated, PA.

"My father often used" Henry L. Raymond to William Pinkerton, undated, PA.

"a man of great" William Pinkerton to Henry L. Raymond, Feb. 21, 1902, PA.

"I was very sorry" William to Robert Pinkerton, Feb. 2, 1902, PA.

"I feel as you do" Robert to William Pinkerton, Feb. 10, 1902, PA.

"keep the matter of his" Robert to William Pinkerton, Feb. 6, 1902, PA.

"we should leave his" ibid.

"I have a letter from Adam" William to Robert Pinkerton, Feb. 9, 1902, PA.

"I hated to say anything" William to Robert Pinkerton, Feb. 7, 1902, PA.

"You cannot get a thing" ibid.

"about as correct as a newspaper" William to Robert Pinkerton, Feb. 9, 1902, PA.

"the most remarkable crime" *New York Sun*, Feb. 9, 1902.

"one of the most celebrated" *Evening Sun*, Feb. 7, 1902.

"one of the most remarkable" *New York World*, Feb. 7, 1902.

"He was personally" *Chicago American*, Feb. 7, 1902.

"the last of a really" *Chicago Tribune*, Feb. 7, 1902.

"In the death of Adam Worth" *Adam Worth*, p. 23.

"Adam Worth is dead" *New York Journal and American*, Feb. 7, 1902.

EPILOGUE

"the robber baron" Gore Vidal, *United States: Essays 1952–1992* (New York, London, 1993), p. 1073.

"Great Dissembler" Robert Gandt, *Skygods: The Fall of Pan Am* (New York, 1995), p. 10.

"at the bottom" Henry L. Raymond to William Pinkerton, undated, PA.

"a man in this city" William Pinkerton to Henry L. Raymond, Feb. 21, 1902, PA.

"We ought to be able" ibid.

"Professional crime among" Morn, p. 140.

"a prime motivation" Horan, p. 497; *World*, April 25, 1920.

"quite obvious that" Guerin, p. 301.

"turning respectable"   ibid., p. 295.

"three men called at"   ibid.

"in trust for the education"   ibid., p. 296.

"Worth knew a lot"   *New York Sun,* May 7, 1902.

"There is nothing"   Note by RAP (Robert Pinkerton), appended to ibid., PA.

"for reasons of sentiment"   *New York Sun,* May 7, 1902.

"Michelangelo, Rembrandt and Whistler"   Morn, p. 133.

"I am what you call"   Brochure for Pinkerton's photographic exhibition, Washington, D.C.

"I don't know the man"   *New York World,* Oct. 15, 1900.

"discovered the secret"   Gallagher, p. 110.

"From the early fifties"   Shinburn, *Safe Burglary,* PA.

"so revealing and instructive"   Morn, p. 138.

"absolutely down and out"   William Pinkerton to George Bangs, Chicago, April 27, 1913, PA.

"a whole lot of ghost"   ibid.

"locked in each other's arms"   Conan Doyle, in "The Final Problem," in Vol. II, p. 317.

"Everything comes in circles"   Conan Doyle, in *The Valley of Fear,* in Vol. I, p. 479.

"an immense and widening"   Allen, p. 113.

"tipsy dowager with"   Wheeler, p. 283.

"his gifts were closely"   Allen, p. 121.

"sporting bids from"   *Daily Telegraph,* July 14, 1995.

"It was just such"   Duke of Devonshire, interview with the author, Sept. 1995.

"There is no technical"   Report on Gainsborough's Duchess of Devonshire by Rica Jones, CHA.

Index